**W9-CKM-362**

# Multicultural America

## Volume III
# The African Americans

# Multicultural America

## Volume III
# The African Americans

Rodney P. Carlisle
GENERAL EDITOR

Facts On File
An imprint of Infobase Publishing

**Multicultural America: Volume III: The African Americans**
Copyright © 2011 by Infobase Publishing

Facts On File, Inc.
An Imprint of Infobase Publishing
132 West 31st Street
New York, NY 10001

**Library of Congress Cataloging-in-Publication Data**
Multicultural America / Rodney P. Carlisle, general editor.
    v. cm.
  Includes bibliographical references and index.
  Contents: v. 1. The Hispanic Americans — v. 2. The Arab Americans — v. 3. The African Americans — v. 4. The Asian Americans — v. 5. The Jewish Americans — v. 6. The European Americans — v. 7. The Native Americans.
  ISBN 978-0-8160-7811-0 (v. 1 : hardcover : alk. paper) — ISBN 978-0-8160-7812-7 (v. 2 : hardcover : alk. paper) — ISBN 978-0-8160-7813-4 (v. 3 : hardcover : alk. paper) — ISBN 978-0-8160-7814-1 (v. 4 : hardcover : alk. paper) — ISBN 978-0-8160-7815-8 (v. 5 : hardcover : alk. paper) — ISBN 978-0-8160-7816-5 (v. 6 : hardcover : alk. paper) — ISBN 978-0-8160-7817-2 (v. 7 : hardcover : alk. paper) 1. Minorities—United States—History—Juvenile literature. 2. Ethnology—United States—History—Juvenile literature. 3. Cultural pluralism—United States—History—Juvenile literature. 4. United States—Ethnic relations—Juvenile literature. I. Carlisle, Rodney P.
  E184.A1M814 2011
  305.800973—dc22          2010012694

Facts On File books are available at special discounts when purchased in bulk quantities for businesses, associations, institutions, or sales promotions. Please call our Special Sales Department at (212) 967-8800 or (800) 322-8755.

You can find Facts On File on the World Wide Web at http://www.factsonfile.com

Text design and composition by Golson Media
Cover printed by Art Print, Taylor, PA
Book printed and bound by Maple Press, York, PA
Date Printed: March 2011
Printed in the United States of America

11 10 9 8 7 6 5 4 3 2 1

This book is printed on acid-free paper.

# CONTENTS

Volume III

# The African Americans

# PREFACE

**AMERICANS HAVE HAD** a sense that they were a unique people, even before the American Revolution. In the 18th century, the settlers in the 13 colonies that became the United States of America began to call themselves Americans, recognizing that they were not simply British colonists living in North America. In addition to the English, other cultures and peoples had already begun to contribute to the rich tapestry that would become the American people.

Swedes and Finns in the Delaware River valley, Dutch in New York, Scots-Irish, and Welsh had all brought their different ways of life, dress, diet, housing, and religions, adding them to the mix of Puritan and Anglican Englishmen. Lower Rhine German groups of dissenting Amish and Mennonites, attracted by the religious toleration of Pennsylvania, settled in Germantown, Pennsylvania as early as 1685. Located on the western edge of Philadelphia, the settlers and later German immigrants moved to the counties just further west in what would become Pennsylvania Dutch country.

The policies of other colonies tended to favor and encourage such group settlement to varying extents. In some cases, as in New Jersey, the fact that each community could decide what church would be supported by local taxes tended to attract coreligionists to specific communities. Thus in the colonial period, the counties of southern New Jersey (known in colonial times as West Jersey) tended to be dominated by Quakers. Townships in New Jersey closer to New York City were dominated by Lutheran, Dutch Reformed, and Anglican churches and settlers.

Ethnicity and religion divided the peoples of America, yet the official tolerance of religious diversity spawned a degree of mutual acceptance. While crossreligious marriages were frowned upon, they were not prohibited, with individual families deciding which parents' church should be attended, if any. Modern descendants tracing their ancestry are sometimes astounded at the various strands of culture and religion that they find woven together.

To the south, Florida already had a rich Hispanic heritage, some of it filtered through Cuba. Smaller groups of immigrants from France and other countries in Europe were supplemented during the American Revolution by enthusiastic supporters of the idea of a republican experiment in the New World.

All of the thirteen colonies had the institution of African slavery, and people of African ancestry, both slave and free, constituted as much as 40 percent of the population of colonies like Georgia and South Carolina. In a wave of acts of emancipation, slaves living in the New England colonies were freed right after the Revolution, soon joined by those in Pennsylvania, New York, and New Jersey. Although some African Americans in the south were free by birth or manumission, emancipation for 90 percent of those living south of Pennsylvania would have to wait until the Civil War, 1861–65. Forcibly captured and transported under terrible conditions overland and across the ocean, Africans came from dozens of different linguistic stocks. Despite the disruptions of the middle passage, African Americans retained elements of their separate cultures, including some language and language patterns, and aspects of diet, religion, family, and music.

Native Americans, like African Americans, found themselves excluded from most of the rights of citizenship in the new Republic. In the Ohio and Mississippi Valley, many Native Americans resisted the advance of the European-descended settlers. In Florida, Creeks and Seminoles provided haven to escaped slaves, and together, they fought the encroachment of settlers. Some of the African Americans living with the Seminoles and other tribes moved west with them on the Trail of Tears to Indian Territory in what later became the state of Oklahoma. Other groups, like the Lumbees of North Carolina, stayed put, gradually adjusting to the new society around them. Throughout scattered rural communities, clusters of biracial and triracial descendents could trace their roots to Native-American and African ancestors, as well as to the English and Scotch-Irish.

The Louisiana Purchase brought the vast Mississippi Valley into the United States, along with the cosmopolitan city of New Orleans, where French exiles from Canada had already established a strong Creole culture. With the annexation of Texas, and following the Mexican-American War (1846–48), the United States incorporated as citizens hundreds of thousands of people of Hispanic ancestry. Individuals and communities in Texas and New Mexico preserve not only their religion, but also their language, cuisine, customs, and architecture.

As the United States expanded to the west, with vast opportunities for settlement, waves of European immigrants contributed to the growth of the country, with liberal naturalization laws allowing immigrants to establish themselves as citizens. Following the revolutions of 1848 in Europe, and famines in Ireland, new floods of immigrants from Central Europe, Ireland, and Scandinavia all settled in pockets.

By the late 19th century, America had become a refuge for political and economic refugees, as well as enterprising families and individuals from many countries. More geographic-ethnic centers emerged, as new immigrants sought out and settled near friends and families who had already arrived. Neighborhoods and whole states took on some aspects of the ethnic cultures that the immigrants carried, with the Italians settling in New York City, San Francisco, and New Jersey; Azoreans and continental Portuguese in Rhode Island and southern Massachusetts; Scandinavians in Wisconsin and Minnesota; Germans in Missouri; and Chinese and Japanese in a number of West Coast cities and towns. San Francisco and Boston became known for their Irish settlers, and Italians joined Franco-Hispanic Catholics of New Orleans. In some other scattered communities, such as the fishing port of Monterey, California, later Portuguese and Italian arrivals were also absorbed into the local Hispanic community, partly through the natural affinity of the shared Catholic faith.

As waves of immigrants continued to flow into the United States from the 1880s to World War I, the issue of immigration became even more politicized. On the one hand, older well-established ethnic communities sometimes resented the growing influence and political power of the new immigrants. Political machines in the larger cities made it a practice to incorporate the new settlers, providing them with some access to the politics and employment of city hall, also expecting their votes and loyalty during election. The intricate interplay of ethnicity and politics through the late 19th century has been a rich field of historical research.

In the 1890s the United States suddenly acquired overseas territories, including Hawaii, Puerto Rico, and Guam. People from the new territories became American citizens, and although the great majority of them did not leave their islands, those who came to the continental United States became part of the increasingly diverse population. The tapestry of American culture and ancestry acquired new threads of Polynesian, Asian, Hispanic, and African-Hispanic people.

During the Progressive Era, American-born citizens of a liberal or progressive political inclination often had mixed feelings about immigrants. Those with a more elite set of values believed that crime, alcoholism, and a variety of vices running from drug abuse through prostitution, gambling, and underground sports such as cockfighting, all could be traced to the new immigrants. The solution, they believed, would be immigration reform: setting quotas that would restrict immigrants from all but Great Britain and northern Europe.

Other reformers took the position that the problems faced by new immigrants could be best dealt with through education, assistance, and social work. Still others approached the questions of poverty and adjustment of immigrants as part of the labor struggle, and believed that organizing through labor unions could bring pressure for better wages and working conditions. Meanwhile, immigrants continued to work through their churches, community organizations, and the complexities of American politics for recognition and rights.

Ultimately, two approaches emerged regarding how different ethnic groups would be viewed and how they would view themselves in America. For some, the idea of a melting pot had always held attraction. Under this way of thinking, all Americans would merge, with ethnic distinctions diminishing and the various cultures blending together to create a new American culture. Such a process of assimilation or integration appealed to many, both among American-born and immigrant groups. Others argued strongly that ethnic or racial identity should be preserved, with a sense of pride in heritage, so that America would continue to reflect its diversity, and so that particular groups would not forget their origins, traditions, and culture.

In 1882 the Chinese Exclusion Act prohibited further immigration of Chinese, and it was extended and made more restrictive in several amendments through 1902. Under the law, Chinese were prohibited from obtaining U.S. citizenship. In 1924 immigration legislation was enacted establishing quotas, based upon earlier census figures, so that the quotas favored those from northern Europe. Under that law, Chinese were excluded, although 1910–40 more than 50,000 Chinese entered under claims they were returning or joining families already in the United States. The racial nature of the Chinese Exclusion and Immigration Acts tended to prevent the assimilation of Chinese into American society, with many cities, particularly in the west, developing defined Chinatowns or Chinese districts.

Whether an individual ethnic group should become assimilated into the total culture, or whether it should strive to maintain its own separate cultural identity, was often hotly debated. For some, like the Chinese, Native Americans, and African Americans, armed power of the state, law, and social discrimination tended to create and enforce separate communities and locales. For others, self-segregation and discrimination by other ethnic groups, and the natural process of settling near relatives and coreligionists led to definable ethnic regions and neighborhoods. Among such diverse groups as African Americans, Asians, Hispanics, Italians, Arab Americans, and Native Americans, leaders and spokesmen have debated the degree to which cultural identity should be sacrificed in the name of assimilation. In the 21st century, the debates have continued, sometimes with great controversy, at other times, the dialogues went on almost unnoticed by the rest of the country.

Armed conflict, race-wars, reservation policy, segregation, exclusion, and detention camps in time of war have shown the harsh and ugly side of enforced separation. Even though the multiethnic and multicultural heritage of the United States has been fraught with crisis and controversy, it has also been a source of strength. With roots in so many cultures and with the many struggles to establish and maintain social justice, America has also represented some of the best aspirations of humanity to live in peace. The search for social equity has been difficult, but the fact that the effort has continued for more than two centuries is in itself an achievement.

In this series on Multicultural America, each volume is dedicated to the history of one ethnocultural group, tracing through time the struggles against discrimination and for fair play, as well as the effort to preserve and cherish an independent cultural heritage.

## THE AFRICAN AMERICANS

The social and cultural history of people of African ancestry in the United States has been surrounded by more controversy than that of any other group within the country. Furthermore issues surrounding the status, economic and social conditions, and cultural contributions of African Americans have been more thoroughly debated and discussed than any other group.

The reasons for this unique status are clear and well known. Unlike other immigrant groups, the vast majority of African immigrants to the United States were brought against their will, purchased as slaves either in Africa or the Caribbean, then sold and dispersed throughout the colonies that became the United States. After 1808 a reduced and illegal slave trade continued, mostly from the Caribbean islands, until just before the beginning of the American Civil War in 1861.

The nature of the slave trade and the slave institution was such that people of African ancestry from a wide variety of societies, speaking different languages, were grouped together, very rapidly breaking up any cultural cohesion. For this reason, within a generation, it was extremely rare for African Americans living in the British colonies of North America or within the states of the early United States to preserve any of the specific language of, or indeed, any knowledge of, their ancestral homelands. Nevertheless some common aspects of custom, religion, bits of vocabulary, cuisine, handicrafts, and other aspects of culture did survive, some of them affecting the broader American society.

Slavery evolved rapidly in the British colonies, and by the late 1600s, black servants in Virginia and elsewhere were treated differently from white indentured servants. They had longer terms of imprisonment for the same crimes, and lived under a variety of measures making their servitude lifelong and inherited by their children, rather than temporary and specific only to an individual. Through the 1700s, the pattern of permanent and inherited servitude became well established, with only a small minority of blacks living as free persons (in most colonies less than 15 percent).

During the American Revolution, the British promised freedom to those slaves who would abandon their owners' plantations and join the British forces attempting to suppress the revolution. A large number, perhaps on the order of 20,000, sought freedom in this fashion. In the northern colonies, however, free blacks joined with the Patriots against the Loyalists. In the years following the revolution, the New England states all passed emancipation laws ending slavery and granting some of the rights of citizenship to former slaves. In the south, those blacks who had sided with the British were evacuated by the British, either to the Bahamas or Nova Scotia.

Thus by 1800 to 1820, a clear division had developed, with the United States divided into slave states (those south of Pennsylvania) and free states from Pennsylvania northward. The expansion of cotton production in the south soon made plantation slavery there highly profitable for the white owners, and tended to make them even more protective of the institution of slavery. The history of the abolition movement and the role of slavery in the secession of the states that formed the Confederacy are well-known aspects of American history. In the decades after the Civil War, the struggle of African Americans to achieve full civil rights within the American social and political system was a dramatic and contentious aspect of American history. At the same time, many African Americans sought to build on their identity. As a consequence, aspects of African-American culture thrived as a vibrant thread in the broader American culture.

In addition as African-American leaders strived to achieve social equity, they debated, and to an extent, continue to debate, the degree to which African Americans should view themselves as a unique and distinct people within the American society. In much of the 20th century, that debate took the form of a tension between advocates of African-American nationalism and advocates of social justice through integration into the mainstream of American society. In the early 21st century, that debate appeared muted with the emergence of successful African-American individuals. The 2008 election of Barack Obama to the presidency of the United States was one evidence of the degree to which the plight of African Americans had come to resemble that of other ethnic groups within the American polity and social structure.

RODNEY CARLISLE
GENERAL EDITOR

# CHAPTER 1

# The Colonial Era: Beginnings to 1776

DIVERSE POPULATIONS THAT had thrived for thousands of years inhabited the continent that would become the Americas. When European explorers embarked for the New World, Africans were among the first visitors. It is reported that cabin boy Diego el Negro accompanied Columbus on his final voyage 1502–04. Since slaves were common in Portugal and southern Spain, nearly every exploration that sailed for the New World from the ports of Andalusia had Africans among the crew. Africans also accompanied the French explorers to regions around the Great Lakes, the Mississippi Valley, and Louisiana. In 1520 about 300 Africans were in the company of Hernán Cortés when he explored the area that would become Mexico. As English colonists began to cast an eye toward expansion, they would transform the demographic, political, and geographical landscape, and Africans would be remade in the image of white settlers.

## SETTLEMENT AND THE INVENTION OF AMERICAN SLAVERY

The first Africans in English North America arrived in 1619, when a Dutch frigate brought a cargo of 20 Africans to Jamestown, Virginia, for sale into bondage. These 20 Africans, including three women, had been purchased from the Dutch by the colonial government and then distributed among private settlers. According to census counts, they were not slaves, but indentured servants. For the first

# Fort Mose and Spanish Florida

Both free and enslaved blacks were present in Spanish Florida from the earliest days of its exploration and discovery, when they accompanied such noted explorers as Pánfilo de Narváez, Hernando de Soto, and Ponce de León. Both the Spanish government and private citizens imported slave laborers into Spanish Florida to serve as seamen, skilled artisans and craftsmen, domestics, and field hands. Florida, however, remained an isolated and neglected part of the Spanish empire throughout its colonial period, negating the need for a large-scale labor force.

Florida slaves lived under less harsh slave codes governing their behavior and had more rights than their counterparts in the British colonies to the north. Florida slaves could also gain their freedom upon sworn allegiance to the Spanish monarch, conversion to the Roman Catholic Church, or entering military service. These factors made Florida an attractive destination for runaway slaves from Britain's American colonies of Georgia and the Carolinas. The fugitives were given sanctuary in Florida by royal decree of Spain's King Charles II in 1693. Because of this decree and the Spaniards' more tolerant attitude toward manumission of slaves, a significant number of free blacks lived in Spanish Florida by the end of the colonial period. Many African Americans also had close relationships with the area's Native-American residents.

African Americans and mulattos played a key role in the defense of St. Augustine after the British establishment of Charles Towne (Charleston) in 1670. They first served in Spanish militia units, and later formed their own militia companies. They also participated in periodic Spanish raids into Georgia and the Carolinas. In 1738 Florida Governor Manuel Montiano established a fortified town for African Americans a few miles north of St. Augustine, in part as a reward for their military service. Officially named Gracia Real de Santa Teresa de Mose, the town was commonly known as Fort Mose. It was the first town of free African Americans to be legally sanctioned in the area of the present-day United States. Here, the town's approximately 100 African-American residents could live as independent frontier farmers and homeowners. The town also aided in the defense of St. Augustine.

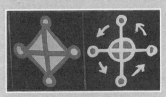

These African symbols representing the position of the sun throughout the day are displayed on tiles at the Ft. Mose National Historic Site.

The town continued to attract new runaways throughout its existence. Ft. Mose was destroyed in British General James Oglethorpe's 1740 attack on St. Augustine, but its residents later rebuilt the fortified town in 1752. It was abandoned for good in 1763 when the British gained possession of Florida at the end of the French and Indian War. Ft. Mose was designated a U.S. National Historic Landmark in 1995.

quarter-century after coming to Jamestown, blacks were designated as indentured servants. Some indentured servants who had completed their indenture were freed and given land. That would change as labor demands made blacks candidates for perpetual servitude. Gradually they were not released after their terms of service had ended.

As a result, black slave labor began to expand, as white indentured labor declined. Colonial legislators created laws to sanction, justify, and administer the emerging slave system. But by whatever term—indentured servants or slaves—blacks were found in every one of the 13 mainland colonies from the beginning of European settlement.

The element of race was almost immediately associated with status (free or enslaved) in the transition from indentured servant to slave. In 1640 John Punch, a black, joined two white servants in running away from Virginia to Maryland. When they were recaptured, four years were added to the period of indenture for the white servants, but Punch was ordered to "serve his master or his assigns for the time of his natural Life or elsewhere." In another case, a mulatto named Manuel had been purchased by Thomas Bushrod "as a Slave for Ever." Although in 1644 it had been declared that he was technically not a slave, it was stipulated that he had to remain with Bushrod for 21 years. By 1662 a Virginia law was already using the term *slaves* to designate black indentured servants.

The Africans who arrived at Jamestown had been baptized, which allowed them to be enfranchised. This implied that they were entitled to certain civil privileges such as the right to vote and, most importantly, the right to be free. The policy that baptism resulted in freedom would soon change in the wake of opposition by slaveholders, and even religious groups. In 1667 Virginia's legislature stated, "the conferring of baptisme doth not alter the condition of the person as to his bondage or freedome." As colonization gained steam, all regions along the eastern seaboard—New England, the mid-Atlantic, and the south—would increasingly import Africans to perform the needed labor of building a world, and complete the conversion from indentured service to slavery.

## NEW ENGLAND COLONIES
Massachusetts Bay Colony first imported Africans in 1637 after enslaving Pequot Indian survivors of the Puritan-Pequot War. The Puritans did not consider Indians to be a good source of slave labor, so they shipped them to the West Indies and South America in exchange for blacks. In 1638 the Salem-registered ship *Desire* landed at Boston with a cargo that included a number of blacks.

Others who disembarked at Hartford, Connecticut followed them. Blacks were used to construct housing and forts that established the colonies. As trade increased, ships leaving from New England carried rum, fish, and dairy products; while slaves, molasses, and sugar were off-loaded from inbound

# The Triangular Trades

The triangular trades is a term used to describe the general pattern ships involved in the modern slave trade followed in response to the demand for a large labor force in some of the European colonies of the New World. Spain, Portugal, and the Netherlands dominated the triangular trades during most of the 17th century, but Britain had become the largest slave trading country by the 18th century. The first leg of the triangular trade was the journey from a home port in Europe to the West Coast of Africa. European slave traders then negotiated with African slave dealers for African slaves largely captured in the continent's interior. Some paid cash, but trade was more common. Common trade goods included weapons and ammunition, alcohol, manufactured goods, and textiles.

The second leg of the triangular trades was the journey from Africa to the Caribbean (West Indies) or the Americas. Slaves were tightly packed into the ships to maximize space, resulting in brutal conditions and high mortality and suicide rates during the infamous Middle Passage. The most common destinations were the tropical Caribbean, Latin America, or the American south, where demand for slave labor was the highest. High mortality rates, harsh living and working conditions, and a surplus of male versus female slaves kept demand for new arrivals steady. Traders would use their profits from the sale of slaves to purchase tobacco, sugar, cotton, and other products to sell upon their return to Europe. The third leg of the triangular trades was the journey back to Europe to re-supply for the next trading voyage.

During the 18th century, a similar triangular trade had developed between Britain's American colonies (later the United States), Africa, and the Caribbean as slavery was legalized and lower mortality rates made higher-priced African slaves preferable to European indentured servants. New England slave traders carried manufactured goods such as rum to Africa to exchange for slaves, which were sold in the Caribbean for molasses to manufacture rum and other products. New England traders also traveled directly to the Caribbean with fish and agricultural products to exchange for sugar and slaves to be sold in the marketplace at Charleston, South Carolina. This trade continued illicitly after the U.S. Congress outlawed the slave trade in 1808. Approximately two million slaves arrived in Britain's American colonies and the United States before the abolition of slavery, most of those to the Caribbean Islands.

ships. After 1720 some New England captains transported slaves directly from Africa to America.

The slave trade meant the commodification of black slaves. Blacks were loaded into the holds of slave ships alongside other cargo. Completely depersonalized and stripped of any identity, slaves were considered merchandise to be sold at auction to the highest bidder. Ironically, blacks not only partici-

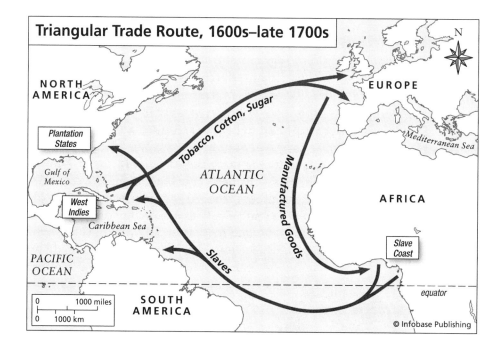

Triangular Trade Route, 1600s–late 1700s

pated directly in the slave trade as traded commodities, but also contributed as shipbuilders, ship hands, and rope makers. The slave trade relied upon Africans who furnished slaves—the spoils of war—to ship captains in exchange for cloth, weapons, distilled liquor (usually rum), and gunpowder. The black population in New England grew slowly as slavery became increasingly entrenched in the region's economic life.

Generally speaking, the slave codes (or rules of behavior) were not as onerous in New England as in the south. In colonial America, indentured servants or slaves were permitted certain legal rights such as trial by jury, suing and being sued, and testifying against whites. They could own property and petition for their freedom. Slaves sometimes cultivated their own garden plots and marketed their produce. Although they had some control over their lives, it was arbitrary—most colonies allowed marriage, but slave marriages were not considered legal and relatives were sold away, thus breaking up families. In 1641 Massachusetts was the first colony to legalize slavery by statute. In 1670 a Massachusetts law declared that the children of slaves could be sold into bondage. This preceded the policy of *partus sequitur ventrem*—where the condition of the child followed that of the mother—which would become widely adopted.

By 1700 slaves accounted for only three percent of New England's population. Part of the reason that the slave population remained small in New England had to do with the climate and soil conditions. Unlike the southern colonies, no crops were worked year-round. New England slaves worked mainly on small farms, although Rhode Island had some larger tracts devoted to tobacco. In addition to agriculture, slaves were involved in raising stock and breeding horses. And many slaves performed both skilled and unskilled varieties of labor, for example, printing, gold- and silversmithing, and cabinetmaking. Both men and women were engaged in domestic service. Slave women were expected to help in spinning, knitting, weaving, and other household chores. Even whites of middle income often purchased a slave to do the cooking, laundry, or maid/butler duty. In fact a family's wealth and status was gauged by the property it owned, including servants.

Although some slaves fled and others rebelled in minor ways, large-scale insurrection was rare. Blacks could still freely associate, for the most part, with each other as well as with whites and Indians. In addition the New England colonies did not expressly forbid slaves from being taught to read and write. In fact some occupations required that blacks acquire at least rudimentary skills in order to perform their work. Just as religion played a role in all avenues of life in New England, so it motivated book-learning for blacks. Judge Samuel Sewall (1652–1730) of Massachusetts wrote the pamphlet *The Selling of Joseph* (1701), which urged masters to provide religious instruction for their slaves while also declaring "Forasmuch as Liberty is in real value next unto Life: None ought to part with it themselves, or deprive others of it, but upon most mature Consideration."

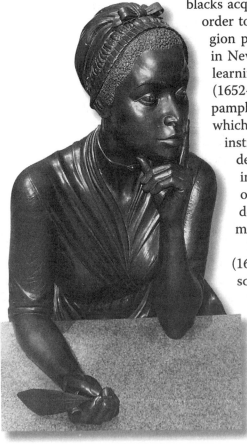

This statue of the poet Phillis Wheatley was dedicated in Boston in 2003.

Puritan clergyman Cotton Mather (1663–1728) established a charity school where blacks could engage in Bible study. And as a result of the interracial permissiveness that often accompanied the condition of slavery, the wives and children of the master—through contact—shared information with slaves. An example of this is Phillis Wheatley, America's first black poet, who was born in Senegal, Africa, in 1753 and sold into slavery at the age of seven to John and Susannah Wheatley of Boston. Raised with the Wheatleys' two children, she learned to read and write English. In 1773 a collection of her poems entitled *Poems on Various subjects, Religious and Moral*, was published in London.

Wheatley's poem *On Being Brought From Africa to America* reads:

*'Twas mercy brought me from my pagan land,*
*Taught my beknighted soul to understand*
*That there's a God that there's a Savior too:*
*Once I redemption neither sought nor knew.*
*Some view our sable race with scornful eye,*
*"Their color is a diabolic dye."*
*Remember Christians; Negroes, black as Cain,*
*May be refin'd, and join th' angelic train.*

## MID-ATLANTIC COLONIES

The Dutch made great profits from transporting slaves to various colonies. In 1624 the Dutch West India Company purchased 16 black slaves from pirates and brought them to the colony of New Netherland (present-day New York, New Jersey, and Delaware), where they worked as farmers and builders, and in aspects of the fur trade. There were large plantations in New Netherland, particularly in the Hudson River valley, and by 1638 many of them were cultivated with slave labor. The Dutch slave code was not elaborate, and manumission was not an uncommon reward for long or meritorious service. In fact 11 of the original 16 slaves were freed in 1644 and given land to establish farms after petitioning the local government and promising to provide produce. Although the demand for slaves exceeded the supply, the number imported by the Dutch was never great enough to arouse white fears.

After England captured New Netherland in 1664, English settlers streamed in with slaves. In 1684 slavery was recognized as a legitimate institution in the province of New York. The black population grew from 2,170 blacks in 1698 to 19,883 in 1771, out of a total population of 168,007. By 1650 New Netherland had become the largest slave importation center in North America, and by 1664 one-tenth of the population was African. When the English ship *Isabella* arrived in 1684, it brought 150 Africans. In reaction the slave code was refined early in the 18th century. In 1706 the colony followed the example of Virginia by enacting a law stating that baptism of a slave did not provide grounds for a claim to freedom. After the English came to dominate New Jersey, slavery was encouraged, and the population grew steadily.

In 1685 William Penn expressed the view that African slaves were more satisfactory workers than white servants, thus encouraging slavery in some

An early image of the slave market in New York as it looked around 1730.

quarters. This was opposed by other members of the Religious Society of Friends (Quakers), however. At a gathering held at a member's house in Germantown, Pennsylvania, on February 18, 1688, a Quaker group spoke against slavery; they invoked the Golden Rule, and drafted a formal remonstrance against "the traffic of men-body." In 1693 George Keith (1638–1716), a Scottish preacher and leader of the Christian Quakers, broke with Penn and remonstrated with Pennsylvanians for holding persons in perpetual bondage. In 1721 the black population of Pennsylvania was estimated at 2,500–5,000. The ambiguity over slavery that existed in Pennsylvania led to an early movement for manumission. Even those who considered slavery acceptable were reluctant to engage in the wholesale and indiscriminate enslavement of blacks. Pennsylvania was not only relatively free of insurrection, but blacks were also able to make some strides in regard to citizenship in the New World. They formed schools and churches, and created a stable social life. The institution of marriage was respected, and the black family achieved a stability unlike that reached by blacks in most English colonies.

Since Delaware was part of Pennsylvania until 1703, the laws of the latter colony applied to Delaware. Afterward the slave population increased in Delaware at a somewhat more rapid rate than it did in Pennsylvania. Eventually Delaware became more closely identified with the interests of its neighboring colonies to the south. Since New York's black population was greater than that of any other colony in the north, its slave codes were harsher. In an attempt to thwart slave conspiracies, New York did not permit more than three slaves to assemble when not working.

Slavery as an institution was never as successful in the middle colonies as it was in the south. The predominantly commercial economy, supplemented by subsistence agriculture, did not encourage the large-scale employment of slave labor. Many of the slaves who entered through the New York and Pennsylvania ports were later sent to the southern colonies. The Dutch, Swedes, and Germans cultivated their farms by themselves or had one to two slaves at most. Finally, the moral issues raised by Quakers against using slaves would become more pronounced during the revolutionary period.

## THE SOUTHERN PLANTATION SYSTEM

In the southern plantation colonies, indentured labor was replaced by slave labor by 1700. As early as 1640, some blacks in Virginia had become bond-men for life. The statutory recognition of slavery came in 1661 in Virginia, but it did not affect blacks who had already completed their indenture. The chartering of the Royal African Company (RAC) in 1672 brought many more slaves. Established by London merchants and led by James, the Duke of York, the RAC allowed England to monopolize the slave trade and transport 5,000 slaves per year to the colonies 1680–86. Slave ships brought cargoes directly from Africa to Virginia, Maryland, and the Carolinas. By the early 1700s southern planters relied almost exclusively on enslaved men and women to tend and harvest huge tracts of cash crops. Whites began to rely exclusively on black labor for several reasons: (1) they feared insurrections such as Bacon's Rebellion in 1676, in which poor whites were joined by free blacks and runaway slaves in the burning of Jamestown; (2) as economic opportunities improved in England, not as many colonists came to the New World, and indentured white servants went to the northern colonies; (3) Virginia and Maryland limited the shipment of white prisoners in 1670 and 1676; (4) the African slave trade was booming because of the quantity available, which made the price of slaves very affordable; and (5) a shortage of white artisans led to the use of slaves.

Economically slavery offered the planters some distinct advantages. The slave code assured that slaves served in perpetuity, and that any offspring belonged to the master and increased his inventory. It was also cheaper to feed and clothe a slave than an indentured servant. The term *negro* would become a synonym for *inferior*. Lists of plantation supplies often described cheap or poorly made items purchased for slaves, such as blankets, as "negro blankets." Although the identification of blacks with slavery occurred gradually elsewhere, it was codified early—by the 1730s—in the south. Unable to get enough white skilled labor, the plantation owners proceeded to train their slaves in the handicraft trades. As self-sufficient economic units, plantations required workers in the wood, leather, cloth, and building trades in addition to field hands.

While it is true that slavery had its roots in economics, the discrimination against blacks by whites actually preceded labor concerns. Skin color made identification (and stigmatization) easy. It was difficult to escape and merge into the general population. Part of the rationale constructed for the justification of slavery was the white belief that blacks could endure a hot climate and were more resistant to malarial diseases than whites. And since black women were considered inferior to white women, planters were justified in assigning them to tasks, particularly work in the fields, that would not be expected of white women. As a result the gender roles of whites and blacks were also stratified and codified. But the code prescribed white behavior

# African Language Survival in the Georgia Sea Islands

African slaves and their descendants have continuously occupied the Sea Islands off the coast of Georgia and South Carolina from the late 17th century. These mainly West African slaves labored on the indigo, rice, and long-staple cotton plantations on the islands and coastal mainland, a region known as the Low Country. The tight-knit Sea Islands slave community formed the majority of the area's population as the prevalence of diseases such as malaria in the swampy environment kept most whites from settling there. Disease also ensured the ongoing integration of new African slaves to replace those who died.

These unique geographic and demographic conditions fostered the development and maintenance of an African-American culture with a strong basis in African customs, traditions, religious beliefs, and language. The Sea Island slaves developed their own English-based language, known as Sea Island Creole, Gullah, or Geechee, terms that are also applied to describe the islanders.

Sea Island Creole was a blending of the pidgin English developed to ease communication between slave traders and their captives along the West African coast, the various West African languages spoken by the slaves, and the English spoken by the South Carolina planters who ultimately purchased them upon their arrival in British America. The result was a new, largely oral language, which became the native language for the Sea Island slave community. Although most of Sea Island Creole's vocabulary is English, a large number of African words are incorporated, and its pronunciation and structure is more similar to that of West African languages. Other African linguistic incorporations include proverbs, oral storytelling, naming practices, and call-and-response-style spirituals.

The Sea Island African-American communities and their unique language have survived into modern times. After the Civil War, they became independent farmers, first in cotton and rice, and later in subsistence farming and fishing. Despite the connections to the mainland established by bridges and causeways, out-migration for employment and education, and an influx of outsiders due to a growing tourism industry, the Sea Islands' distinctive African-American community has sought to preserve its African-based culture and language. Many modern Sea Islanders still reside on the same land that has been inherited from generation to generation. Although Sea Island Creole has evolved over the centuries, its African linguistic roots have survived. Certain Sea Island Creole words have also been adopted into common English usage, mainly in the southeastern United States.

as well as black. In Virginia a white who mingled socially with blacks faced censure. In 1630 the court ordered Hugh Davis to be whipped for "defiling his body in lying with a negro." In 1680 a law was passed prohibiting blacks from having a white indentured servant.

By 1756 blacks outnumbered whites in many communities. They were located mostly in colonies that were adapted to slave labor such as those that produced tobacco, rice, and later, indigo. South Carolina was the greatest rice producer, and Virginia was the leading tobacco colony. Although some whites tried to prohibit the importation of slaves, those who had the most to gain from their commercial interests ignored the protests. As the numbers of slaves grew, white fears grew in direct proportion. Finally, the Virginia slave code, borrowed heavily from practices in the Caribbean, was formalized. Slaves were not permitted to leave plantations without permission. They could be hanged for murder or rape, and lashed, pilloried, whipped, branded, or maimed for lesser offenses. As Virginia's population grew, the connection between race and slavery became solidified in a series of laws meant to regulate the lives of Africans—adults and children—who were sold into lifelong slavery.

Other colonies followed suit. In Maryland slavery came into existence shortly after the first settlements were founded in 1634. In 1659 the colony passed laws relating to the return and treatment of fugitive slaves. The law of 1663 reduced all blacks in the colony to slavery, even though some were already free, and sought to impose slave status on all blacks born in the colony, regardless of the free status of their mothers. In 1671 the legislature declared that the conversion of blacks to Christianity did not affect their status. Planters could now import them, convert them, and still hold them in slavery. By 1750 the population consisted of 40,000 blacks and 100,000 whites.

There was no question that slaves would be imported into the Carolinas, since four of the proprietors of the colony were members

This c.1780s newspaper advertisement offered slaves, some with immunity to smallpox, at Ashley Ferry near the slave-trading hub of Charleston, South Carolina.

of the Royal African Company. Plantation slavery was a cornerstone of the colony's economy, which was based on the cultivation of rice and the processing of indigo. Charleston would become a slave-trading hub. In 1663 the proprietors offered to the original settlers 20 acres for every black male slave and 10 acres for every black female slave brought into the colony in the first year. Twenty years after the original settlements, the black population in the Carolinas was equal to that of the white population. In South Carolina whites adopted slave laws patterned after those of Barbados and Jamaica. In South Carolina in 1698 whites were required to purchase one white servant for every six blacks, which was a form of social control prevalent in the Caribbean sugar islands. As early as 1686 the Carolina colony forbade blacks to engage in any kind of trade, and enjoined them from leaving their masters' plantations without written authorization. In 1724 there were three times as many blacks as whites. Although slave rebellions rarely became full-blown insurrections, the increased population of slaves provoked a few memorable incidents, and exacerbated white fears.

Georgia was the only important New World colony established by England in the 18th century. Originally founded as a colony for poor English, it was to grant no free land titles, permit no use of alcoholic beverages, and allow no slavery. From the time of its establishment in 1733, though, each of these proscriptions was subjected to enormous pressure from the settlers, and one by one the restrictions collapsed. In 1750 the prohibition against slavery was repealed, and from that point on, slavery flourished. Georgia's slave code, adopted in 1755, echoed that of South Carolina. By the time of the American Revolution, blacks outnumbered whites in Georgia.

## THE STONO REBELLION

In 1739 the Stono Rebellion (also known as Cato's Conspiracy) began 20 miles west of Charleston, South Carolina. Led by an Angolan named Jemmy, 20 slaves (most of them newly arrived from Africa) killed two guards in a warehouse, secured weapons, and then went on a crusade to destroy slavery in that area. Eventually comprised of about 100 slaves, they then headed for the Florida territory, then under the Spanish, who welcomed and freed escaping slaves from the British colonies as a military buffer against British incursion into Spanish territory. The uprising was quelled by the colonial militia with the help of Native Americans, but not for several days, and not before 30 whites and 44 blacks lost their lives.

Although the reasons remain unclear, the Stono Rebellion may have been sparked by the soon-to-be enacted Security Act, which required all white men to carry firearms to church on Sundays—traditionally a time when slaves were given release from labor. In reaction to Stono, whites quickly passed a Negro Act that prohibited slaves from growing their own food, assembling in groups, earning their own money, or learning to read.

# Slave Rebellions in the Colonial Period

Slave rebellions in the colonial period, also known as revolts or insurrections, were smaller in size than their 19th-century counterparts such as Nat Turner's 1831 rebellion. Slave rebellions were more common in the Spanish and Portuguese colonies in Central and South America, and the European colonies in the West Indies, than in British North America. Although deliberately slow work, breaking tools, stealing, feigning illness or injury, running away, and other tactics were more common methods by which slaves avenged their captivity; full-scale rebellions were the most dreaded. Groups of slaves most likely to rebel included field hands, who generally worked under the most brutal conditions; slaves who enjoyed relative freedom, which gave them more opportunity to plan; and slaves in areas where they formed a majority of the population.

The most well known colonial rebellions occurred in New York City and South Carolina. The 1712 New York City rebellion began when several dozen armed slaves set fire to a building and ambushed any whites who responded, killing several. Militia put down the rebellion and pursued the survivors, some of whom committed suicide. Twenty-seven people were eventually charged, with 21 executed. The ensuing fear was still present when a series of robberies and arsons plagued the city in 1741; this led panicked residents to believe another rebellion had begun. Over 150 slaves and 25 whites were charged, with many of the accused slaves either executed or sent to the West Indies. During the 1739 Stono Rebellion in South Carolina, approximately 100 armed slaves attempted to escape to Spanish Florida, gathering new recruits as they traveled. Militia put down the revolt, which resulted in the deaths of more than 40 slaves and 30 whites.

Although there were few notable colonial slave rebellions, the possibility spread fear among the white population, especially in southern colonies where slaves were in the majority. Many colonies passed harsh legal slave codes governing behavior and punishment, in part as a response to this fear. The first slave codes appeared in the West Indies, while the first mainland British colony to enact a slave code was Virginia in 1682. Slaves were required to carry passes when traveling off the plantation, and forbidden from meeting in large numbers to aid in the prevention of rebellions. Free blacks, viewed as bad examples, also faced restrictions and accusations of fomenting rebellions. Common punishments for planning or participating in a rebellion included castration, branding, or being burned alive.

## THE ROOTS OF ABOLITIONISM

In London in 1701 the Anglican Church founded the Society for the Propagation of the Gospel in Foreign Parts (SPG), one of whose purposes was missionary work among blacks and Native Americans. The SPG missionaries tried to raise the level of living both among whites and blacks. They suggested that slaves be given time to study the scriptures, and learn to read and write. In many cases they taught slaves themselves. Four years after its founding the society established a black school in New York City. This was followed 40 years later by the Charleston, South Carolina, Negro School, in which two former slaves (Harry and Andrew) owned by the SPG became teachers, having been trained and freed for that purpose. The SPG also cooperated with another Anglican group to establish schools in Philadelphia, Williamsburg, and Newport, aided in part by support from Benjamin Franklin. Since the SPG sanctioned slavery, planters did not object to the activities of the SPG. More forceful voices would, however, soon continue to humanize slaves through education, and directly attack the immorality of the slave trade.

## QUAKER REFORMERS

As early as 1700 three leading Friends (Quakers) publicly advocated taking steps for the mental improvement of the slaves: Quaker founder George Fox, proprietor William Penn, and George Keith of Philadelphia, whose followers had published the first antislavery tract in British America in 1693. Unique to Quakers among denominational groups was the belief that religious instruction was a step toward physical emancipation, as well as a means of spiritual salvation. During the first half of the following century, a half-dozen Quaker reformers, the greatest of whom was John Woolman, sounded the condemnation of slavery. Woolman had toured the southern colonies in 1746 and traveled extensively in an effort to convince fellow religionists of their Christian obligation toward their slaves. He expressed his deep reservation in his 1753 publication *Some Considerations on the Keeping of Negroes,* and recorded his feelings in his journal, in which he wrote:

> *My employer, having a negro woman, sold her, and desired me to write a bill of sale, the man being waiting who bought her. The thing was sudden; and though I felt uneasy at the thoughts of writing an instrument of slavery for one of my fellow-creatures, yet I remembered that I was hired by the year, that it was my master who directed me to do it, and that it was an elderly man, a member of our Society, who bought her; so through weakness I gave way, and wrote it; but at the executing of it I was so afflicted in my mind, that I said before my master and the Friend that I believed slave-keeping to be a practice inconsistent with the Christian religion.*

Woolman's close friend and coworker was Anthony Benezet. The leading antislavery propagandist in pre–Revolutionary War America, Benezet compiled and distributed abolitionist books and pamphlets. But perhaps his greatest passion was preparing blacks for their freedom by teaching them to read and write. Benezet, a school-teacher of poor white children by day and black children by night, denounced slavery. He was the key figure in the operation of a school for slaves founded in Philadelphia in 1770. The school had a handful of white students—six out of 46 in 1775—but its basic reason for existence remained that of discharging a duty "to those oppressed people." He may also have been the first to equate black cognitive ability with that of whites by demonstrating that blacks could learn. The influence of Quakers also led Rhode Island in 1784, in freeing its slaves, to stipulate that their children be taught to read and write.

In the south, Quakers in North Carolina urged the establishment of regular meetings of slaves, and Quaker slaveholders were urged to treat their blacks well. Since North Carolina had a small black population and a considerable Quaker population, no significant slave insurrections took place there during the colonial period. Before the end of the colonial period there was some sentiment among Quakers to discourage members from purchasing slaves. Finally, in 1770 the organization described the slave trade as "an iniquitous practice" and sought its prohibition. The Quakers would continue to struggle with abolition, however. In some states yearly conferences would eventually split over the issue of slavery and abolition.

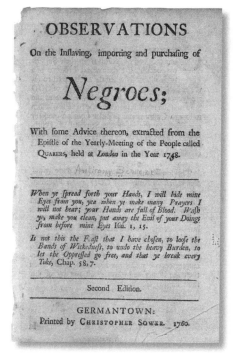

This antislavery pamphlet by Anthony Benezet was published in 1760.

## THE LEGAL INVENTION OF AMERICAN SLAVERY

Gradually the slave codes would be reinforced by cases that were processed through the legal system, providing a history of the invention of American slavery through case studies. In Virginia in 1641, John Graweere was a slave for William Evans. Evans permitted Graweere to keep hogs for himself, but he had to give half of the "increase" to Evans. Graweere had a young child by a black woman, who belonged to Lieutenant Robert Sheppard, whom he wanted to Christianize. He bought the child's freedom and the court ordered that the child was to be free of Evans and raised by Graweere. This is significant, as Graweere had to purchase the child's freedom before Christianizing him. In

1641 freedom preceded baptism, instead of resulting from it as was previously the case. And if Graweere had been white, no such court proceeding would have been required to confirm his right to purchase property and deny his master the right to it.

Race-based punishments and privileges began in 1630, when Hugh Davis was whipped for having intercourse with a black woman. These early punishments against whites reflected religious and cultural practices that were in force at the time. As the slave codes of the various colonies became codified, the conditions of relations between blacks and whites and the evisceration of the rights of slaves were refined and expanded. In Maryland in 1664, all blacks already in servitude were ordered to serve forever, along with their children. Although slave status and racial boundaries were originally fluid, they became hardened with the increase in the numbers of slaves and the identification of race with slavery. When this latter occurred, even free blacks faced restrictions. It was ultimately left up to the colonies, presaging the tradition of states' rights, to establish rules of conduct for black slaves. As a result slave codes varied according to local cultural and religious norms. For example, although South Carolina developed the most severe racial code in English North America, it tolerated interracial sex, but only sex between black women and white men.

## AFRICANS BECOMING AMERICAN

Gradually African traditions merged with Christian practice and beliefs to create new kinds of religious communities and expressions of faith. The Great Awakening, a religious movement during the 1730s and 1740s, offered inspirational messages and promises of salvation made by itinerant preachers. Traveling to remote areas, these preachers spurred enthusiasm among people who wanted to Christianize slaves. The Awakening left a legacy of a type of religion that was more evangelical and emotional than earlier Calvinistic forms. The informal camp meetings of the Great Awakening included singing and dancing, and the preaching conveyed a more comforting and hopeful message than that of earlier Protestant sects.

Blending African traditions with this new American expression, the songs of slaves gave birth to slave spirituals, which would eventually become known as negro spirituals. Slaves who came from cultures in Africa relied on drumming as a means of communication and personal expression. Whites feared this, so slaves were not allowed to play drums. On slave ships, slaves would use the wood of the hull to communicate with others and appeal to the ancestors. Eventually they began to use their bodies as an instrument. Over time, the hand clapping, foot stomping, body thumping, and thigh slapping evolved into a dance called *patting juba*. It was performed by whites adorned in blackface in minstrel shows, which lampooned African Americans. This was not the only tradition that whites would borrow. In

South Carolina, whites drew on slaves' knowledge of rice cultivation, much like earlier settlers in New England had drawn upon Native-American agricultural knowledge.

## STIRRINGS OF AFRICAN-AMERICAN PATRIOTISM

On the eve of the Revolutionary War, there was growing hostility to the slave trade and resistance on the part of blacks themselves. Opposition to the slave trade was rooted in the fear of slave insurrections. When blacks became numerous enough to endanger the status quo, colonial legislatures acted to prohibit the foreign slave trade outright, or to place heavy import duties on it. This, however, widened the rift between England and the colonies because the parliament and British shipowners did not want to do this. In the years preceding the war, colony after colony expressed displeasure concerning slave importations from abroad. The Massachusetts legislature passed anti–slave trade measures in 1771 and 1774, but the royal governor prevented them from becoming law. In 1774 both Rhode Island and Connecticut voted to prohibit the slave trade. In 1773 Pennsylvania levied a stiff duty on each imported slave. Three southern colonies passed restrictive measures in 1774 and 1775.

There were several reasons for this: (1) any increase in the number of slaves increased white fears of an uprising; (2) it was an attempt to strike back at the English Parliament for passing objectionable laws that the colonists were forced to obey; and (3) the beliefs and rhetoric of a philosophy of human freedom were now gaining momentum as the foundation was laid for separation from England. Slaves were not immune from this philosophy and political ferment. The slogans of liberty, especially in New England, influenced the slaves to use freedom suits and petitions to gain their freedom.

In freedom suits, the slave, charging that his liberty was being "restrained," took his master to court. The best known of these suits was the Jenny Slew case in 1766. Born about 1719 to a white woman and a black man, she was living as a free woman in 1762 because her mother was free. But then she was kidnapped and enslaved. Her owner said that since she had been married, she couldn't sue on her own behalf independently of a husband. But she had been married to slaves, so any marriage was not considered legal. Slew successfully brought charges against her owner, and the court awarded her "the sum of four pounds lawful money of this Province" as damages. The procedure had its drawbacks. It was expensive, slow, and individual. It did not establish a broad principle of universal freedom, since the verdict extended only to the parties immediately involved.

In Massachusetts in 1773, a group of slaves petitioned the legislature to liberate them, rightfully claiming: "We have no Property! We have no Wives! We have no Children! No City! No Country!" In 1774 slaves in Massachusetts sent another petition to Boston, stating that they had a right to their freedom. But neither the governor nor the legislature was inclined to grant relief, and the

At the Boston Massacre on March 5, 1770, former slave Crispus Attucks became a martyr for the patriot cause.

legislature tabled both requests. Beyond suits and petitions, a more direct way to obtain liberty was by taking part in the struggle between the colonies and England in 1775. To become a soldier was one way to gain one's freedom. Since manpower shortages often outweighed white reluctance to give blacks a gun, it was entirely possible that blacks would be allowed to bear arms. In fact blacks had set a precedent by serving in the colonial militia. In the French and Indian War, both northern and southern colonies used black soldiers. Colonial clergyman and historian Jeremy Belknap (1744–98) expressed the belief that in Massachusetts the number of slaves had declined by 1763 "because in the two preceding wars, many of them were enlisted either into the army or on board vessels of war, with a view to procure their freedom."

On the night of March 5, 1770, a crowd of blacks and white sailors in Boston started taunting the guard at the customhouse. The action might have been precipitated three days earlier, when a fight broke out between Boston rope makers and British soldiers. When seven other redcoats came to his rescue, the crowd started throwing snowballs and brickbats at the British regiment. When the soldiers fired into the crowd, a runaway slave named Crispus Attucks was the first to die. His fame and that of the other four victims was fanned by the public funeral held three days after the tragic event. Patriots dubbed the event the Boston Massacre, and its victims became symbols of liberty. During the court trial Attucks was accused of being a rabble-rouser, rather than a patriot. Nevertheless he became an early martyr of the coming revolution.

The words of the Declaration of Independence, which suggested that the war was being waged to extend the boundaries of human freedom and the rights of men, must have conveyed hope to enslaved blacks. Approved by the Continental Congress on July 4, 1776, its soaring rhetoric appealed to the oppressed. It stated that all men were created equal and endowed with certain rights that could not be taken away, among them life, liberty, and the pursuit of happiness. It was a message that blacks could apply to their personal situations, rather than to a largely symbolic king. If blacks did take up the cause against the king, it was likely that they associated him with the English slave trade and the middle passage. However only in New England did the alliance of blacks with the patriot cause lead to emancipation; in Virginia, by contrast, blacks were enlisted in the Loyalist cause, further defining their changing status in the post-revolutionary period.

## CONCLUSION

In 1991 the African Burial Ground in Manhattan, dating back to 1690, was unearthed during a construction project. It is estimated that approximately 15,000 enslaved and free Africans had been buried at the site over the course of 100 years. Similar sacred grounds have been unearthed in Portsmouth, New Hampshire (in 2006), and Shockoe Bottom, Richmond, Virginia. In Shockoe Bottom the Burial Ground for Negroes was used from the late 1700s to the early 1800s. Now a private parking lot owned by a real estate firm, the calls to protect the site are insistent. These silent spaces continue to bear witness to the history and experience of Africans becoming African Americans during the colonial period.

JAYNE R. BEILKE
BALL STATE UNIVERSITY

## Further Reading

Adler, Mortimer J., ed., et al. *The Negro in American History, Vol. III, Slaves and Masters, 1567–1854.* New York: Encyclopedia Britannica Educational Corporation, 1969.

Berlin, Ira. *Many Thousands Gone: The First Two Centuries of Slavery in North America.* Cambridge, MA: Harvard University Press, 1998.

Gates, Henry Louis, Jr. *The Trials of Phillis Wheatley: America's First Black Poet and Encounters with the Founding Fathers.* New York: Basic Civitas Books, 2003.

Greene, Lorenzo J. *The Negro in Colonial New England, 1620–1776.* New York: Columbia University Press, 1942.

Jackson, Maurice. *Let This Voice Be Heard: Anthony Benezet, Father of Atlantic Abolitionism.* Philadelphia: University of Pennsylvania Press, 2009.

Morgan, Philip D. *Slave Counterpoint: Black Culture in the 18th-Century Chesapeake and Lowcountry.* Chapel Hill: University of North Carolina Press, 1998.

Rediker, Marcus. *The Slave Ship: A Human History*. New York: Viking, 2007.

Shorto, Russell. *The Island at the Center of the World: The Epic Story of Dutch Manhattan and the Forgotten Colony that Shaped America*. New York: Doubleday, 2004.

Thornton, John. "The African Experience of the '20 and Odd Negroes' Arriving in Virginia in 1619." *William and Mary Quarterly*, v.55/3 (July 1998).

# CHAPTER 2

# The American Revolution: 1775 to 1783

**BY 1775 SLAVES** in the American colonies totaled some 500,000—about one-fifth of the total colonial American population. There may have been as many as 40,000 free blacks as well, most in the north, but some living south of the Mason-Dixon line separating Pennsylvania and Maryland. African Americans participated in every phase of the American Revolution, from the polarizing events of the Boston Massacre in 1770 to the surrender of British general Lord Cornwallis at Yorktown, Virginia, in 1781. Regardless of their contribution, African Americans would participate little in the gains of the American Revolution, which tended to reward white, property-owning, adult males.

For most of the colonial era, blacks had fought alongside whites in a series of conflicts. In South Carolina they had fought against Native Americans and Spanish and French troops. The Stono slave rebellion of 1739, however, sparked fear of arming slaves, and South Carolina prohibited black militia service. In other colonies the practice continued. African Americans saw extensive service in the French and Indian War. Many slaves served in both army regiments and naval units as a way to earn their freedom; free blacks used service as a way to improve social status. Historian Jack Foner said black service in the war "explained the decline in the number of slaves in Massachusetts by 1763." Much of the African-American involvement in the early stages of the American Revolution came from New England.

In 1774 the First Continental Congress approved the creation of "minutemen" regiments in the Massachusetts militia. These quick-response units would provide a first line of defense if British troops, then massing in greater numbers in Boston, moved aggressively into the Massachusetts interior. Massachusetts permitted enlistment of blacks, and many quickly enrolled. African Americans were present at the battles of Lexington and Concord on April 19, 1775, the first day of the American Revolution. Noted African-American historian Benjamin Quarles said that among them were the black soldiers "Pomp Blackman, who later served in the Continental army, and Prince Eastabrook, a casualty." African Americans also helped white militiamen besiege redcoats in Boston following those fights.

## AFRICAN AMERICANS AT THE BATTLE OF BUNKER HILL

African Americans distinguished themselves again at the Battle of Bunker Hill on June 17, 1775. In fact as much as five percent of the American army there may have been African American. American militia had bottled up British troops outside Boston by taking high ground encircling Boston Harbor and confining the redcoats to the lower expanses near the water. The standoff was not entirely a siege because the British could have boarded naval vessels and left. However British commander William Howe refused such a move, not wanting it to appear to be a cowardly retreat. Rather he massed his forces and, in a series of attacks on June 17, attempted to push Americans off the heights. The Americans left, but only after inflicting heavy casualties on Howe's troops and in the face of a British flanking maneuver. The British claimed a victory, but they had paid dearly for it.

Among the American combatants was an African American named Salem Poor, a member of the Fifth Massachusetts Regiment. He had joined the unit five days after the war began. His exact activities at Bunker Hill remain unclear, but they were heroic enough to draw the attention of his white commanders. Colonel Jonathan Brewer and 13 other officers drafted a petition of commendation to send to the Massachusetts state legislature "in justice to the Caracter of so Brave a Man." They said that to "set forth the Particulars of his Conduct would be 'tedious;' however, Poor acted like "an Experienced officer, as well as an Excellent Soldier ... We would only begg leave to Say in the Person of the Negro Centers a Brave and gallant Soldier." They left any reward for Poor up to the congress. Some scholars have argued that in spite of the commendation, the officers' petition bears a latent hint of racism, in that singling out Poor for such a commendation indicates a measure of surprise that an African American could execute such heroism in battle.

Also at Bunker Hill was an African American with a similar name, Peter Salem. Salem had been a slave in Framingham, Massachusetts, and had recently joined the rebel militia. Salem has long been credited with killing British Major John Pitcairn, a Royal Marine commander, during the battle. He reportedly fired the fatal shot as Pitcairn bounded to the top of a battlement shouting, "the day is ours!"

While Salem's act has never been fully substantiated, the identity of the victim may actually help to validate it. Pitcairn was the commander of British troops who had fired on American militiamen at Lexington on April 19, starting the Revolutionary War. Thus, Pitcairn was considered something of a villain throughout New England. That a generation of American rebels willingly credited the death of this man to an African American lends truth to the story.

Salem Poor and Peter Salem were not the only African Americans fighting at Bunker Hill. Historians Franklin and Moss describe the others as "Caesar Brown of Westford, Massachusetts, who was killed in action; Barzillai Lew, a fifer and drummer; Titus Colburn and Alexander Ames of Andover; Prince Hall, later an abolitionist and Masonic Leader, and many other Massachusetts Negroes: Cuff Hayes, Caesar Dickerson, Cato Tufts, Grant Cooper, and Sampson Talbert."

## CONGRESS DISALLOWS AFRICAN AMERICANS

Meritorious service at Bunker Hill did not necessarily guarantee African Americans full participation in the Revolution. The colonial practice of granting freedom to slaves who gave armed service scared revolutionary-era slaveholders into opposing their use in the new war. On May 20, 1775, the Massachusetts Committee of Safety passed a resolution prohibiting the enrollment of slaves as "inconsistent with the procedures that are to be supported." In short, the enlistment of slaves and their potential manumission ran counter to one of the pillars of Locke's Natural Rights for which the colonists were fighting—the right to own property. Historian Foner notes that "other colonies followed the example of Massachusetts."

The move to ban African Americans from service soon became national. On June 17, 1775, the very day of Bunker Hill, the Second Continental Congress took control of all patriot armies

James Armistead, an African-American slave who volunteered to spy for the patriots, appears beside General Lafayette in this 1783 painting.

This 1853 illustration shows George Washington at Mount Vernon with his slaves, who are harvesting grain. Washington at first tried to ban African Americans from fighting in the Revolution.

in an attempt to unify their efforts. At the suggestion of Massachusetts delegate John Adams, the congress appointed Virginian George Washington as general-in-chief of the entire army. Washington was a respected plantation owner, businessman, surveyor, and statesman with experience in the Virginia colonial militia, the French and Indian War, and the Virginia House of Burgesses.

A slaveholder himself, Washington agreed with the exclusion of slaves from the patriot armies. Washington well understood the manpower problems the new army would face; he also did not question African Americans' willingness or ability to fight. He did, however, know that distinguishing a free black from a runaway slave would always be difficult. So on July 9, 1775, Washington issued an order for recruiters and mustering agents to not allow "any stroller, Negro, or vagabond" into the Continental ranks. He did not say anything about discharging blacks already in service.

On October 8 Washington and a council of his top generals took up the issue again, this time more vigorously. The officers agreed that they should make no "distinction between such as are slaves and those who are free," and they moved to "reject negroes altogether." Two weeks later, the Second Continental Congress affirmed that action.

Something else fueled these exclusionary decisions—sectionalism. Adams had suggested Washington to lead the Continental army in part because, among his other qualifications, he was a southerner. Adams knew, as did Washington and Benjamin Franklin, that to succeed, American efforts had to be continental, not regional. New Englanders could not hold the line against British troops if southerners were only to turn their backs on those gains. There would be no quicker way to alienate southerners from the revolution than to make southern troops march side-by-side with African Americans, whom they considered inferior. The issues of slavery and racism, as it would be so many times in American history, would have to be put off until later.

## LORD DUNMORE'S GAMBIT

The British understood the potentially divisive nature of American slavery as well as the colonials. In late 1775 they moved to exploit it. As early as June 1775, General Thomas Gage, the chief British commander in Boston, suggested to Lord William Barrington, British secretary-at-war, that they "avail ourselves of every resource" and enlist African Americans, either runaway slaves or freemen who felt no part of the revolution, into the British army.

Nothing came of the suggestion until November 1775, when John Murray, Lord Dunmore, the royal governor of Virginia, put the suggestion into effect. As revolutionary fervor swept Virginia, Dunmore abandoned his quarters in Williamsburg and set up office aboard the HMS *William* at anchor off Norfolk, Virginia. From there he drafted an invitation to colonial blacks to join the British army—any slaves who bolted from their masters and joined would receive their freedom. Dunmore reasoned that such a move would pad the British army's superior manpower, deprive the Continentals of a potential manpower pool should they decide to use it, and demoralize southern colonials, perhaps to the point of capitulation.

"I do hereby ... declare," wrote Dunmore, "all indented servants, Negroes, or others, (appertaining to Rebels), free, that are able and willing to bear arms, they joining His Majesty's troops, as soon as may be, for the more speedily reducing this Colony to a proper sense of duty to His Majesty's crown and dignity." He signed the proclamation on November 7, 1775.

African-American response to Dunmore's proclamation was immediate. By December, at least 300 runaways had joined Dunmore's newly created Ethiopian Regiment. Their British uniforms were adorned with the phrase "Liberty to Slaves." The significance of Dunmore's proclamation was long term. Thomas Jefferson estimated that Virginia lost more than 30,000 slaves by 1778; historians have estimated that South Carolina lost some 25,000 slaves, and Georgia about 11,250 during the war.

## BATTLE OF GREAT BRIDGE

Dunmore put his Ethiopian Regiment into combat December 9, 1775, in what came to be known as the Battle of Great Bridge. Seeking to capitalize on Tory sympathy in Norfolk, Dunmore returned to shore. Learning that Americans were massing south of the town, he opted to fortify a bridge some 10 miles south of Norfolk and meet the colonials there if they attacked. The Americans also moved closer and built their own defenses. Dunmore, who had only 409 men including the runaway slaves, did not realize that the Americans numbered more than 850. In fact, he had fallen victim to an African-American double agent whom the Americans had sent into his lines to feed him false information about the colonials' strength. In the ensuing fight, Americans decimated Dunmore's army and forced Dunmore to abandon the town and again take refuge on a ship. In early January 1776, American sniping from Norfolk prompted Dunmore to order a shelling of the town, which virtually destroyed it.

Dunmore ultimately took refuge on Gwyn Island in the Chesapeake, from where he attempted to launch desultory raids against rebellious Virginia. In early June Americans took the island and dispersed Dunmore and his remaining force. Among the wreckage of Dunmore's camp, the Americans found a muster sheet from late May indicating that Dunmore had at least 150 African-American soldiers remaining, as well as 50 African-American women who had been

One of Lord Dunmore's Ethiopian Regiment is shown at left in combat alongside British troops in this 1784 painting by John Singleton Copley. The soldier wears the regiment's distinct uniform, which was said to be embroidered with the phrase "Liberty to Slaves."

# Black Loyalists

During the American Revolutionary War, the British offered black slaves in the American colonies the opportunity to gain their freedom if they successfully escaped to the British lines and served the British military effort. Later offers also promised grants of land and provisions to aid in postwar resettlement. These men and their families became known as Black Loyalists. Some Black Loyalists served in royal and provincial military units, but the majority served in civil units as combat troops, scouts, guides, drummers, trumpeters, laborers, servants, and other support positions. Well known Black Loyalist units included the Ethiopian Regiment, the Black Pioneers, and the Black Brigade. When the war ended in 1783, those Black Loyalists who had not been recaptured into slavery left with the British and white Loyalists for other parts of the British Empire. The largest group of Black Loyalists, numbering approximately 3,500, resettled in the British colony of Nova Scotia.

Nova Scotia struggled to incorporate the large wave of Loyalist settlers in the postwar period. Many Black Loyalists established their own communities, while others settled in predominantly white Loyalist settlements. The Black Loyalist settlement known as Birchtown became the largest free black town outside of Africa. The distribution system for the land grants and provisions promised to all Loyalists was based on both race and class, and marred by governmental corruption and incompetence. Consequently most Black Loyalists did not receive any benefits. Those that received land had difficulty establishing successful farms because of the small grants, poor soil, and harsh climate. Those who worked for white employers faced high unemployment rates, lower wages, and other forms of discrimination. Community leader Thomas Peters, already well known for his military service, submitted several failed government petitions for better treatment. He then began recruiting for the new British colony of Sierra Leone in West Africa.

British businessmen and former abolitionists had established the Sierra Leone Company in part to aid those blacks who had been suffering from similar poverty, unemployment, and discrimination in Britain. Sierra Leone's first settlers, recruited from Britain, arrived in 1778 facing harsh conditions, short supplies, and disputes with various local tribes. The original settlement was destroyed in 1789. The Sierra Leone Company then turned to Nova Scotia for new settlers to repopulate the colony with the aid of Thomas Peters. Approximately 1,200 Black Loyalists from Nova Scotia sailed for Sierra Leone on January 15, 1792, aboard 15 ships. The new arrivals established the settlement of Freetown. Descendents of the original Black Loyalists remained in both Nova Scotia and Sierra Leone in subsequent generations.

following the Ethiopian Regiment. The regiment disbanded with Dunmore's departure. By that time, however, Americans had begun calling African Americans who had enlisted with the British army the Black Banditti.

## CONTINENTAL ARMY RELAXES ITS POLICIES

American responses to Lord Dunmore's enlistment of African Americans were immediate. In Virginia the colonial government guaranteed full pardons for runaway slaves who returned from Dunmore's lines. At Continental army headquarters, Washington also softened his position. Realizing that many of the black veterans of the first months of the Revolution whom he had turned out of the army were now dissatisfied and threatening to join the British, Washington reversed his policy and agreed to allow them to reenlist. On January 16, 1776, the Second Continental Congress agreed, making it clear the enlistments would only include free blacks who had served in the Boston area.

Those policy reversals ignited a string of similar moves at the state level, which effectively changed the character of the Continental army. The Continental Congress approved something of a quasi-draft to ensure state manpower quotas, and in 1776 New York agreed that free African Americans could act as substitutes for drafted whites. Later New York approved freedom for slaves who served three years in the army, as well as land payments to their former masters. New Hampshire offered enlistment bounties to free blacks and land bounties to owners who would free slaves who then enlisted as freedmen. Rhode Island, Connecticut, and Massachusetts all followed suit with similar enlistment plans. In the south, Virginia and North Carolina began allowing free African Americans into service; however South Carolina and Georgia remained opposed to black service. Nevertheless these steps would allow some 5,000 African Americans to serve in the Continental army during the war.

## WITH WASHINGTON CROSSING THE DELAWARE

Washington changed his opinion of blacks in military service early in the war. He took at least one with him on one of his most famous exploits of the war: crossing the Delaware River to attack Hessian mercenary soldiers at Trenton, New Jersey.

Washington had spent most of 1776 in retreat. He had lost Long Island and New York City to the British in August, and spent the autumn evading them in New Jersey and Pennsylvania. In truth he was smartly handling his army, part of what he called a "strategic defensive." He knew that his small army could not go head-to-head with the British and win. Rather he would take advantage of his more mobile force, periodically engage the British, then disperse to fight again. If it worked, the continentals might wear out the British army, effectively negating their larger size, training, and resources. But it was not good for American morale; nothing satisfied quite like a battlefield victory.

*Emanuel Gottlieb Leutze's famous painting* Washington Crossing the Delaware. *Leutze depicted African-American soldier Prince Whipple among the rowers at the bow of the boat.*

Washington saw his opportunity at Trenton. Recognizing that the Hessians garrisoned there would likely be less than effective after Christmas celebrations, he determined to attack them on the morning of December 26. That entailed crossing his army to the New Jersey side of the ice-choked Delaware River on Christmas night. The crossing was difficult and time consuming, but it worked, and the American army beat the Hessians at Trenton that morning.

Making the crossing with Washington were possibly two African Americans who have become famous in the lore of African-American soldiers. Their names were Prince Whipple and Oliver Cromwell.

Cromwell had been born free in Black Horse, New Jersey, in 1752. At the beginning of the war he joined the Second New Jersey Regiment. He subsequently campaigned with Washington's army at Trenton, Princeton, Brandywine, Monmouth, and Yorktown. Washington commended Cromwell upon the latter's dismissal from the army in 1783.

Whipple's story, however, is less clear. Generations of historians have accepted that Whipple also crossed the Delaware with Washington, but recent information suggests otherwise. Whipple, unlike most of that generation of African Americans, had actually been born in Africa. He had become a bodyguard of a General Whipple from New Hampshire, and had thus found his way into Continental service. He had been on Washington's retreat from Long Island.

Whipple's notoriety comes from the fact that 19th-century romantic painter Emanuel Gottlieb Leutze included him in the famous painting *Washington Crossing the Delaware*. Leutze positioned Whipple at the bow of Washington's boat, straining with an oar along with other oarsmen to make the crossing a remarkable success.

In an article for the 225th anniversary of the crossing, historian Richard S. Walling says that although Whipple was involved in Washington's other campaigns, he was not on the crossing or at Trenton. Other popular sources support that interpretation. Walling says the story of Whipple on the crossing originates with 19th-century historian William C. Nell who, in 1855, wrote *Colored Patriots of the Revolution.* At that time disputes over slavery were driving the United States toward civil war, and Nell sought out hundreds of stories to prove that blacks had been central to the American Revolution. He submitted that Whipple had been with Washington on the crossing.

Leutze, the painter, took the story and embedded it in the American psyche when he painted Whipple in the bow of Washington's boat. The German-born Leutze was a liberal in the European democratic revolutions of the mid-19th century. As Walling writes, "Leutze sought to both pay homage to the first modern democratic revolution, and to inspire his fellow Europeans by the idealism of the American Revolution." Thus Whipple took a seat at the front of the boat. Walling says Nell and Leutze "used symbolism [Whipple] to inspire and remind Americans of the vision of a nation of free men and women."

## RADICAL RHODE ISLAND

1776 and 1777 saw the United States officially declare its independence from Great Britain, lose New York and Philadelphia to British troops, and ultimately win the support of France by beating the British at the Battle of Saratoga. By the end of 1777, George Washington's arm of the Continental army was encamped at Valley Forge near Philadelphia; despite advances in the war, manpower was a huge problem for the Americans. Enlistment of blacks certainly helped, but it was scattershot. As historian Fritz Hirschfeld has noted, "to Rhode Island belongs the credit for being the first state to meld successfully a cohesive group of slaves into the overall war effort."

On January 2, 1778, Brigadier General James Varnum, a Rhode Island attorney who had commanded troops from that state since the beginning of the war, suggested to Washington that the recruitment of a "Battalion of Negroes" would go far in helping Rhode Island meet its manpower quota. Varnum's suggestion was radical. He did not advocate mixing blacks into white regiments, which Continentals had spent two years becoming accustomed to, but rather a battalion composed almost entirely of African Americans. They would continue to be officered by whites, but Varnum's idea was a milestone, one that was no doubt informed by Dunmore's Ethiopian Regiment two years earlier.

Washington quickly endorsed the plan and forwarded it to Nicholas Cooke, governor of Rhode Island. Cooke, in turn, gave it to the Rhode Island Gen-

# Establishing the First Rhode Island Regiment

In February 1778, the Rhode Island General Assembly passed a milestone act creating the first all-African-American battalion in the Continental army. The assembly's proclamation read, in part:

. . . whereas, history affords us frequent Precedents of the wisest, the freest, and bravest nations having liberated their Slaves, and inlisted them as Soldiers to fight in Defence of their Country; and also, whereas, the Enemy, with a great force, have taken Posession of the Capital and of a great Part of this State; and this State is obliged to raise a very considerable Number of Troops for its own immediate Defence, whereby it is in a Manner rendered impossible for this State to furnish Recruits ... without adopting the said Measure so recommended:

It is Voted and Resolved, that every able-bodied negro, mulatto, or Indian man slave, in this state, may inlist ... to serve during the continuance of the present war with Great Britain: that every slave so inlisting shall be entitled to and receive all the bounties, wages, and encouragements allowed by the Continental Congress to any soldier inlisting into their service.

It is further Voted and Resolved, That every slave so inlisting shall, upon his passing muster before Col. Christopher Greene, be immediately discharged from the service of his master or mistress, and be absolutely FREE, as though he had never been incumbered with any kind of servitude or slavery.

A French soldier and artist made this watercolor image of a black soldier in the First Rhode Island Regiment in the early 1780s.

eral Assembly, which adopted it in February. The resulting all-black unit was designated the First Rhode Island Regiment of 1777. Connecticut soon followed suit with the creation of the Second Company of the Fourth Connecticut Regiment.

Just as his army was changing, George Washington was changing as well. Although he would have met the suggestion with a resounding "no" in 1775, now the exigencies of war made him more practical. Historian Hirschfeld writes that "Washington, a Southerner himself, demonstrated his ability to rise above certain inborn and ingrained prejudices." That ability allowed him to listen to "young liberal-minded progressives [like Varnum and others who] argued convincingly in favor of recruiting African Americans as soldiers, organizing them into military units, and eventually freeing them."

## THE FIRST RHODE ISLAND IN COMBAT

By July 6, 1778, the First Rhode Island numbered 19 commissioned officers, 144 noncommissioned officers, and men grouped in four companies. The later addition of another company raised total enlistments to 226. Colonel Christopher Greene was their commander. Greene had successfully led black troops in combat against Hessian mercenaries near the Delaware River the previous year.

Within two months, Greene's First Rhode Island was in combat against British regular troops and Hessian mercenaries hired to help the British in the Revolution. The British troops had been consolidating in Rhode Island, largely on Aquidnek Island, to move either southwest against New York City, or north against New England. To check the threat, General Nathanael Greene, one of George Washington's most trusted lieutenants and a cousin of Christopher Greene, took an element of the Continental army, including the First Rhode Island, to engage the British.

The ensuing Battle of Rhode Island on August 29, 1778, saw the Continentals disperse the British and Hessians, but not until after seven hours of hot, brutal fighting. The African-American soldiers in the First Rhode Island Regiment clashed with wave after wave of Hessians. In an oft-recounted telling of the battle, historian Samuel G. Arnold writes, "It was in repelling these furious onsets, that the newly raised black regiment, under Col. Greene, distinguished itself by deeds of desperate valor. Posted behind a thicket in the valley, they three times drove back the Hessians who charged repeatedly down the hill to dislodge them." Arnold's account would seemingly have the black troops turning the tide of battle all alone. However subsequent historians have clarified the regiment's role in the battle, and it was strong generalship by Nathanael Greene that carried the day.

The First Rhode Island Regiment of African Americans remained constituted until the war's end. On May 4, 1781, the regiment fought a Tory unit at Points Bridge on the Croton River in New York. There the regiment suffered a dreadful blow when Colonel Greene fell mortally wounded. Historian George Livermore colorfully writes that, "the sabers of the enemy reached ... [Greene's] body only through the limbs of his faithful guard of blacks, who hovered over him and protected him, every one of whom was killed, and whom he was not ashamed to call his children."

Lieutenant Colonel Jeremiah Olney commanded the First Rhode Island Regiment for the rest of the war. Their service included a turn in the trenches at Yorktown, Virginia, where Washington's army defeated the British under

# African Americans at Sea

African Americans also found service in the navy of the new United States. Both state and Continental navies enlisted black sailors, and they accepted both slaves and freemen. Some of the slaves served on promise of freedom, some as substitutes for white draftees, and all of them because the navies suffered the same manpower shortages as the infantry. Navies, however, were not as squeamish about black enlistment as land forces.

As Washington had foreseen and feared at the start of the war, military service could offer runaway slaves sanctuary; such was certainly true of the navies. Service at sea offered distance from authorities tracking runaways. Likewise, service

*An unidentified African-American sailor wearing a navy uniform in a portrait from around 1780.*

on a privateer—a private ship that the government sanctioned as a warship to augment its own navies—offered blacks even more safety than state-owned ships.

Privateers also offered more opportunity for blacks. On privateers blacks could serve at the sailor's rank of seaman, or even as a ship pilot. On Continental ships, they remained in support jobs or galley jobs, usually below decks. The U.S. Navy retained that practice through World War II.

One such African American sailing on a privateer was James Forten, a free black. Born to free parents in 1766, James signed on with the privateer *Royal Louis* at the age of 13 or 14. The British captured him and held him on a prisoner ship for seven months in New York Harbor before exchanging him and others for British prisoners held by Americans. Forten became a successful American entrepreneur, and he fought for the abolition of slavery until his death in 1842.

General Charles Cornwallis in the last major battle of the war. The First Rhode Island was mustered out of service on June 13, 1783.

## ARMING BLACKS IN THE SOUTH

The advancements in arming African Americans for war came initially in the north where slavery was on the wane, if not already dead. It came late in the

# Alexander Hamilton's Letter

When John Laurens appealed to the South Carolina legislature in 1779 to allow the arming of African Americans to fight the British in the south, he took with him an eloquent letter from Alexander Hamilton supporting the cause. Hamilton's letter foreshadows his passionate work on the U.S. Constitution. It read, in part:

*I frequently hear it objected to the scheme of embodying negroes that they are too stupid to make soldiers. This is so far from appearing to me a valid objection that I think their want of cultivation (for their natural faculties are probably as good as ours) joined to that habit of subordination which they acquire from a life of servitude, will make them sooner become soldiers than our White inhabitants. Let officers be men of sense and sentiment, and the nearer the soldiers approach to machines perhaps the better.*

*I foresee that this project will have to combat much opposition from prejudice and self-interest. The contempt we have been taught to entertain for the blacks, makes us fancy many things that are founded neither in reason nor experience; and an unwillingness to part with property of so valuable a kind will furnish a thousand arguments to show the impracticability or pernicious tendency of a scheme which requires such a sacrifice. But it should be considered, that if we do not make use of them in this way, the enemy probably will; and that the best way to counteract the temptation they will hold out will be to offer them ourselves. An essential part of the plan is to give them their freedom with their muskets. This will secure their fidelity, animate their courage, and I believe will have a good influence upon those who remain, by opening the door to their emancipation. . . .*

South Carolina repeatedly refused the plan, prompting George Washington to comment that the spirit of freedom to which Hamilton had appealed had vanished. "That spirit of Freedom which at the commencement of this contest would have gladly sacrificed every thing to the attainment of its object has long since subsided, and every selfish Passion has taken its place; it is not the public but the private Interest which influences the generality of Mankind nor can the Americans any longer boast an exception."

war to the slaveholding south. It also did not happen until the British shifted their focus to the southern colonies (after the disastrous Battle of Monmouth largely closed their northern efforts in 1778), and they began inciting southern Tories and Native Americans to fight the American rebels. Even so black soldiers may not have appeared in the south without encouragement from Washington's headquarters.

Washington had on his staff a volunteer aide named John Laurens, son of South Carolina planter Henry Laurens, who himself was the third president of the Continental Congress. As early as 1778, John Laurens had become convinced that the arming of blacks was an essential ingredient of American victory. He wrote to his father, "I would solicit you to cede me a number of your able bodied men slaves, instead of leaving me a fortune." He would then train them to fight.

"I would bring about a two-fold good," he wrote. "First, I would advance those who are unjustly deprived of the rights of mankind to a state which would be a proper gradation between abject slavery and perfect liberty, and besides I would reinforce the defenders of liberty with a number of gallant soldiers." Laurens concluded, "if I could obtain authority for the purpose, I would have a corps of such men trained, uniformly equip'd and ready in every respect to act at the opening of the next campaign."

When his father, Henry, asked what Washington thought of the plan, John soon had an answer. Washington had become convinced of the value of African-American soldiers over the past three years, and he told the younger Laurens that they comprised a southern resource that "should not be neglected." Henry Laurens proved as enlightened as his son and as dynamic as Washington, and he consented to the plan.

In early 1779, hard-pressed by the British southern campaign, South Carolina representatives fairly begged the Continental Congress for more troops. Equally hard-pressed by the needs of war, the congress replied they had none to give and that southern states should look to slaves to augment their troops.

John Laurens seized the opportunity and went to Charleston, South Carolina, to make his case. He took with him an impassioned letter from Alexander Hamilton, then a member of Washington's staff, pressing the case for arming blacks and letting them participate in the cause of freedom.

The South Carolina legislature, not surprisingly, refused. In fact Laurens entreated the assembly on several occasions over the next three years with the same result. In August 1782 Laurens died in a minor skirmish with the British south of Charleston, having seen no positive response to his entreaties.

## CONCLUSION

While hundreds of African Americans fought for the United States during the Revolutionary War, their service to country would first retreat before it advanced further. By the time of the Civil War in 1861, blacks were not allowed to fight in either army, north or south. Not until the U.S. Congress passed the Enrollment Act in 1862 would that change. Then blacks could serve but, just as they had in the Revolution, only under white officers. Blacks would go on to serve in segregated units during the Indian Wars, the Spanish-American War, and World Wars I and II. Not until the civil rights era of the 1950s would they fight in desegregated units with some measure of racial equality.

STEVE JONES
SOUTHWESTERN ADVENTIST UNIVERSITY

# Further Reading

Adams, Gretchen. *"Deeds of Desperate Valor:" The First Rhode Island Regiment.* Available online, URL: http://www.americanrevolution.org/blk .html. Accessed August 2009.

Adler, Mortimer J., ed., et al. *The Negro in American History, Vol. III, Slaves and Masters, 1567–1854.* New York: Encyclopedia Britannica Educational Corporation, 1969.

Fishel, Leslie H., Jr., and Benjamin Quarles. *The Negro American: A Documentary History.* Glenview, IL: Scott, Foresman and Company and William Morrow and Company, 1967.

Foner, Jack D. *Blacks and the Military in American History: A New Perspective.* New York: Praeger, 1974.

Franklin, John Hope, and Alfred A. Moss, Jr. *From Slavery to Freedom: A History of Negro Americans*, 6th ed. New York: McGraw-Hill, 1988.

Hirschfeld, Fritz. *George Washington and Slavery: A Documentary Portrayal.* Columbia: University of Missouri Press, 1997.

National Historic Landmarks Program. "Site of Battle of Rhode Island." Available online, URL: http://tps.cr.nps.gov/nhl/. Accessed October 2008.

Nell, William Cooper, "The Colored Patriots of the American Revolution, With Sketches of Several Distinguished Colored Persons: To Which Is Added a Brief Survey of the Condition And Prospects of Colored Americans, 1855." Available online, URL: http://docsouth.unc.edu/neh/ nell/nell.html. Accessed July 2009.

"Oliver Cromwell." Available online, URL: www.co.burlington.nj.us/tourism /history/african/cromwell.htm. Accessed July 2009.

Quarles, Benjamin. *The Negro in the Making of America.* New York: Collier Books, 1964.

Robinson, J. Dennis. "Prince Whipple and American Painting." Available online, URL: http://www.seacoastnh.com/Black_History/Black_History_of_the_Seacoast/Prince_Whipple_and_American_Painting/3/. Accessed August 2009.

Walling, Richard S. "Prince Whipple: Symbol of African Americans at the Battle of Trenton." Available online, URL: http://www.whipple.org/ prince/princewhipple.html. Accessed July 2009.

# CHAPTER 3

# The Early National Period and Expansion: 1783 to 1859

AFTER THE REVOLUTION, Americans began to wonder what the outcome would mean for them. African Americans, in particular, were hopeful that the rhetoric of the Revolution emphasizing liberty and freedom would apply to them. They soon realized, however, the contradiction of fighting a war in the name of liberty, while people remained in slavery. It would not be the last time that African Americans would feel betrayed after fighting in a war to assure—or protect—freedom. In the case of the Revolutionary War, the "compromise of 1787" was used to justify the accommodation of slavery.

Ratified in 1788, the U.S. Constitution defined millions of Americans as property. There have been various explanations as to why the Constitution did not include a national abolition plan. Historians offer the following reasons: (1) the vulnerability of the new nation, which struggled with the tension between freedom and order; (2) the regionalism apparent among the New England, mid-Atlantic, and southern colonies that might inhibit a national cohesion; and (3) the economic reliance of the new nation on the fortunes of a plantation system. As the new nation tried to create an American identity, slavery would move to the forefront of a great debate.

The concept of states' rights that allowed individual regions to chart their own course also included policies and practices regulating slavery. Not until 1857 was a consistent national policy forged in regard to the status of African

Americans in the new nation. In the meantime, a developing Code Noir not only prescribed the treatment of slaves, but associated skin color and facial features with social status. In the absence of any mention in the Constitution of race, it would eventually fall to abolitionist societies, churches, and benevolent organizations to mount a protest. In the meantime, slavery would expand and African Americans—both free and enslaved—would undergo a social and political transformation.

Despite the efforts of organizations such as the American Colonization Society (ACS), the great majority of blacks chose to remain in America, rather than to return to Africa. Formed in 1817, the ACS sought the aid of Congress in seeking a colony in Africa to which blacks who were captured in the illegal slave trade could return. In 1822 the colony of Liberia, on the west coast of Africa, was formed under the auspices of the ACS, assisted by the federal government. But by 1852 fewer than 8,000 blacks had gone to Liberia. The mass of blacks considered America—not Africa—their home. Even after the passage of the Fugitive Slave Act in 1850, there was little interest in returning to Africa.

## AFRICAN AMERICANS IN BONDAGE

The framers of the Constitution took into consideration the demands of southern planters and politicians to protect the foreign slave trade for three reasons: (1) to offset the number of slaves who had left the United States with the British for relocation in Nova Scotia, the Bahamas, or other British colonies after the war; (2) to replace fugitives who had run away from their masters; and (3) to include slaves in the census enumeration for purposes of representation in Congress. The Constitution specified a 20-year grace period during which planters could import slave labor and retrieve fugitives from northern states and Canada. Finally, the Constitution defined African Americans as "three-fifths of all other persons" as it related to representation in the House of Representatives and for purposes of direct taxation of the population. Many of those who crafted the Constitution, such as Thomas Jefferson, were influenced by the fact that they were also slave owners.

In addition to geography and politics, distinct patterns of slavery emerged according to the labor economy. In the Chesapeake Bay area, which by the mid-19th century was called the Upper South, tobacco emerged as a staple crop. In the Deep South, crops included rice, indigo, sugar, and hemp. It was King Cotton, however, that would fuel the "peculiar institution" (as John C. Calhoun referred to slavery) for the next several decades and lead to the creation of the American plantation system in its most fully realized form. It was, after all, not the crop that would define the peculiar institution; rather it was the system of social relations.

Cotton began to prevail in the Deep South after the invention of the cotton gin in 1793. The term *gin* is derived from the word engine. The cotton gin was

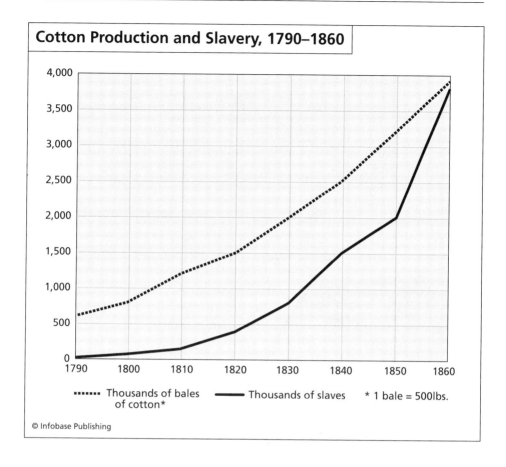

## Cotton Production and Slavery, 1790–1860

······ Thousands of bales of cotton*     ▬▬▬ Thousands of slaves     * 1 bale = 500lbs.

© Infobase Publishing

a labor-saving device that sped up the process of removing cotton seeds from the cotton bolls after they were hand-picked. By removing this bottleneck in the production process, the invention greatly expanded the capability of southern plantations to produce cotton, and hence, ironically, this labor-saving machine created a great demand for slave labor. Although it is attributed to Eli Whitney, slaves created prototypes of a wooden box with a roller that pulled the fibers from cotton bolls.

However blacks could not file for patents, so whites such as Whitney could claim credit for his model of the machine. The cotton gin increased eightfold the amount of cotton that was shipped abroad and used domestically. It is estimated that the south produced 75 percent of the world's supply of cotton 1835–60: 100,000 bales a year.

Modeled after the plantation system of the medieval Mediterranean, southern plantations were feudalistic in nature. They were entirely self-sufficient, isolated from other plantations and urban centers, and the authority of the owner was absolute. Everyone contributed to the factory that was the plantation—men, women, and children. For slaves who were field hands, the lowest rung of the labor ladder, the labor was unrelenting and the living conditions were particularly brutal.

Although the foreign slave trade was outlawed in 1808, slave ships (called Guineamen) continued to bring cargoes from Africa and the West Indies to the United States. In addition states that did not have cotton as their primary cash crop, such as Virginia, Maryland, and Kentucky, had a surplus of slaves. Slaves were taken to slave markets held throughout the south and mid-Atlantic. They were paraded in front of buyers, evaluated for physical health, temperament, and age, and sold to the highest bidder. There was no attempt to keep families together. Each person was a piece of property that was purchased to fill a need on the plantation.

The next stop was often the bustling city of New Orleans, which was the epicenter of the slave trade and the portal to the Deep South. Being "sold down the river" became a dreaded prospect for African Americans who knew what awaited them. According to historian Ira Berlin, the number of slaves sold per year from 1820 to 1860 was 7,500. This estimate is low, however, because it

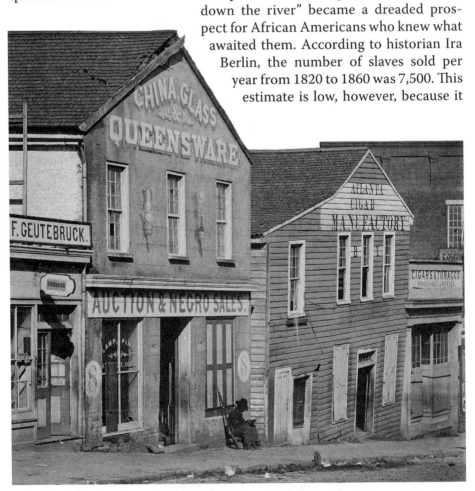

A sign reading "Auction & Negro Sales" on Whitehall Street in Atlanta, Georgia, in the mid-19th century. According to one estimate, 7,500 slaves were sold every year in the United States from 1820 to 1860.

# J.J. Roberts and the Development of Self-Government in Liberia

Joseph Jenkins (J.J.) Roberts was born in Norfolk, Virginia, in 1809 and grew up in the free black community of nearby Petersburg with his mother, stepfather, and six brothers and sisters. As a child, he learned to read and write, and acquired an understanding of the basics of business from his stepfather. Desiring citizenship and civil rights unavailable in the antebellum United States, Roberts immigrated to the colony of Liberia in West Africa in 1829 along with his wife Sarah and infant child. His mother and most of his siblings also immigrated.

Roberts's wife and child both died shortly thereafter and he remarried Jane Rose Waring. The American Colonization Society (ACS) had founded Liberia as a place for free blacks to escape the racism and discrimination that limited their opportunities in the United States, and as a Christian missionary outpost, both goals that Roberts supported.

Roberts achieved economic success in Liberia through a trading partnership with a free black from Virginia named William Colson, but gained lasting renown for his political leadership. His brothers Henry, a trader and physician, and John, a bishop in the Methodist Episcopal Church, also played important roles in Liberia's development. Roberts served as high sheriff, chief justice, and lieutenant governor before becoming the first African-American governor of Liberia in 1840. By the late 1840s, Liberia's leaders desired independence for the country in order to further their political and economic goals. Roberts was instrumental in establishing Liberia as an independent republic in 1848. A constitution and bill of rights modeled on those of the United States were created.

Roberts was elected Liberia's first president, serving until 1856, and later returned to the presidency 1871–76. He was a member of Liberia's Republican Party, opposed by the True Whig Party. As president Roberts's interests and accomplishments included diplomatic recognition and the establishment of relations with European nations, fundraising, territorial expansion, continued emigration from the United States, the development of agriculture and education, and an end to the African slave trade.

Roberts also served as the president of Liberia College. Supporters praised his political leadership, while critics claimed he was simply a privileged mulatto who only supported those of his position. Roberts died in Monrovia, Liberia, in 1876. Both during his lifetime and afterward, Roberts became a symbol of African Americans' abilities in political, economic, religious, and educational leadership, and his example challenged the era's prevailing racist beliefs.

This print illustrates the idealized paternalistic relationship some slave owners believed they had with their slaves.

does not take into consideration the informal private transactions that were made, or those who hired out the labor of their slaves to others on a part-time basis. This was especially the case for slaves who were skilled craftsmen such as carpenters. They were allowed to work for others in order to bring in extra income to the owner.

The economic need for slavery as an institution was justified by the creation of a social construct that designated slaves as inferior to whites morally, intellectually, and physically—particularly in regard to skin color. Within the hierarchy of this construct, it was only natural that inferior blacks should serve superior whites. It was necessary for whites to subscribe to this psychologically. Another rationale was aimed at not only convincing blacks that slavery was a reflection of the natural order, but that paternalism was the peculiar burden of whites. "Happy Darkies" were portrayed as being well cared for by a benevolent white social structure. It was reinforced that whites ruled divinely from God. Bible passages read to slaves focused on obedience, docility, gratefulness, and the value of work. In addition a system of slave codes was established in each southern state and in some border and northern states that prescribed the conduct of blacks vis-à-vis whites.

Slavery, however, was not monolithic. In both the north and the south, slaves could more easily control their lives in urban areas than in the isolated plantation system. As Frederick Douglass pointed out, it was easier for slaves to hire their time out in urban areas. Similarly slaves who worked in the Big House, or plantation manor, generally received better care and experienced less onerous labor. They were often given the clothing hand-me-downs of the owners. Black children could associate with white children until the onset of puberty. House, or domestic, slaves had better access to information exchanged by whites and to education. In defiance of the slave codes, white owners would sometimes provide house slaves with a rudimentary education. Craftsmen had to be taught some literacy and math in order to perform their jobs adequately. House slaves often accompanied the

# National Negro Conventions
# Before the Civil War

African-American men and women held a series of national Negro Conventions from 1830 through the early 1860s in order to organize and give full expression to their goals. African Americans had actively participated in abolitionist and other reform organizations, but were frequently denied leadership roles, and many felt a larger role in securing freedom and equality was essential.

Political organizations were one of the few avenues open to African Americans in the antebellum period, as slaves had no rights, and free black suffrage was severely limited. The first national Negro Convention was held on September 20, 1830, in Philadelphia, Pennsylvania.

Issues taken up by the national Negro Conventions included civil rights, suffrage, education, economic self-sufficiency, women's rights, temperance and other moral reforms, and an end to economic, legal, and social discrimination. Although most participants lacked the power to achieve direct political action, they were able to issue resolutions and petitions to local and state governments, as well as the U.S. Congress.

The national Negro Conventions also provided organizational guidance to the large number of national, state, and local African-American committees, churches, mutual aid societies, and insurance groups. Negro Convention participants also debated the issue of black separatism within the United States. Those who believed that the paternalistic, racist beliefs of many whites would prevent African Americans from achieving political, social, and economic equality within mainstream American society supported the creation of separate black institutions.

Some participants supported the efforts of groups like the American Colonization Society, which aided free black emigration to the West African colony of Liberia, while others were strongly opposed to leaving their home. The participation of wealthy free blacks like Philadelphia sail maker James Forten and his family lent reinforcement to the economic argument for abolitionism that free blacks could become productive U.S. citizens when given the chance.

A deteriorating political climate brought on by the Fugitive Slave Act of 1850, the 1854 Kansas-Nebraska Act, and the Supreme Court's 1857 Dred Scott decision led the national Negro Convention movement to further distance itself from the work of white abolitionist and other reform groups. The national Negro Convention movement was reorganized into the National Equal Rights League in 1864.

owner on travel to northern states and cities, which allowed them a glimpse at life in free states.

In addition to economic imperatives, a revolution in Haiti increased the dread of slave rebellion in the United States and prompted white retaliation. When revolution broke out in France in 1789, free blacks on the island of St. Domingue (later known as Haiti) also claimed their rights. In 1791 a slave named Boukman led a rebellion against the slave system. It was a conflict between white Haitians and enslaved Africans, who outnumbered their owners. In 1793 French planters and merchants fled the island, seeking refuge in U.S. coastal cities.

A republic of African people was established on January 1, 1804, in Haiti. They had forced the withdrawal of the British as well as the French and Spanish armies. In the process, they had planted the seed of fear on another continent. As word of the rebellion spread, citizens of the new nation feared that insurrection would inspire blacks in the United States to rebel. It would also spur the sale of the Louisiana Territory to the United States, which doubled the size of the United States in 1803, and created the opportunity for the spread of slavery.

The Missouri Compromise led to further expansion of slavery in new states and territories. Since 1798 Congress had admitted new states to the Union on an equal basis—one slave state for each free state. This was done in order to maintain the balance of congressional representation between north and south. But in 1819, the Missouri territory applied for statehood with explicit guarantees to permit slaveholding. This would spread slavery west of the Mississippi River for the first time. After several months of debate, Congress crafted a compromise. It admitted Maine as a free state to balance the admission of Missouri as a slave state, thus maintaining the representational balance. A second problem arose, however, when the Missouri state constitution forbade the entry of free black Americans into the new state. This raised the issue of black citizenship. Finally the matter was left to local option—that is, the legal status of Missouri's free blacks would be decided by local and state courts. Missouri subsequently passed a law banning the admission of free black people.

## RESISTANCE

Resistance to slavery took many forms. Slaves tried to flee, but they were rarely successful. They feigned sickness, slowed down the work, and pretended to be incapable of learning or doing a job competently. Masters encountered resistance in the form of countless small acts such as ruined meals, broken tools, pilfered livestock, and sabotaged crops. Rarely, slaves organized revolts against the ruling class. In 1822 a free black named Denmark Vesey organized a revolt in Charleston, South Carolina that struck fear into the hearts of whites. Vesey and his followers planned to raid two

# HORRID MASSACRE IN VIRGINIA.

This 1831 woodcut depicts Nat Turner's followers attacking men, women, and children in Virginia with axes and other weapons. The insurrection resulted in the deaths of 55 whites.

arsenals on a Sunday night in July, when many whites would be away on vacation. After a slave turned informer, Vesey and 35 others were tried and subsequently hanged.

Nat Turner, a slave preacher, attributed an apocalyptic vision to God, directing him to lead a rebellion just as Moses had led slaves out of bondage. On August 22, 1831, Turner's soldiers killed his master and family, then marched to Jerusalem, Virginia. Altogether they killed 55 men, women, and children with axes and clubs. As word spread, white militia groups descended on them. Most of the insurrectionists were hunted down, captured, or killed, until only Turner and three companions remained at large.

Turner was finally captured on October 30, 1831, and hanged. But while the Turner insurrection had failed, he suggested in his "confessions" to a white lawyer that a Christian God had motivated him to seek justice for slavery. Their fears exacerbated, southern whites reinforced slave codes and increased the numbers of lynchings and burnings of blacks who had committed infractions, prohibited reading, and banned free African Americans from preaching to slaves. In addition slaves were not permitted to fraternize with each other, or to form groups of three. Armed patrols (often referred to as "paterollers") roamed the countryside, much like vigilante groups.

But blacks, too, were spurred to action. The first black newspaper, *Freedom's Journal*, was printed in New York City in 1827 and edited by Samuel Cornish, a black Presbyterian minister. It exhorted whites and blacks to oppose slavery. Although slaves could not assemble, free blacks found the newspaper to be a forum for political views and exchange of information related to new churches, schools, fraternal organizations, and mutual aid societies. Political events were debated and information was shared across regions. All the while, a clandestine operation assisted slaves who tried, against all odds, to escape by running to freedom via the Underground Railroad.

The Underground Railroad was a loosely organized community of blacks and white allies who transported slaves from the south to freedom in Ohio, Pennsylvania, and New York, and ultimately to Canada, Europe, and Mexico. It was at its most active during the 1850s as the rhetoric over slavery intensified. It was metaphorically called a "railroad" because it was a secret (underground) passageway from the south to the north, guided by "conductors" who gave slaves rest and comfort along the way. One of the most famous was Harriet Tubman, who made as many as three dozen trips back into slave territory to lead hundreds of slaves to freedom. She had engineered her own escape into Pennsylvania from Maryland. Although it is estimated that about 100,000 former slaves traveled the Underground Railroad 1820–60, that is a small fraction of the millions who were held in slavery. After reaching Canada, the cold climate, lack of jobs, racism, and loneliness were small comfort. In conjunction with the Underground Railroad, individual acts of courage created a canon of escape narrative. Three of the best known discuss the Crafts, Henry "Box" Brown, and Margaret Garner.

## SLAVE NARRATIVES

In 1848 William and Ellen Craft escaped from their Georgian master. William disguised himself as a servant to the light-skinned Ellen, who dressed as a man and posed as the slave owner's sickly son. The Crafts traveled by steamboat and stayed in fine hotels along the way. After their successful escape, they published their story in 1851 and became popular antislavery speakers.

Escaped slave Henry "Box" Brown arriving at the office of the Pennsylvania Anti-Slavery Society.

In another sensational case, with help from a northern Vigilance Committee, Henry "Box" Brown packed himself into a two-foot-square crate, with air holes and food, and shipped himself from Richmond, Virginia, to William Johnson, a black abolitionist in Philadelphia. Others who published their stories include Harriet Jacobs (*Incidents in the Life of a Slave Girl*, 1861), Frederick Douglass

(*Narrative of the Life of Frederick Douglass,* 1845), and Sojourner Truth. Truth published her life story, *Narrative of Sojourner Truth,* in 1850 and traveled widely on the antislavery lecture circuit. Described by some as "the only colored woman to gain a national reputation as a speaker in the years preceding the Civil War," Truth's message melded gender rights (including women's suffrage) with antislavery rhetoric.

Margaret Garner's story in 1856 was partially the inspiration for Toni Morrison's novel *Beloved.* Garner fled slavery with her husband Simeon, their four children, and Simeon's parents and took refuge in Ohio. When U.S. marshals closed in to return the family to slavery, Garner slit the throat of her infant daughter and struck two of her sons with a shovel in an effort to prevent them from being hauled back into slavery. Garner threw herself and one or perhaps more of her children into the Ohio River. She was captured anyway, and sold into the Deep South, perishing soon afterward from disease.

## FREE BLACKS

In 1790 there were 59,557 free blacks. By 1860 this number had increased to 488,070. Of that number, almost 250,787 were in the south. Some were freed as a result of their service during the Revolutionary War. Others may have run away, although they lived with the threat of recapture after passage of the Fugitive Slave Act in 1850. And others may have secured manumission from conscience-stricken owners. According to the slave code, the children of women who were enslaved inherited that condition. But slave masters who had impregnated their slaves would sometimes free the woman and her children. These decisions were made on an individual basis. Freed slaves could also be those who immigrated to the United States and had never been enslaved. Finally, slaves could purchase their own freedom with money they earned from hiring themselves out. This was particularly true of blacks who lived in urban areas.

The status of free blacks, however, was not without its constraints. Although free, they were expected to adhere to the black codes. They could not vote, testify against whites, or strike a white person even when provoked. They could not buy liquor or own a gun except by special permission. Neither could they hold office or assemble except for church. Some states went so far as to restrict the entry of blacks. In 1807 Ohio passed a law requiring that blacks could not enter the state unless they could furnish a bond of $500 as a guarantee of good conduct. Illinois required an incoming black to post a bond of $1,000; Indiana's constitution of 1851 prohibited blacks from coming into the state to reside. Since states associated skin color with social status, dark-skinned blacks were automatically assumed to be slaves. The onus was on blacks to prove that they were free by being able to produce a certificate of freedom or manumission. Even African-Americans with pale skin could be arrested and sold.

*Frederick Douglass in a photograph from around 1860.*

After the passage of the Fugitive Slave Act in 1850, there were few hospitable destinations for free black people in the United States. Some black leaders advocated that free blacks leave the country. Founded by Martin Delany and James Holly, the American Emigration Society endorsed Canada as a destination, along with the West Indies, Liberia, Haiti, and Central America. After Holly met white abolitionist James Redpath, however, Holly began recommending Haiti because he and Redpath had persuaded the government to give free land to African-American settlers.

Motivated by the hope that the new black communities would provide a buffer zone between white Canadians and rebellious Indians, the Canadian government offered citizenship and the franchise to black immigrants after three years' residency. By 1860 about 5,000 black immigrants had moved to Canada, but found it difficult to find work, and ended up in stereotypical occupations such as domestic service and barbering. The schools provided for blacks were inferior to those of whites.

While some blacks chose emigration, others like Frederick Douglass explored political methods to end slavery and gain citizenship. In 1840 Douglass joined the Free Soil Party, a coalition of Americans in the east led by New England abolitionists who wanted any territory obtained from Mexico to be non-slave. Though black men could vote in only a few states, Douglass was able to help design the party's platform. Douglass argued that the U.S. Constitution guaranteed African Americans citizenship. He remained committed to staying within the United States and urged black organizations to work with—but not within—white reform organizations.

Nevertheless blacks were able to progress economically, and a free black class began to emerge. Blacks who had developed skills as artisans or craftsmen benefited from growing industrialization. Particularly in the south, blacks did not face the competition from white immigrants, who arrived in the millions 1830–60. In cities, free blacks did most of the work in the mechanical trades. In Charleston, South Carolina in 1850, there were 122 carpenters, 87 tailors, and 30 shoemakers among the city's 700 free, employed black males. When opportunities opened in manufacturing, blacks provided a ready labor supply for mills and factories. By 1860 over one-third of the rural black heads of families had become owners or renters of land. Prosperous black farmers were not uncommon. In Rush County, Indiana in 1857, 46 black heads of families owned a total of more than 3,000 acres. These farmers often supported schools and churches, and contributed to the growth of pioneer communities.

## CHURCHES, MUTUAL AID, AND BENEVOLENT SOCIETIES

As the population of free black people increased from nearly 60,000 in 1790 to more than 233,000 in 1820, social organizations formed the infrastructure of a free black society. In 1792 former slave Richard Allen remembered being evicted from St. George's Methodist Church in Philadelphia when church officials decided to relegate black worshippers to a segregated section. He would eventually found the African Methodist Episcopal Church (AME) in 1816. It became the largest denomination of black Christians in the United States, and Allen became the first bishop. Part of its mission was the abolition of slavery. Much like community centers today, churches were a haven for African Americans where they could celebrate their identity unimpeded by whites. In urban areas such as Philadelphia and New Orleans, blacks founded mutual aid and benevolent societies, schools, and community organizations. Allen formed the Free African Society of Philadelphia (FAS), a mutual aid society. Mutual aid societies provided food and clothing to the needy, burial fees, and financial assistance. They organized schools, assisted the poor, and provided spiritual help.

Allen also organized the first black Sunday school in America in Philadelphia in 1795. Later, Allen established the Society of Free People of Color for Promoting the Instruction and School Education of Children of African Descent. Other cities, such as Charleston, South Carolina, and Baltimore, Maryland, followed suit. Black Americans held education in esteem as the surest path to success. Only the children of the tiny black middle class, however, were able to attend

*Juliann Jane Tillman, shown above, was a female preacher in the African Methodist Episcopal Church in the 1840s.*

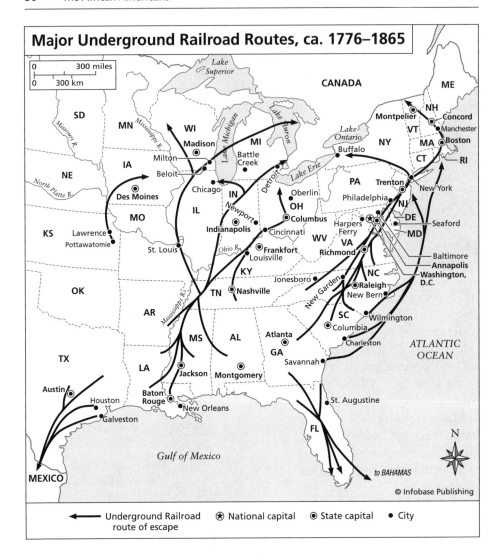

Major Underground Railroad Routes, ca. 1776–1865

Underground Railroad route of escape    ★ National capital    ◉ State capital    • City

© Infobase Publishing

school for any extended period. Like the rest of the country during this period, schooling was intermittent. In rural areas, school attendance was dictated by the agricultural calendar and the demands of the farm.

Both whites and blacks started abolitionist societies. In the case of whites, some of the first abolitionist societies included the Pennsylvania Society (1775). Local groups also were founded that attempted to prevent free slaves from being sold into slavery, and to assist those who were already slaves. Although their main goal was the abolishment of slavery, they provided freed slaves with basic necessities and employment. Once again, education was viewed as instrumental to the cause. In 1787 the New York Manumission Society founded the African Free School.

When it came to white churches, the Religious Society of Friends (Quakers) was on the forefront of antislavery activity. Although not all Quaker meetings subscribed to this political view, historically they have been aligned with efforts to assist freed slaves and to aid the escape from slavery for those who were held. Their efforts were instrumental in making Pennsylvania the first state to abolish slavery in 1780. As Quakers emigrated from the east coast to the Midwest, their efforts continued in Indiana, Ohio, and Michigan, from which slaves could cross into Canada and freedom. Blacks, however, rarely joined Quaker meetings. Despite their opposition to slavery, Quakers did not go so far as to advocate racial equality. Blacks who did attend meetings were relegated to the "Negro Pew."

## RADICAL ABOLITIONISM

By 1830 abolitionism had turned radical as reformers were prepared to break laws, directly confront slaveholders, and even commit violence. It solidified with the 1833 founding of the American Anti-Slavery Society in Philadelphia, which was led by William Lloyd Garrison along with influential blacks such as James Forten, a prosperous sail maker. In particular they opposed the clause in the Constitution that counted a black person as only three-fifths of a citizen. In an effort to attract supporters, lectures were given in which former slaves gave testimonials as to the brutality of the plantation system, to which many outside the south were oblivious. Lecturers dispersed literature, presented slave testimony, and gathered signatures for petitions. The most widely read literature included Garrison's newspaper *The Liberator* and Lydia Maria Child's *An Appeal in Favor of that Class of Americans Called Africans* (1833). One of Garrison's most important converts to abolitionism was Frederick Douglass. Born on a Maryland plantation in 1817, Douglass was the son of a slave woman and a white father. The planter's wife helped him learn to read as a child. In 1838, disguised as a sailor, Douglass escaped to New Bedford, Massachusetts. He hired out his labor to the shipyards and emigrated to England until American abolitionists could raise enough money to purchase his freedom. Freed by 1845, he was an imposing figure at antislavery gatherings.

The African-American population jumped from 2.3 million in 1830 to 3.6 million in 1850. However the percentage of free African Americans dropped from 15.9 to 13.6 percent, meaning the addition of 1.3 million more slaves. Part of this can be attributed to the decrease in manumission. By 1820 only the border states of Delaware, Maryland, and Kentucky allowed slaves to be manumitted (freed). In addition the high fertility rates of enslaved women added to the population, even though the infant mortality rate was high (27 percent) and life expectancy was low. And despite the prohibition, illegal importation of slaves continued. Free blacks tended to congregate in urban areas like Charleston, Mobile, Louisville, New Orleans, Baltimore, Savannah, and Richmond. By mid-century, Baltimore had the nation's largest black community—over 20,000 free African Americans. Black northerners tended to live in Philadelphia, New York, Boston, Pittsburgh, and Cincinnati.

The California gold rush qualified the territory for statehood by 1850, after thousands of Americans—black and white—headed west to capitalize on the 1848 discovery of gold. But admitting California as a free state would upset the free state/slave state balance. President Zachary Taylor invited California and the New Mexico Territory to apply for statehood, touching off a bitter congressional debate. The solution came in the form of the Compromise of 1850, which contained four provisions: California was admitted as a free state; territorial governments were created in New Mexico and Utah, giving the right to the settlers to decide whether or not to permit slavery; legislators abolished the internal slave trade in Washington, D.C., but not slavery itself; and the Fugitive Slave Act allowed federal commissioners to adjudicate fugitive slave cases, rather than giving them a jury trial. It also compelled northern citizens to help apprehend runaways: now it was not only illegal to assist a fugitive slave, but one could be prosecuted for refusing to assist slave catchers.

In 1851 Edward Gorsuch, accompanied by a federal marshal, journeyed to Christiana, Pennsylvania, to reclaim Joshua Kite and six other African-American fugitives. Kite and the others had escaped from Gorsuch's farm two years earlier, and were living in a community populated by 3,000 free and fugitive blacks. Gorsuch hired slave hunters to help him track down the group. But as he approached Christiana, Kite and dozens of his black neighbors had been forewarned and waited for Gorsuch at the home of William and Eliza Parker. Parker would not capitulate, and his wife threatened the slaves with a corn cutter if they tried to surrender. Within minutes, Gorsuch was shot to death, and his son was badly wounded. Kite, Parker, and a few others escaped to Canada. Known as the Christiana Riot, it both inspired African Americans and frightened slaveholders. Officials responded by arresting nearly three dozen people, white and black, who were charged with conspiracy and treason. In a reaction to the Fugitive Slave Act, white jurors, however, acquitted one man and dropped the charges against the rest. White northerners who had been indifferent about slavery now associated antislavery action with the right to make their own laws. White

This 1850 illustration titled "Effects of the Fugitive Slave Law" depicts escaping slaves shot in the back by their pursuers.

# Black Participation in the Underground Railroad

African Americans were the primary force behind the operation of the Underground Railroad, which was made up of secret networks designed to transport fugitive slaves to safety. Underground Railroad networks primarily existed in the north and upper south, most notably in Michigan, Ohio, Pennsylvania, and New York. Many African-American participants were free blacks, while others were fugitive slaves. Both men and women, and all classes from the wealthy to the working class, lent their aid in a variety of ways. Some aided the Underground Railroad through the collection of food and clothing, financial support, leadership and legal assistance, and networking among influential businessmen and politicians. Some participated through organizations such as churches, abolitionist societies, and urban vigilance committees. Others played a direct role in aiding the flight and resettlement of fugitive slaves.

Most fugitive slaves carried out their initial escape, but could not have successfully avoided recapture and made their way to a safe destination without the aid of Underground Railroad operatives. Secret messages carried in slave spirituals such as Go Down, Moses offered encouragement and information. Although fugitives came from all demographics and slave states, most were young males from border or upper southern states. These fugitives were called passengers in the Railroad's metaphoric terminology. Engineers or conductors directed or personally led passengers to known safe houses called stations. The owners of these houses, which provided temporary food and shelter, were known as agents or stationmasters. Common final destinations included Canada, the north, and Spanish Florida, where the fugitives often settled in African-American communities.

Underground Railroad operatives warned of the presence of slave catchers and attempted rescues of recaptured fugitives after the passage of the Fugitive Slave Act of 1850. Well-known African-American participants included Harriet Tubman, the "Moses of her people" who led hundreds to freedom as a conductor; Frederick Douglass, the former fugitive slave turned renowned orator, editor, and author; and William Still, who organized the network around Philadelphia, aided fugitives, and recorded their stories. African-American participation in the Underground Railroad served as an important challenge to the proslavery argument that Africans were content under slavery's paternalistic system and incapable of sustaining themselves in freedom. Underground Railroad activities ended with 1863's Emancipation Proclamation freeing slaves in the rebellious Confederate territories, and the end of the Civil War with the subsequent abolition of slavery in the United States.

southerners increasingly felt betrayed by the federal government. Even if they didn't own slaves, they felt it their duty to defend the institution.

## A LITERARY BLOW

It would fall to Harriet Beecher Stowe to strike a literary blow against slavery with publication of her novel *Uncle Tom's Cabin*. Based on a serialized newspaper story, it immediately sold 300,000 copies. Stowe's characters humanized slavery, particularly for northern whites. Incorporating religious overtones and drawing on the capacity for human sympathy, she also exposed the myth of a "kinder form of slavery." The book did not place blame on slaveholders, who alleged that they were as much victims of the system as blacks. And much to the chagrin of black leaders like Martin Delany, she perpetuated the "good Negro" stereotype. Southerners charged that folks like Stowe were uninformed.

*This poster was made for an 1886 theatrical production of* Uncle Tom's Cabin.

In 1854 Congress passed the Kansas-Nebraska Act. Sponsored by Illinois Senator Stephen A. Douglas, it proposed that white Americans would decide—by popular referendum—whether to have slavery in their communities. This act forged a battleground for proslavery and antislavery confrontation. Eventually the area was known as Bleeding Kansas due to rioting and skirmishes. As Congress debated whether to admit Kansas to statehood in 1856, Massachusetts's abolitionist senator Charles Sumner delivered an impassioned speech about the "crime against Kansas." He was attacked two days later by South Carolina Congressman Preston Brooks in the Senate, and injured so severely that he could not return to Congress for three years.

Meanwhile the U.S. Supreme Court was considering a suit that had meandered through the courts for more than a decade. It centered on Dred Scott, a Missouri slave whose master had taken him from slave territory into Illinois and Wisconsin Territory in the 1830s and then back to the south. When the master died in 1846,

*John Brown and his men en route to Harpers Ferry in an engraving from the November 26, 1859,* Harper's Weekly *magazine.*

his widow's brother, an abolitionist, helped Scott sue for his freedom on the grounds that he had lived on free soil. Before the passage of the Fugitive Slave Act, Missouri's courts had judged him to be free. But after five more years of litigation, in 1857, the U.S. Supreme Court handed down three important rulings: first, the Court said that Scott was not free, because to free him would deprive this owner of property without due process of law. Second, the Court declared that slaves were not entitled to use the courts, as only citizens had that right. Finally, the justices maintained that neither slaves nor their descendants could ever be citizens. The Court used Scott's case to define the Missouri Compromise as unconstitutional, because Congress could not make a policy that could deprive citizens of their property just because they moved to a different region of the United States.

On October 16, 1859, John Brown ordered his 21-man army to "Get on your arms; we will proceed to the ferry." Brown was a religious zealot who was dedicated to purging society of slavery. He represented abolitionists who believed that violence was the only solution. Brown proceeded to Harpers Ferry, Virginia, intending to raid a federal armory to get rifles to arm local slaves for an uprising. Brown's army consisted of 16 white men and five black men, only one of whom—Shields Green—had once been a slave. Local African Americans—mostly women working as domestic servants—did not participate. Most of Brown's soldiers, including two of his sons, were killed. The only black man among the five who escaped, Osborne Anderson, returned to Canada. On December 2, 1859, Brown and others went to the gallows for treason.

## CONCLUSION

The Harpers Ferry raid sparked fears of a larger conflict. Black and white abolitionists began describing Brown's raid as "noble," and Brown became a martyr. Hundreds of thousands of black Americans, weeping, lined the tracks as the train carried Brown's remains home from Virginia through Philadelphia to his farm in New York's Adirondack Mountains. As the national period drew to a close, African Americans would prove to be a decisive factor in the preservation—or dissolution—of the nation.

JAYNE R. BEILKE
BALL STATE UNIVERSITY

## Further Reading

Adler, Mortimer J., ed., et al. The Negro in American History, Vol. III, Slaves and Masters, 1567–1854. Encyclopedia Britannica Educational Corporation, 1969.

Berlin, Ira. Many Thousands Gone: The First Two Centuries of Slavery in North America. Cambridge, MA: Harvard University Press, 1998.

Carson, Clayborne, Emma J. Lapsansky-Werner, and Gary B. Nash. African American Lives: The Struggle for Freedom. New York: Pearson Education, 2005.

Douglass, Frederick. Narrative of the Life of Frederick Douglass, An American Slave. New York: Bedford/St. Martin's Press, 2002.

Fishel, Leslie H., Jr., and Benjamin Quarles. The Negro American: A Documentary History. Glenview, IL: Scott, Foresman and Company and William Morrow and Company, 1967.

Foner, Jack D. Blacks and the Military in American History: A New Perspective. New York: Praeger, 1974.

Franklin, John Hope, and Alfred A. Moss, Jr. From Slavery to Freedom: A History of Negro Americans, 6th ed. New York: McGraw-Hill, 1988.

Jones, Jacqueline. Labor of Love, Labor of Sorrow: Black Women, Work, and the Family from Slavery to the Present. New York: Basic Books, 1985.

Quarles, Benjamin. The Negro in the Making of America. New York: Macmillan, 1969.

# CHAPTER 4

# The Civil War to the Gilded Age: 1859 to 1900

**WITH THE ELECTION** of Republican candidate Abraham Lincoln to the presidency of the United States in November 1860, the simmering crisis over the issue of slavery finally erupted. The Deep South states seceded, fearful that a "Black Republican" president would seek to end slavery. In February 1861 the Confederate States of America was formed. Tensions continued to mount, leading to the bombardment by Confederate forces on Fort Sumter in Charleston Harbor on April 12. Lincoln's call for volunteers led to the secession of the Upper South states, which joined the Confederacy in turn.

Only war would determine whether or not the Union would be restored, and what type of Union it would it be. The latter issue was especially important to African Americans. If the four decades leading up to John Brown's 1859 raid at Harpers Ferry had been of crucial importance for building to a showdown on slavery, then the four decades following Brown's execution would lead to profound changes for African Americans. Slavery would be destroyed, but African Americans would struggle to build their lives on their own terms. After the demise of Reconstruction, conditions would gradually deteriorate, as black Americans slowly lost many of their newfound and hard-won freedoms. Nevertheless black institutions would grow, providing a strong base for identification and endurance.

## TOWARD A FEDERAL POLICY

After the outbreak of the Civil War, northern blacks were eager to assist the federal cause. Many sought to enlist in the army, but were initially denied the opportunity. At the time the Civil War erupted, the U.S. Army prohibited the enlistment of African Americans; as the states began to raise volunteer regiments and battalions to supplement the small regular army, these policies did not change. Nevertheless northern blacks threw themselves into various activities to support the U.S. war effort.

A question hovered over all early federal efforts: what to do about southern slaves as Union forces moved deeper into the south. On the surface, the answer would seem easy: free the slaves. Northern abolitionists, both black and white, saw the conflict from the beginning as an opportunity to end the hated institution. For President Lincoln, however, the issue was not so easy. Like other Republicans Lincoln detested slavery, but he was not a member of the radical wing of the party that sought immediate action on abolition. Further, like many other white opponents of slavery, Lincoln felt some ambivalence toward the role of free blacks in American society; even through the early part of the war, he seemed to favor colonization in Africa as a desirable goal for American blacks. As president, Lincoln saw his primary responsibility as restoration of the Union. He also had to prevent the situation from growing worse, as four southern states (the "border states" of Maryland, Delaware, Kentucky, and Missouri) remained in the Union, but contained strong pro-Confederate elements in their population; any wrong moves on the part of his administration might precipitate a secessionist response, with disastrous results. Further, many northern white Democrats were unsympathetic toward anything that smacked of abolitionist tendencies in U.S. policy, and Lincoln required the support of enough of them to keep the war effort going.

Thus Lincoln felt that he had to move cautiously on issues related to slavery. As is often the case in a war, however, matters took on a life of their own, as many southern slaves and some Union commanders in the field took action. As soon as the conflict started, more and more slaves in the regions bordering federal zones of control fled toward the hoped-for shelter of Union lines. This situation forced local officers to make their own decisions, such as when Major General Benjamin Butler in southeastern Virginia declared runaway slaves to be "contraband of war," thus in effect confiscating them from their former masters as a war measure. Such efforts were not always approved by the authorities in Washington. Gradually, however, federal policies changed. In August 1861 the U.S. Congress passed the Confiscation Act, which authorized the seizure of any property that Confederate slaveholders could use for the support of the war effort; this included their slaves.

By the summer of 1862, Lincoln was debating the issuance of a preliminary emancipation proclamation, giving the Confederate states one last chance to return to the Union, or face the consequences. Under the terms of the proclamation, if the southern states did not come back to the Union by January 1, 1863, then all the slaves within the portions of the Confederacy not under federal military control by that time would be permanently freed, an idea that would become reality as the U.S. forces continued to advance. With the failure of the Confederate drive into western Maryland, Lincoln felt that the military situation was sufficiently propitious to issue the document on September 23, 1862. Critics both north and south jeered the document, which exempted slaveholders in areas under federal control and in the border states, and which was put forward primarily as a military strategy, rather than as a humanitarian measure. Nevertheless Lincoln had initiated a major shift in governmental policy, one that had both short-term and long-term consequences. As news of the proclamation spread through the south, more and more slaves were encouraged to flee their owners, while others would be freed by the advancing Union armies.

## AFRICAN-AMERICAN SOLDIERS

When the Emancipation Proclamation was issued on January 1, 1863, it provided for the enlistment of blacks into the federal army. Already, however, some progress had been made toward enlisting African Americans into the federal ranks. In October 1862 the 1st Regiment South Carolina Volunteers was organized from former slaves along the coast of that state, and by the end

*African-American soldiers in action near Dutch Gap, Virginia, in November 1864. As many as 179,000 African Americans served in the military during the Civil War.*

# A Black Soldier at Battery Wagner

George E. Stephens was a prominent black abolitionist from Philadelphia. He had worked as a cabinetmaker before serving a brief stint on a U.S. naval warship (an occupation that almost led to his enslavement when the ship touched port in Charleston and he was seized by local authorities). By the outbreak of the Civil War, Stephens was a newspaper correspondent for the *Weekly Anglo-African*. In early 1863 he became a recruiter for the 54th Massachusetts Infantry, one of the first black regiments. He served in the regiment as 1st sergeant of Company B. Stephens continued to act as a correspondent for the *Weekly Anglo-African* while in the army, providing a very valuable collection of letters of life in a black regiment. Here are excerpts from his letter to the editor for July 21, 1863, recounting the part played by his regiment on July 18 in assaulting Battery Wagner, an important fortification on Morris Island in Charleston Harbor. The 54th Massachusetts' role in this battle was dramatized in the 1989 film *Glory*. Stephens's account captures the horrors of Civil War combat, including the confusions accompanying a night attack:

*About sundown we were ordered to advance at the double quickstep, cheering as if going on some mirthful errand. The rebs withheld their fire until we reached within fifty yards of the work, when jets of flame darted forth from every corner and embrasure, and even Fort Sumter poured solid shot and shell on our heads. The 54th, undaunted by the hellish storm, pushed up the work, down into the moat, and like demons ascended the parapet, found the interior lined with rebel soldiers who were well sheltered and fought here for one hour before we were re-enforced; and when the regiment reached us ... they ... emptied their rifles into us...*

*Some few entered the fort, and when they got in, it was so dark that friends could not be distinguished from foes, and there is no doubt but that many a Union soldier was killed by his comrades.*

*On the whole, this is considered to be a brilliant feat of the 54th. It is another evidence that cannot now be denied, that colored soldiers will dare go where any brave man will lead them. Col. [Robert Gould] Shaw, our noble and lamented commander, was the bravest of the brave. He ... led the column up to the fort, and was the first man who stood on the parapet...*

*When he reached it he said, "Come on men! Follow me!" and he either received a mortal wound and fell over the wall, or stumbled into the Fort and was killed...*

*[Brig.] Gen. [George Crockett] Strong [the 54th's brigade commander], seeing that the rebels were in too great a force, ordered the retreat ... The only good approach to the fort is by the beach. The tide was low, when we made the charge, and before we could rescue our dead and wounded the tide came up, and such as could not crawl away were drowned.*

THE GALLANT CHARGE OF THE FIFTY FOURTH MASSACHUSETTS (COLORED) REGIMENT

*The 54th Massachusetts Infantry charging Battery Wagner on Morris Island in Charleston Harbor on July 18, 1863, in an important battle involving the African-American regiment.*

of the following month Major General Butler had organized three regiments of Louisiana Native Guards. With the release of the proclamation, the process accelerated. In January 1863 the first African-American unit to be organized in a northern state mustered into federal service as the 1st Regiment Kansas Colored Volunteers. Soon afterward, the 54th Regiment Massachusetts Infantry was formed. Many more units were to follow. By the end of the war, some 179,000 African Americans had seen military service.

Black soldiers encountered many problems in the federal armies. Racial prejudice was an ever-present factor, even among some of their own white officers. Many northern whites doubted whether black soldiers could or would fight effectively, and preferred that they be used either for military labor or for garrison duty to free up white troops for combat. African-American troops were also often poorly armed, uniformed, and equipped through 1863, and faced a long struggle over equal pay for service that did not end until Congress passed a law on the subject in June 1864, after much protest by the soldiers, their officers, and abolitionists.

A deadlier issue was the possible fate that awaited black soldiers when they encountered the enemy. The Confederates viewed the recruitment of African-American soldiers by the U.S. government as an encouragement to slave rebellion. Black soldiers and their white officers were all too often shown no quarter, even after surrender or capture. There were several large-scale

*African-American soldiers from the 2nd Louisiana Regiment launching the assault at Port Hudson, Louisiana, on May 27, 1863. Confederate troops are shown attacking and killing black soldiers in fierce hand-to-hand combat.*

incidents where African-American soldiers were massacred by victorious Confederates, most notoriously at Fort Pillow in western Tennessee on April 12, 1864, and during the Battle of the Crater at Petersburg, Virginia, on July 30, 1864. Surviving black prisoners were sometimes sold into slavery. Only threats of retaliation by the Lincoln administration began to rein in some of the more flagrant abuses.

Despite all of the problems they faced, African-American troops quickly made an impact on the federal war effort following their introduction into combat. The performance of black troops at the battles of Port Hudson, Louisiana, in May 1863; at Milliken's Bend, Louisiana, in June 1863; and at Battery Wagner in Charleston Harbor in July 1863 did much to silence white northern critics and shore up support for the use of African Americans as combat soldiers.

Throughout the south as the war progressed, slaves understood that the plantation and slavery system was collapsing. In effect they achieved freedom "with their feet," simply walking away from plantations. Where possible, they joined Union lines, where they were treated as "contrabands of war" from 1861. As this policy was regularized under the Confiscation Acts of 1862 and 1863, it only gave governmental sanction to something that slaves already understood: if they went on strike by walking away from the plantations in tens of thousands, the system would come to an end. This fact of self-liberation is often overlooked in historical works that prefer to give all the credit for liberation to Union generals or Lincoln.

*Troops opening fire on a crowd in an attempt to quell the draft riots in New York City in July 1863.*

## RACIAL TENSIONS IN THE NORTH

While the war raged on, African Americans in the north endured troubles of their own, including urban riots. The worst occurred in July 1863 in New York City, beginning just five days before the 54th Massachusetts Infantry made its famous assault on Battery Wagner. The causes of the riot were complex, but racial tensions were a major component. Resentment had been building for some time among urban white northern laborers when employers used blacks as strikebreakers.

This exacerbated fears already held among some white urban workers that the end of slavery would lead to a mass migration of blacks to the north that would result, in turn, in economic troubles and unemployment. As a result, there were several violent incidents perpetrated against blacks in major cities during 1862 and 1863.

The institution of a draft for the federal armies in March 1863 added fuel to the fire: in the minds of many, white laborers were being coerced into military service for the cause of freeing the slaves. In the late spring, a major longshoreman strike in New York City led to the employment of black strikebreakers. Acts of violence against black laborers in the city grew. On July 13, full-scale rioting broke out, directed against African Americans and the institutions of conscription. Over the next five days, black businesses, homes, and aid associations were destroyed, and many lives were lost. Order was restored only after troops from the Army of the Potomac, recently victorious at Gettysburg, were sent to put down the riots. The draft riots were a troubling revelation of the racial divide that lay within northern society, and a possible omen that postwar support for African-American rights by white northerners might not endure.

## TOWARD RECONSTRUCTION

The United States emerged victorious over the Confederate States of America in April 1865. The collapse of the Confederacy ushered in a new era for African Americans. Yet questions remained about what role blacks would play in post-

This group of former slaves gathered for a photograph in June 1865. The damaged buildings of Richmond, Virginia, are visible in the background.

war society; what civil rights they would hold, and how former slaves would support themselves. These issues were already coming to a head while the fighting raged.

As early as 1862, some officers charged with administering occupied portions of the south dealt with issues related to a large, newly free population, and a number of policies were devised to deal with the matter to varying degrees of success and failure. Certain issues emerged that would echo throughout the postwar era: the freedmen (as the former slaves were called) wanted land, and they wanted to work for themselves. In some places, lands abandoned by Confederates were granted to slaves.

In order to address these and related problems, the U.S. War Department created the Bureau of Refugees, Freedmen, and Abandoned Lands in March 1865. Under the leadership of Major General Oliver Otis Howard, the Freedmen's Bureau attempted to resolve the knotty problems posed by the postwar chaos. Both white and black refugees were resettled. The bureau attempted to protect African Americans in their right to work, and to negotiate fair wages with their white employers. The bureau also often tried to regulate standards of labor for the former slaves in a well-intentioned, but patronizing effort to keep them occupied and economically useful. The former slaves had their own ideas on how to manage their labor, especially

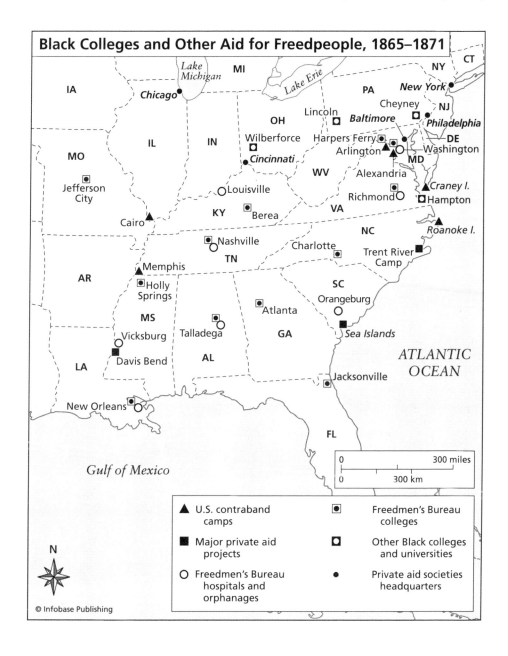

**Black Colleges and Other Aid for Freedpeople, 1865–1871**

U.S. contraband camps (▲)

Major private aid projects (■)

Freedmen's Bureau hospitals and orphanages (○)

Freedmen's Bureau colleges (◉)

Other Black colleges and universities (□)

Private aid societies headquarters (●)

© Infobase Publishing

when dealing with employers who, as former slave owners, were anxious to restore as much of the old work schedules and disciplines as the new reality allowed.

The outcome of these issues depended to a large extent on the political climate. Abraham Lincoln's reconstruction policy was still evolving at the time of his assassination in 1865. He had come to realize that the idea of colonization was unwelcome to blacks, and had cautiously begun to throw his support behind the idea of suffrage for some black men (especially the educated and those who had served in the war). Lincoln was also anxious to restore peace within the reunited nation, and proposed a policy of readmission to the Union for the Confederate states, which his more radical critics considered too lenient.

Lincoln's successor, Vice President Andrew Johnson, soon attempted to move the country in a direction quite different from what the former slaves and their Republican supporters wanted. Although a fierce wartime Unionist who had long detested the southern planter elite, Johnson was also a virulent racist.

What surprised many was his eagerness to gain the good opinion and support of those same wealthy slaveholders whom he had once hated and denounced as traitors. He thus pursued an even more lenient policy toward the former Confederates than Lincoln's, and was hostile toward the aspira-

In this illustration from July 1868, an official from the Freedman's Bureau is depicted as a peacemaker between opposing sides of whites and blacks.

tions of the freedmen. Soon ex-Confederates were returning to their former lands, displacing blacks who had been living and working on them, or attempting to subjugate them into harsh labor conditions often little better than slavery.

It was becoming increasingly obvious that only the full rights of citizenship would protect the interests of African Americans. Even before the end of the war, the first major step had been taken in that direction. The Thirteenth Amendment to the U.S. Constitution that would end slavery was proposed in 1864. By the beginning of 1865 it had passed Congress. With its ratification in December 1865, slavery was ended in those remaining sections of the country not covered by the Emancipation Proclamation.

This poster was made to celebrate the short-lived rise of a number of black politicians "from the plantation to the Senate" during Reconstruction.

African Americans and their white supporters realized, however, that freedom in and of itself would have little meaning without the right to vote. That reality became all too plain when congressional and state elections were held in 1866. Many former Confederates were back in office at both the federal and state levels, allied with an increasingly isolated President Johnson against the radical wing of his own party. African-American rights could hardly flourish in such an environment, and southern state governments were soon passing laws placing severe limitations on the freedoms of blacks.

In December 1865 the radical Republicans in Congress instituted measures to take control of Reconstruction away from Johnson. This was the beginning of a long struggle that climaxed with the president's impeachment in 1868. Ulysses S. Grant was elected the new Republican president in the same year.

Although Grant was no radical and favored a policy of reconciliation with the southern states, he had no patience with efforts by former Confederates to suppress the rights of former slaves. The tensions between these two themes in Grant's government, as northerners grew increasingly weary of the aftermath of the war, would prove problematic over time.

In the meantime the Fourteenth Amendment to the Constitution was introduced in 1866 and ratified in 1868. It prohibited states from depriving U.S. citizens of the right to vote, thus granting some degree of protection for African Americans. Among its other measures, the amendment removed the former Confederates from office, although a clause allowing reversals by congressional vote allowed the possibility of their eventual return. The Fifteenth Amendment, ratified in 1870, prohibited the denial of citizenship rights to any American citizen, regardless of racial heritage or former status as a slave, and gave Congress the power to enforce it. Taken together with the Thirteenth Amendment, the Fourteenth and Fifteenth Amendments effectively ended the antebellum order, although due to the political compromises that had gone into their creation and their sometimes ambiguous wording, they did not initially bring about the permanent protection of equality hoped for by many African Americans.

## ACCOMPLISHMENTS OF RECONSTRUCTION

Reconstruction revolutionized the lives of both northern and southern African Americans in numerous ways. The black family was strengthened as an institution, without the debilitating threat of family members being sold. The black church grew and flourished openly, and new black denominations were established, while older ones such as the African Methodist Episcopal Church saw a tremendous increase in membership. African Americans established their own aid associations and businesses. Many rural blacks in both the north and the south moved to the cities, joining the growing labor force.

For the first time African Americans were elected to state legislatures and Congress, providing an opportunity for public service and a chance to play a direct role in shaping national and local policies. Others pursued careers in the army. Although most of the black regiments from the Civil War were rapidly disbanded as part of a general postwar demobilization, a few regiments were retained and reorganized. They saw occupation duty in the south or served in the west, where they participated in the wars against the Native Americans. African-American veterans of the Civil War established their own posts within the Grand Army of the Republic, the postwar Union veterans' association.

Educational opportunities for African Americans exploded after the war. The Freedmen's Bureau played a major role in establishing schools for African Americans in the south. Southern blacks eagerly embraced education as a chance to advance themselves and better secure their freedoms. Teachers included many northern black and white men and women who moved south for this purpose, but many former slaves founded local schools of their own. Reconstruction in fact marked a brief period of education expansion in the south in general, far beyond the activities of the bureau. Some integrated schools were established, and there were some efforts to integrate

*The Zion School for Colored Children in Charleston, South Carolina, shown in this December 1866 engraving, was part of the expansion of educational opportunities for African Americans immediately after the war.*

colleges or universities. Other institutions of higher learning were established throughout the nation for black students, such as Howard University in Washington, D.C.

## THE END OF RECONSTRUCTION

White southerners looked upon the postwar world with dismay. Some began to institute a violent response to Reconstruction with the goal of forcing blacks back into a condition as close to slavery as possible. Efforts were also directed against the *carpetbaggers* (white northerners who moved into the postwar south for business purposes, to assist the former slaves, or both) and the *scalawags* (white southerners who supported Reconstruction). The Ku Klux Klan, founded in 1866 in Tennessee as a social club for ex-Confederates, soon became the forerunner of more sinister things to come. The Klan quickly evolved and spread as an underground terrorist organization, targeting supporters of Reconstruction.

By 1870 the Klan and other groups with similarly strange names were active in many rural districts of the south. Usually acting at night, the Klan and their counterparts committed beatings, murders, mutilations, and rapes, and burned the homes of African Americans, white supporters of Reconstruction,

Two members of the 1860s Ku Klux Klan wearing early versions of Klan hoods in 1868.

and schoolhouses. Violence and intimidation were used to prevent blacks from voting. In addition, former Confederates in southern cities sometimes staged riots in efforts to accomplish similar purposes.

Response to the Klan and its imitators varied. Some state governments attempted to suppress the night riders, with varying degrees of success. Other state Reconstruction governments succumbed, as Klan violence in support of the Democratic Party led to their collapse and the restoration to power of former Confederates. The federal response under Johnson was virtually nonexistent. Thus African Americans often had to protect themselves as best they could, arming themselves and acting individually or in groups.

Congressional hearings led to the passage of a series of laws in 1870 and 1871 that targeted the night-riding groups and their supporters, leading to the arrest of many members. The Klan formally disbanded, and their imitators gradually followed suit. In truth, however, the night riders did not completely fade away, as similar groups continued to operate in one form or another after Reconstruction.

In the meantime the former Confederates continued to chip away at Reconstruction, as the federal government gradually relaxed the restrictions preventing them from voting and holding office. More open forms of violence and intimidation replaced the night-riding activities of earlier years, and were used to tip elections toward the Redeemers (as the anti-Reconstruction ex-Confederates called themselves). The north was tired of Reconstruction and of supporting black rights, as the old Radicals and abolitionists had died or retired. New Republican leaders were more concerned with economic development. Corruption ruled as the Gilded Age of American history took hold. Although politicians of both political parties indulged in graft, enemies of Reconstruction were successful in painting their black and white opponents as the personification of all corruption, a stereotype that persisted well into the next century. Many African-American political leaders, particularly those in office, were also successfully and unfairly stereotyped as ignorant and incompetent.

The crisis came to a head with the presidential election of 1876. By this time only three southern states were still under Reconstruction governments and occupied by federal troops. The Democrats campaigned openly for the end of Reconstruction. The race between Republican candidate Rutherford B. Hayes and Democrat Samuel J. Tilden ended in dispute over voting totals. An electoral commission decided in favor of Hayes by one vote after the Republicans promised to end Reconstruction and withdraw the last federal troops. Reconstruction formally ended in April 1877, with the departure of the last soldiers.

## THE COMING OF SEGREGATION

The closure of Reconstruction did not lead to an automatic end to all of the freedoms that African Americans had gained. Nor did the era of segregation begin suddenly with the U.S. Supreme Court decision in *Plessy v. Ferguson* (1896). The loss of black civil rights in the south was a gradual process, as laws were slowly put into effect that inhibited or prohibited black voting through literacy tests and similar measures, as well as by violence and intimidation. African Americans were not the only victims of these actions, however, as poor southern whites increasingly became targets as well. Rural blacks and whites found some common cause through the Farmer's Alliance and the Populist Party. African Americans were able to return to political office at the local and state level in parts of the south. The political renaissance proved short-lived, however. Whites reacted with uneasiness to these new developments, and the Populist Party did nothing to secure or utilize black support. By the mid-1890s the agrarian movement had faded. By that time, increasing efforts were under way to more openly and thoroughly disenfranchise African Americans.

The social status of African Americans was imperiled as well. Beginning in the last years of Reconstruction, some southern states had begun to gradually introduce laws segregating blacks and whites. These laws were also on the rise by the mid-1890s, thanks in large part to an 1883 Supreme Court decision that for all intents and purposes gutted the Fourteenth Amendment. No support could be counted on from Republicans or white northerners. Racism and Republican disinterest were only part of the problem. In the last decades of the 19th century, a steady lessening of the sectional hostilities associated with the Civil War was evident throughout the country. A romanticized view of the conflict as a "brothers' war" in which the courage of both sides was celebrated had taken hold. These views became entangled with patriotism surrounding the Spanish-American War of 1898, in which some former Confederates participated; the fact that African-American troops participated as well went largely ignored. Old white veterans of the Civil War came to symbolize the conflict; the role played by slavery in the origins of the war was muted, and the participation of black soldiers in the Union war effort

# Plessy v. Ferguson

Homer Plessy was a young shoemaker of mixed (but predominantly white) racial ancestry. According to the laws of Louisiana, however, he was black. In June 1892 Plessy decided to challenge the Jim Crow laws of his state by defying the Separate Car Act, passed two years earlier to segregate streetcars. He boarded a car reserved for whites only, announced his identity to the conductor, and refused to leave for the car reserved for blacks. This led to Plessy's arrest. In October he was tried in the Louisiana criminal district court under Judge John H. Ferguson. Plessy based his case on the Thirteenth and Fourteenth Amendments to the U.S. Constitution, arguing that he enjoyed the same rights as other citizens, regardless of racial heritage. In November Ferguson refused to dismiss the case on the grounds that segregation was legally permissible to promote public order. Plessy's attorney filed an appeal. Thus a series of actions was initiated, culminating in the U.S. Supreme Court decision *Plessy v. Ferguson*, issued on May 18, 1896.

Writing for the majority, Justice Henry B. Brown wrote that it was "too clear for argument" that the Louisiana law did "not conflict with the Thirteenth Amendment, which abolished slavery and involuntary servitude, except as punishment for crime." While admitting that the Fourteenth Amendment "was undoubtedly to enforce the absolute equality of the two races before the law," he contended that "in the nature of things, it could not have been intended to abolish distinctions based upon color, or to enforce social, as distinguished from political, equality, or a commingling of the two races upon terms unsatisfactory to either . . . We consider the underlying fallacy of the plaintiff's argument to consist in the assumption that the enforced separation of the two races stamps the colored race with a badge of inferiority. If this be so, it is not by reason of anything found in the act, but solely because the colored race choose to put that construction upon it."

In the lone dissent, Justice John Marshall Harlan argued that the Thirteenth Amendment "not only struck down the institution of slavery as previously existing in the United States, but it prevents any imposition of any burdens or disabilities that constitute badges of slavery or servitude. It decreed universal civil freedom in this country," while the Fourteenth Amendment "added greatly to the dignity and glory of American citizenship, and the security of personal liberty . . . These two amendments, if enforced according to their true intent and meaning, will protect all the civil rights that pertain to freedom and citizenship."

*Plessy v. Ferguson* codified at the national level the concepts of segregation that were already in effect at the state and local levels in the south, and paved the way for them to be expanded further. It would remain national law until overturned by the U.S. Supreme Court in 1954 in *Brown v. Board of Education of Topeka*.

was conveniently forgotten. By 1900 the United States was well into the era of Jim Crow, the segregation laws nicknamed after a character in the racially stereotypical minstrel shows.

As the realities of the Jim Crow era settled in, African Americans found the new barriers affected every aspect of their lives. Young whites and blacks might play together, but sooner or later a black child would realize the limitations of those friendships, or face their end altogether. African-American children might also face the prospect of watching the humiliation of their elders at the hands of whites, or even see violence perpetrated against them. Growing into adulthood, many young blacks had to face the narrowed horizons of low-wage jobs with little or no chance of advancement. Angry feelings about the situation had to be kept clamped inside, as signs of anything smacking of "disrespect," let alone rebelliousness, could have serious consequences.

## CONCLUSION

In spite of discrimination, African Americans in the 1890s continued to build their own path within the circumstances that they faced, drawing upon the strength of their own institutions. African-American churches continued to interpret Christianity in light of the black experience, giving a strong voice to justice in the face of oppression. African Americans continued to establish their own colleges to provide for higher education that young blacks would otherwise be unable to obtain. Among the pivotal figures in African-American education to arise in this period was Booker T. Washington. A former slave and the founder of Tuskegee Institute in Alabama, Washington preached a message of self-reliance for blacks. He also emphasized, however, that blacks should seek to accommodate themselves to American society as defined by whites, and focused his educational goals on training young blacks for "useful" work in such fields as agriculture and mechanics.

Washington's message was welcomed by many whites,

African-American leader and educator Booker T. Washington in a photograph from the 1880s.

especially after his appearance at the Cotton States and International Exposition of 1895 in Atlanta. There he gave a speech accepting segregation and racial inequality for the present, while asserting that the immediate goal of African Americans should be to focus on economic equality through hard work. Although Washington's speech reflected the realities under which African Americans lived, it angered and disappointed many blacks with its tone of acquiescence. Chief among these was a young African-American professor at Atlanta University named W.E.B. Du Bois. Over the next several years Du Bois would become Washington's most important black critic, asserting that African-American political equality was as essential to success as economic equality. In the decades that followed the turn of the century, a new generation of African Americans would follow the lead of Du Bois and others who believed in racial equality.

MICHAEL COFFEY
NORTH CAROLINA OFFICE OF ARCHIVES AND HISTORY

# Further Reading

Bernstein, Iver. *The New York City Draft Riots: Their Significance for American Society and Politics in the Age of the Civil War*. New York: Oxford University Press, 1990.

Blackmon, Douglas A. *Slavery by Another Name: The Re-Enslavement of Black Americans from the Civil War to World War II*. New York: Doubleday, 2008.

Blight, David W. *Race and Reunion: The Civil War in American Memory*. Cambridge, MA: The Belknap Press of Harvard University Press, 2001.

Fireside, Harvey. *Separate and Unequal: Homer Plessy and the Supreme Court Decision that Legalized Racism*. New York: Carroll and Graf Publisher, 2004.

Foner, Eric. *Reconstruction: America's Unfinished Revolution 1863–1877*. New York: Harper & Row, 1988.

Franklin, John Hope, and Alfred A. Moss, Jr. *From Slavery to Freedom: A History of African Americans*. New York: Alfred A. Knopf, 2000.

Glathaar, Joseph T. *Forged in Battle: The Civil War Alliance of Black Soldiers and White Officers*. New York: Free Press, 1990.

Hahn, Steven, et al., eds. *Freedom: A Documentary History of Emancipation, 1861–1867*. Chapel Hill: University of North Carolina Press, 2008.

Jones, Jacqueline. *Labor of Love, Labor of Sorrow: Black Women, Work, and the Family from Slavery to the Present*. New York: Basic Books, 1985.

Kinshasa, Kwando M. *Black Resistance to the Ku Klux Klan in the Wake of the Civil War*. Jefferson, NC: McFarland & Co., 2006.

Litwack, Leon F. *Been in the Storm So Long: The Aftermath of Slavery.* New York: Alfred A. Knopf, 1998.

Packard, Jerrold M. *American Nightmare: The History of Jim Crow.* New York: St. Martin's Press, 2002.

Shaffer, Donald R. *After the Glory: The Struggles of Black Civil War Veterans.* Lawrence, KS: University Press of Kansas, 2004.

Smith, John David, ed. *Black Soldiers in Blue: African American Troops in the Civil War Era.* Chapel Hill: University of North Carolina Press, 2002.

Steward, T.G. *Buffalo Soldiers: The Colored Regulars in the United States Army.* New York: Humanity Books, 2003.

Ward, Andrew. *The Slaves' War: The Civil War in the Words of Former Slaves.* Boston, MA: Houghton Mifflin Company, 2008.

Yacovne, Donald, ed. *A Voice of Thunder: The Civil War Letters of George E. Stephens.* Chicago: University of Illinois Press, 1997.

# CHAPTER 5

# The Progressive Era and World War I: 1900 to 1920

**FOR MANY AFRICAN** Americans the Progressive Era did not have the same positive identity as it did for the white middle-class reformers who were working to combat such social ills as poverty, crime, poor health and sanitation, and corruption. Instead the final decades of the 19th century and the early decades of the 20th century represented an erosion of the citizenship rights of most African Americans. The clearest evidence of this decline was the 1896 *Plessy v. Ferguson* Supreme Court decision that justified the separate-but-equal basis of legal segregation. The impact of this decision was most immediately felt by the two-thirds of the United States' over 10 million African Americans who in 1900 lived in the south. Because of poor conditions and discrimination in the south, over 200,000 African Americans left the south as economic and social migrants from 1890 to 1910. Eastern and Midwestern cities attracted most African Americans, with the single largest migration occurring during World War I, when an estimated 500,000 to 1 million people moved from the south.

Violence reflected the growing racial tensions of the era. The most notorious example of this violence was lynching, the mob murder of those accused of crimes or violations of the social order. As many as two blacks a week were lynched between 1883 and 1903. The most popular film of the Progressive years—1915's *The Birth of a Nation*—even featured and seemingly accepted

A lynching victim in Alabama in January 1889. By 1918 an estimated 3,000 African-American men had been lynched.

lynching as a form of legitimate justice. The film was based on the explicitly racist fiction found in Thomas Dixon's *Clansman,* published in 1905. The film's legendary director, D.W. Griffith, presented the Klan as the saviour of white people.

Although the height of lynching was at the end of the 19th century, the practice nevertheless continued to be a serious issue throughout the Progressive years, with President Theodore Roosevelt formally denouncing the practice in 1903. Concern continued to the point that federal legislation in the form of the Dyer Anti-Lynching Bill was introduced in 1918. However final passage of the bill had to await the 1920s. A further example of the dire straits facing African Americans during these years was seen in the revival of the Ku Klux Klan, with a membership after 1915 that grew rapidly as racial tensions increased. In the face of the many problems of these years, a number of African-American leaders arose to become effective advocates for change.

## BOOKER T. WASHINGTON'S LEGACY

Booker T. Washington (1856–1915) was born into slavery in Franklin County, Virginia. In time he became an African-American leader and educator of influence and national prominence. Washington escaped poverty through intelligence, hard work, and ambition. After gaining an education, he headed—from 1881 until his death—the Tuskegee Institute in Tuskegee, Alabama, a famed African-American educational establishment. Tuskegee was initially geared to vocational education programs that prepared black students for self-reliance and success in the midst of a segregated and discriminatory world.

Washington's autobiography *Up from Slavery*, published in 1901, became a classic tale of self-improvement during the Progressive era. Over time his position was such that he advised presidents Theodore Roosevelt and William Howard Taft, as well as the key industrialists of the day, Andrew Carnegie and John D. Rockefeller, on racial issues, making him one of the most visible African Americans of the period. Such impressive contacts, along with his belief in laissez-faire capitalism, Christian morality, and middle-class aspirations and values helped him curry favor and raise funds from the national elites.

His ability to gain donations as well as white approval provided the endowments needed for Tuskegee's success.

Washington was freed from slavery in 1865 at age 16, and gained entry to the Hampton Normal and Agricultural Institute in Virginia founded in 1868 by Union General Samuel Chapman Armstrong. Here he received teacher training and worked his way through school, graduating in 1875. From 1878 to 1879 he attended Washington's Wayland Seminary and returned to teach at the Hampton Institute. His many talents so impressed Armstrong that he recommended Washington for the Tuskegee position.

Washington's approach to the affairs of the age was that of an "accommodationist," meaning that he accepted some aspects of the divided racial society that confronted him. His concentration on economic progress over social and political reform created tensions among certain African-American leaders such as W.E.B. Du Bois (1868–1963), William Monroe Trotter (1872–1934), and others in the Niagara Movement. They opposed Washington's racial stance, arguing that disenfranchisement and full civil rights had to be achieved before justice and equality could ever be established for African Americans. Booker T. Washington's Atlanta Exposition Address of 1895, which reflected his stature as a national spokesperson for African Americans, had seemingly accepted

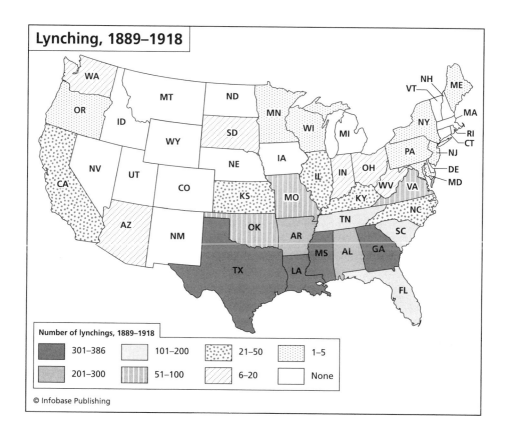

Lynching, 1889–1918

Number of lynchings, 1889–1918

301–386  101–200  21–50  1–5
201–300  51–100  6–20  None

© Infobase Publishing

the present segregationist reality. However Washington's public image represented only the surface of a more complex figure. He did see the evils and inequalities of the times as seriously as many of his critics. He often operated behind the scenes to use the courts to overthrow Jim Crow, and cooperated with W.E.B. Du Bois in such efforts, even co-authoring a joint project in 1907, *The Negro in the South*.

Washington's approach brought him much recognition, including an honorary degree from Harvard in 1897. His advocacy of self-help was an important attribute, and fit well within the conservative side of Progressivism. It was a commonly shared ideal that good deeds, education, and hard work brought their own rewards. Opportunity and success increased an individual's voice and influence, even in an age of institutional racism. Washington nevertheless was able to look past current reality toward a future of equality. His approach helped loosen the purse strings of many white donors, securing needed funds that maintained African-American institutions during insecure times.

## W.E.B. DU BOIS

W.E.B. Du Bois was born in Great Barrington, Massachusetts. He came from a Haitian mulatto background, and was raised in a largely white community where he faced muted, but not brutally overt, racism. Academically talented and introverted, he developed an early interest in his race. Although capable, he lacked the initial resources to enter Harvard and instead attended Fisk College (now University) in Nashville, Tennessee, helped by a scholarship and various forms of family support. His time there from 1883 until 1885 introduced him to the realities of southern institutional discrimination, and stimulated what became a lifelong hatred of all forms of inequality.

Du Bois was finally admitted to Harvard in 1888, supported by a scholarship that saw him through completing his degree in 1890. He immediately began graduate work and received a grant to study at the University of Berlin, where he spent two years before returning to Harvard to complete his doctorate in 1895 with a dissertation titled *The Sup-*

*W.E.B. Du Bois, the first African-American Ph.D. graduate from Harvard, in an undated photograph.*

# Marcus Garvey

Marcus Garvey (1887–1940) was born in Jamaica and was a printer by training. He later became a publisher, orator, and organizer of extreme skill, as well as an entrepreneur of considerably less success. He traveled from Jamaica to Central America and then to London, before settling in New York in 1916.

Garvey developed in these years a belief that the only way forward for African Americans as well as others of African descent was through a truly Pan-African movement that preached a unity that would reach all levels of the community. Their goal was a single political profile for all Africans. To accomplish such an ambition, in 1914 he formed the United Negro Improvement Association and African Community League (UNIA-ACL). Through lectures and rallies, Garvey built up UNIA as a social, economic, and political force that in 1919 claimed a membership of four million, making it the most significant African-American organization of the day.

From 1918 UNIA circulated its message through the *Negro World* edited by Garvey. Speaking in Madison Square Garden in 1920, Garvey drew a crowd of over 25,000, making him the seeming voice of the African-American community. To build further and lasting strength he advocated numerous moneymaking ventures that would bring self-reliance and wealth to African Americans and others of African descent wherever they lived. His was a truly Pan-African movement that saw a return to Africa as a way to reclaim not only black rights, but black also wealth from the imperialist powers that controlled Africa at this time.

Garvey's increasing influence raised the hackles of many, including the U.S. Justice Department, which eventually tried Garvey for mail fraud. The charges stemmed from 1919 stock sales involving the creation of the UNIA-owned Black Star shipping line. Although protests claiming his innocence were mounted, Garvey was convicted in 1923 and given five years imprisonment. His sentence began in 1925, but in 1927 it was commuted by President Calvin Coolidge and Garvey was deported. Garvey continued his campaigns from outside the United States, eventually settling in London after 1935, where he died of a stroke in 1940.

*pression of the Slave Trade in the Americas.* He was the first African American to earn a doctorate from Harvard.

His career first appeared destined for teaching and academic research with positions at Wilberforce in Ohio and the University of Pennsylvania. At Pennsylvania he produced an important early sociological investigation in *The Philadelphia Negro* (1899). He then went to Atlanta University, where he expanded his interests in things African and began to challenge the Booker T.

Washington accommodationist approach to race relations. Du Bois felt that only a complete struggle for civil and political rights and economic security was acceptable. In part as a response to Washington, Du Bois published his *Souls of Black Folks* in 1903.

## DU BOIS AND HIS CONTEMPORARIES

Du Bois and other advocates such as his contemporary and fellow Harvard graduate William Monroe Trotter felt that a stronger stand for African-American rights was in order, and in 1905 created the Niagara Movement to challenge the status quo. Members of this organization, with the exception of Trotter, would in 1909 form the core, along with others such as Mary White Ovington and Oswald Villard, of what became the National Association for the Advancement of Colored People (NAACP). Trotter instead founded the National Equal Rights League.

Like Du Bois, Trotter was an important critic of Washington, but he had a more confrontational approach to activism, which included political action such as protesting outside theatrical performances of *Birth of a Nation* in Boston. Trotter founded the newspaper the *Guardian* in Boston in 1901, which was one of a growing number of black newspapers in this era. The paper was highly critical of Washington's standpoints. Trotter also personally confronted President Woodrow Wilson over racial discrimination in government jobs at the White House in 1914, and was banned from further visits there during the Wilson administration as a result.

Du Bois, even with certain policy reservations, took charge of publications and research and edited the NAACP's house journal *Crisis* for 25 years. He indicted U.S. society for its injustices against African Americans, and his rhetoric accepted few compromises. He was strident in all of his efforts, for he saw a talented tenth of African Americans as natural leaders of their race who would raise the civilized threshold for all African Americans. In this regard, and as the years passed, he increasingly argued for more exclusively African-American leadership in organizations such as the NAACP.

Toward the end of the Progressive period Du Bois's struggles took him to the wider causes of black people, such as the Pan-African movement that linked Caribbean, Latin-American, African-American, and African political aspirations. Du Bois helped organize the first Pan-African Congress in Paris, which was held at the same time as the Versailles Conference peace treaty negotiations in 1919. In his later years, although fully engaged in many pursuits, his politics took him further leftward, eventually into the hands of the communists and an exiled life in Ghana, where he took up citizenship and died in 1963. Du Bois's voice was one of the most important heard during the Progressive period. He represented many of the reform ideals of the generation and argued for the extension of civil rights and equality to all Americans.

Du Bois's activity in the Pan-African movement eventually led him into direct conflict with Marcus Garvey over the correct approach to black nationalism. Garvey emerged as an influential name in the latter years of Progressivism, and became a symbol of another aspect of African-American development during this period. Garvey was clearly a popular rival to other African-American organizations such as the NAACP. His style and approach stressed a form of black supremacy, rather than simply equality. This clearly resonated in parts of the African-American community. In addition the return-to-Africa movement diverted attention from the painful racial divides that affected the United States. However Garvey's manner failed to impress Du Bois, who remained a harsh critic of Garvey and his enterprises, even though he shared Pan-African dreams. In return Garvey argued that it was his authentic blackness that angered Du Bois.

## BLACK WOMEN'S CLUBS

From the 1890s to the end of the Progressive Era, the African-American women's club movement became a central force in a number of campaigns, particularly against lynching. The seriousness of this latter issue was clear. By 1918 more than 3,000 African-American men had been lynched. Led by women such as Ida B. Wells, they denounced lynching through national addresses, lectures, and press reports. Clubs such as the Neighborhood Union of Atlanta, under the direction of Lugenia Burns Hope, extended the antilynching campaign to include other reforms that could impact the local community.

As racism and discrimination were more strongly confronted, calls came to improve other aspects of the African-American experience. These calls fell into line with the Progressive ideals of the day involving issues such as health, education, hygiene, sanitation, and suffrage. To gain more influence, several black women's clubs united in 1896 to form the National Association of Colored Women's Clubs (NACW), initially led by Mary Church Terrell.

Other initiatives reflecting the spirit of the age such as participating in the settlement house movement, expanding educational opportunities, and creating benefit societies were popular undertakings. These endeavors offered many needed services that were lacking for African Americans. Support was also given to union organizing efforts that addressed the conditions affecting African-American female workers, many of whom worked in service industries.

The massive migrations of the period raised new demands in northern and Midwestern cities. To meet these needs, the National League for the Protection of Colored Women was founded. Through later mergers with other organizations, this association became an essential ingredient in the creation of the National Urban League in 1910. Under the early leadership of Ruth

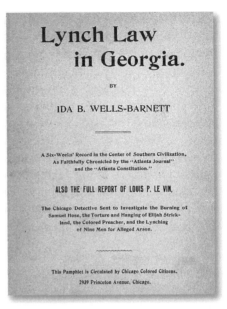

Lynch Law
in Georgia.

BY

IDA B. WELLS-BARNETT

A Six-Weeks' Record in the Center of Southern Civilization,
As Faithfully Chronicled by the "Atlanta Journal"
and the "Atlanta Constitution."

ALSO THE FULL REPORT OF LOUIS P. LE VIN,

The Chicago Detective Sent to Investigate the Burning of
Samuel Hose, the Torture and Hanging of Elijah Strick-
land, the Colored Preacher, and the Lynching
of Nine Men for Alleged Arson.

This Pamphlet is Circulated by Chicago Colored Citizens.
2939 Princeton Avenue, Chicago.

*Ida B. Wells and her 1899 report "Lynch Law in Georgia." Wells was one of a number of female activists who worked toward improving conditions for African Americans in the early 1900s.*

Standish Baldwin and Dr. George Edmund Haynes, the league first operated under the name National League of Black Men and Women. Other organizing efforts created African-American YWCA branches to provide additional services for recent urban arrivals. Protection was particularly needed in light of difficult industrial and economic conditions.

From these social organizations a notable number of prominent African-American women emerged who very much identified with the Progressive zeal for association-led improvement. For example Mary McLeod Bethune formed the National Council of Negro Women, the South-eastern Federation of Colored Women's Clubs, and the Bethune-Cookman Institute, all uplift organizations. Nannie Helen Burroughs founded the National Training School for Women and Girls in Washington, D.C., as part of the general drive for improvement. This organization provided African-American women migrants with education and housing benefits, as well as practical guidance and survival skills. Further Maggie Lena Walker, the first African-American bank president and head of a successful mutual benefit society, showed how economic progress could be achieved.

Throughout these years African-American women led the drive for civic reform and justice. They were initially motivated by the wide range of abuses blacks encountered such as lynching, disenfranchisement, and the social segregation that affected all walks of life. These concerns expanded over time and embraced the full gamut of standard Progressive causes such as health, child care, education, recreation, and public services. Although these initiatives reflected similar issues found in white women's associations, African-American women did not experience the same level of access to politicians, or for that matter even the support of like-minded white associations.

## NATIONAL ASSOCIATION FOR THE ADVANCEMENT OF COLORED PEOPLE

The formation of the National Association for the Advancement of Colored People (NAACP) in 1909 (incorporated in 1911) evolved from the earlier work of Thomas Fortune and those in the Niagara Movement. Figures such as W.E.B. Du Bois and journalist Ida B. Wells pushed for an association that would differ from the Booker T. Washington approach to racial affairs. The NAACP was structured very much like other associations that reflected the Progressive reform and social consciousness.

The 1908 Race Riot in Springfield, Illinois, symbolized the tensions that made such an organization necessary. However even in the midst of a wide range of reform-minded associations, none of these met the specific needs of African Americans whose lives were worsened through the rise of Jim Crow disenfranchisement and a multitude of other discriminatory practices. These were in addition to the brutalities associated with lynching and mob justice.

The NAACP's early leadership was racially and religiously mixed, and drew upon the liberal orientation of many white reformers such as Oswald Villard, Mary White Ovington, and Moorfield Story (NAACP president 1909–15). These individuals were instrumental not only in launching the organization, but also were essential in the fundraising drives that enabled the NAACP to succeed. Membership numbers reached 6,000 in 1914, and numerous city and regional branches were created. By 1919 the organization's membership exceeded 90,000.

In the Progressive years, the focus of the NAACP's campaigns was consumed with court challenges against the parade of restrictions that denied full civil rights to African Americans. These campaigns included pressuring the federal government for legislation to combat lynching, and after 1913, attempting to curtail President Woodrow Wilson's segregationist employment practices in federal jobs. Appeals to the Supreme Court were seen as the best method to defeat segregation, which, although slow in producing results, did bring some partial victories such as *Buchanan v. Warley* in 1917, which attacked city residential segregation policies. During World War I, when the draft called African Americans for military service, the NAACP worked to guarantee the creation of officer status and training for African-American soldiers.

## AFRICAN AMERICANS AND WORLD WAR I

Wilsonian idealism, shaped by Progressive values, influenced America's entry into World War I. The United States did not go to war for simple material gain, but was joining the fight to spread democracy and end the possibility of future conflicts. It was believed that the peace that followed the defeat of the Central powers in 1918 would introduce an age of fairness and universal harmony, guaranteeing the self-determination of nations and the arbitration of disputes. Cooperation would replace big-power rivalry.

African Americans wanted to be a part of this achievement, and after the introduction of the draft, close to 370,000 African Americans came to serve in four units. However the units were marked by Jim Crow segregation that followed them to the battlefront. Further the African-American units such as the 24th and 25th Infantry and the 9th and 10th Cavalry were led by white commanders. In addition large numbers of African-American soldiers were assigned service roles in supply units and labor battalions.

However there were two African-American divisions, the 92nd and 93rd, that saw much active combat. The severity of the fighting was seen in the 35 percent casualty rate that afflicted the 93rd. In the end over 40,000 African-American troops saw action.

Upon arrival in France, the soldiers lacked significant preparation, and were placed under French command for both training and combat operations. This followed a British refusal to train African-American soldiers, which led the U.S. commander, General John J. Pershing, to protest.

Part of this division, the 369th Infantry regiment, particularly distinguished itself serving on the front lines for over six months, longer than any other U.S. unit. Their combat took them to some of the most vicious fronts such as the

*African-American soldiers of the 24th Infantry marching during preparations for the Spanish-American War in 1898. Large numbers of African Americans served in that conflict, and though their contributions went largely unrecognized, this experience soon paved the way for their participation in World War I.*

*This poster published in Chicago in 1918 commemorates the service of African-American troops in World War I while invoking the memory of Abraham Lincoln and the Civil War.*

Argonne, Chateau Thierry, and St. Mihiel, among other battle zones. Their fighting prowess was recognized with 171 French Legions of Merit, which reflected individual bravery and sacrifice under fire, in addition to numerous unit citations. Sergeant Henry Johnson of the 369th received the Croix de Guerre, as did Private Needham Roberts.

*More than 40,000 African-American troops saw action during World War I, including these black soldiers hurling grenades during trench warfare in France.*

The 369th regiment also benefited from the services of Lieutenant James Reese Europe, who led the famous 369th regimental band. The African-American musical contribution, particularly with each regiment having its own band, was critical in introducing both ragtime and early jazz to Europe. Reese was a prominent musician, whose syncopated beat proved very popular in France with both the French and the American troops. Vaudeville star Noble Sissle also served in the band, and helped spread jazz performance styles to Europe.

The 369th unit was known to the Germans as the Hell Fighters, and to the French as the *Enfants Perdus*, or lost children, due to the fact that they existed outside the American mainstream and faced constant discriminatory practices. An example illustrating the outsider status occurred when the 15th New York Guard unit that made up part of the 369th Regiment was not permitted to participate in the New York City departure parade in 1917.

The strict racial codes of the south were informally and privately promoted at the highest military level by General Pershing, even though he officially appreciated the usefulness and valor of the African-American soldiers. Fear of unrest and rebellion by white U.S. soldiers was a major reason behind the strict adherence to segregation. In the Navy, African-American enlistment was

# Jack Johnson

If any figure symbolized the place of African Americans in American popular culture during the Progressive Era, it was Arthur John "Jack" Johnson (1878–1946), who was born in Texas, the son of former slaves. Jack Johnson's triumphs as a boxer made him the most famous and controversial African American in the world. As world heavyweight champion 1908–15, he presented an alternative image to both Booker T. Washington and W.E.B. Du Bois. Although clearly different, he was just as significant.

He gained the championship in 1908 by defeating the champion, Tommy Burns, in Australia in front of a crowd of 20,000. This victory shocked the white community and started a campaign to find a "great white hope" to reestablish the notion of white dominance and superiority. This clamor would finally lead to the former, undefeated white champion James J. Jefferies coming out of retirement to face Johnson. This "fight of the century" occurred on July 4, 1910, in Reno, Nevada, in front of a crowd of 22,000. After being knocked down for the first time in his career, the Jefferies's corner stopped the fight in the 15th round, making Johnson the undisputed champion and a rich man. The reaction across the African-American community was one of universal jubilation that poured onto the streets, to the dismay of many white Americans. The celebrations were soon classified in many quarters as racial riots that resulted nationally in the deaths of 23 African Americans and two whites.

Following this victory Jack Johnson emerged as a famous figure, and perhaps the first celebrity sportsman in an age when professional sports were taking off. As criticism of his success mounted, Johnson added to the controversy with provocative remarks and published commentary. Most importantly in this heightened racial age, Johnson bravely ignored the sexual taboos of the period as he entered repeatedly into interracial marriages and affairs that inflamed white society, making him an even-greater target for abuse. The degree of hatred was such that some even called for his lynching. To escape the controversy, Johnson traveled to Europe.

However it was his heavyweight championship that inflamed most white passions. In order to reverse this uncomfortable reality, a championship bout was arranged in Havana for April 5, 1915. His opponent, Jess Willard, made use of the oppressive heat and eventually wore Johnson down through body punches, finally knocking him out in the 26th round.

Johnson's troubles did not end with the loss of the crown. In 1920 he faced moral charges under a Progressive Era reform, the Mann Act, which was designed to protect women from sexual exploitation if they were transported across state lines for immoral purposes. Johnson's many affairs finally caught up with him, and he was convicted and sentenced to a year in Leavenworth Prison. He gained his release in July 1921.

rejected unless it was restricted to mess service. Yet even in the face of such discrimination, over 5,000 African Americans gave their lives in the conflict.

On the home front during World War I, African-American patriotism was seen in many domestic arenas. From 1917 on, key support was found in African-American Liberty Bond drives to raise war funds. In addition women such as Eva D. Bowles served as Secretary of Colored Women's War Work in the Cities, and coordinated many useful war efforts. She made use of her considerable experience drawn from her Colored YWCA work. Alice Dunbar Nelson drew African-American women to the Council of National Defense, and Louise J. Ross made significant contributions toward the work of the American Red Cross in New Orleans.

The war also created employment opportunities for many African Americans who joined the wartime industries, particularly as munitions workers. Other African Americans contributed by working for the Department of Labor, National Food Administration, and the Women's Motor Corps, which were all engaged in various support or fundraising projects to aid the war effort.

## RACE RIOTS

One particular reflection of the rising tensions that came to the surface in the Progressive period was the racially charged riot. As black populations moved into urban areas and as social tensions increased, rioting became an expression of the mounting fears and frustrations felt by both sides of the racial divide.

The Atlanta race riot of September 22–25, 1906, revealed what could happen when emotions became overly heated. In this case the situation was inflamed by claims of an African-American crime wave, particularly one that suggested frequent attacks or assaults on white women. In addition the heated 1906 gubernatorial campaign between Hoke Smith and Clark Howell made the circumstances worse, as they each exploited white fears of African-American domination that could only be stopped by further disenfranchisement. Others have argued that the increasing entrepreneurial success of Atlanta's African Americans raised suspicions and resentment among lower-class whites. Whatever the background, black citizens were attacked on the streets and days of rioting followed, leaving 25 African Americans and two whites dead.

Atlanta's riots created a familiar pattern in these supposedly Progressive decades. Generally this pattern reflected indiscriminate white attacks on entire black communities. Such violence was attributed to the rapid urbanization that followed black migration northward. By 1920 over two million African Americans—out of a population of over 10 million—had moved to the cities of the north and the Midwest. This increased African-American presence created divides over housing, competition for jobs, and threatened the sense of racial superiority held by many white residents. As violence escalated, casualties were felt on both sides but, in most cases, African Americans suffered most.

Rioting became worse in the years leading up to World War I and its immediate aftermath as social tensions arose, particularly as more Africans Americans wanted an end to their second-class status. After Atlanta there were riots in Springfield, Illinois in 1908 that left six people dead, and later in East St. Louis. The 1917 East St. Louis riot began when striking white workers attacked, fearing that African Americans would take over their jobs at a local aluminium plant. The whites struck at black neighborhoods with an indiscriminate vengeance, destroying property and homes. In the end hundreds were injured, and the official report stated that 39 blacks and nine whites were killed. The NAACP questioned these figures, and argued that African-American deaths numbered in the hundreds.

However in 1919, in the immediate aftermath of war and as the Progressive Era nominally ended, the worst riots occurred. During the summer of 1919 there were 26 riots across the nation in such places as Washington, D.C.; Charleston, South Carolina; Knoxville and Nashville, Tennessee; Omaha, Nebraska; Elaine, Arkansas; and Longview, Texas. The worst, though, was in Chicago, Illinois. The Chicago riot began in late July 1919 when an African-American youth entered a white swimming area, which provoked a white reaction that ultimately led to his drowning. This sparked a 13-day orgy of violence with thousands participating, destroying property and lives. In the end 15 whites and 23 African Americans were killed, and hundreds on both sides were wounded.

Some historians have attributed the increasing postwar violence to the refusal of returning African-American soldiers, who had just participated in a war for democracy, to accept second-class treatment. Others suggested that the causes behind the riots were less lofty and more local, tied to the rising social tensions and competition that resulted when migration brought the races together in crowded urban terrains, where rumor and individual acts could spark mass violence.

## CULTURAL DEVELOPMENT

More successful examples of African-American achievement during the Progressive Era were evident in the cultural arena. In the early years of the 20th century, poet Paul Dunbar and novelist Charles W. Chesnutt gained recognition. Other African-American writers who emerged at this time were Claude McKay, Weldon Johnson, and Carter Woodson. Some published their work in early issues of the NAACP journal *Crisis*. Although making a living from writing remained difficult, a degree of notice and popularity did come to these authors. Dialect was often the preferred form used in these works, and racial issues were often confronted.

*A wide variety of important American musical styles emerged from the work of African-American musicians in the early 20th century. This mostly black musical ensemble of six men posed with their instruments in Atlanta, Georgia, around 1899.*

In music the decade saw the emergence of ragtime, which was the creation of African-American pianists such as Scott Joplin, and it became a key feature of the period's popular minstrel shows. Likewise jazz shaped by musicians such as Charles Bolden spread from New Orleans up the Mississippi as African Americans migrated north. In this way rhythm gained even more importance in American music, a factor that greatly influenced white musicians who copied and adopted these African-American styles for their own compositions. After 1910 W.C. Handy's music introduced the blues to the United States, and musicians such as Jelly Roll Morton spread the new music to wider audiences. Although blacks were denied free and equal integration into most aspects of U.S. life, music was one area of expression that was accepted on a free and equal footing. This musical victory was at least one area during this period where African-American endeavors were not seen as inferior.

A changing economy also brought success to entrepreneurs such as Sarah Breedlove, whose marketing persona was Madame C.J. Walker. These years introduced new industries, some of which were tied to the rising roles of women in American life. Fashion and cosmetic businesses, fueled by growth in the advertising industry, became important reflections of Progressive modernity. Breedlove pioneered products such as pomades for straightening hair, and built a business that included manufacturing laboratories and a sales force that was known throughout the African-American community. By the time of her death in 1919, she was a millionaire and a philanthropist.

## CONCLUSION

African-American intellectuals and cultural figures made important strides in the Progressive Era, building organizations such as the NAACP that would go on to play important roles in the struggle for civil rights throughout the rest of the 20th century. Black women leaders, especially, began to publicly address social issues such as lynching and discrimination, though they suffered from a lack of attention and support from mainstream society. Toward the end of the era, the experience of African Americans in World War I increased the urgency of the search for justice at home. This search led even more African Americans to join the move away from rural farms in the south and into the industrial cities of the north, contributing to a massive population shift that would continue into the 1920s and 1930s.

THEODORE W. EVERSOLE
NORTHERN KENTUCKY UNIVERSITY

# Further Reading

Barbieu, Arthur E., Florette Henri, and Bernard C. Nalty. *The Unknown Soldiers: African American Troops in World War I*. Cambridge: MA: Da Capo Press, 1996.

Berry, Mary F. "Repression of Blacks in the South, 1890–1945: Enforcing the System of Segregation," In *The Age of Segregation: Race Relations in the South, 1860–1945*. Ed. by Robert Haws. Jackson: University Press of Mississippi, 1978.

Buenker, John D., and Joseph Buenker. *Encyclopedia of the Gilded Age and the Progressive Era*. Armonk, NY: M.E. Sharpe, 2005.

Cooper, Michael L. *Hell Fighters: African American Soldiers in World War I*. Hialeah, FL: Dutton, 1997.

Diner, Steven J. *A Very Different Age: America during the Progressive Era*. New York: Hill and Wang, 1998.

Dittmer, John. *Black Georgia in the Progressive Era, 1900–1920*. Champaign: University of Illinois Press, 1977.

Frankel, Noralee, and Nancy S. Dye, eds. *Gender, Class, Race & Reform in the Progressive Era*. Lexington: University Press of Kentucky, 1991.

Gould, Lewis L. *America in the Progressive Era, 1890–1914*. Harlow, UK: Pearson Educational, 2001.

Harlan, Louis R. *Booker T. Washington: The Making of a Black Leader, 1856–1901*. New York: Oxford University Press, 1975.

———. *The Wizard of Tuskegee, 1901–1915*. New York: Oxford University Press, 1986.

Harley, Sharon, and Rosalyn Terborg-Penn, eds. *The Afro-American Woman: Struggles and Images*. Port Washington, NY: Kennikat, 1978.

Jones, Jacqueline. *Labor of Love, Labor of Sorrow: Black Women, Work, and the Family from Slavery to the Present*. New York: Basic Books, 1985.

Lewis, David L. *W.E.B. Du Bois: Biography of a Race 1868–1919*. New York: Holt, 1994.

McGerr, Michael. *A Fierce Discontent: The Rise and Fall of the Progressive Movement in America, 1890–1920*. New York: Oxford University Press, 2005.

Meier, August. *Negro Thought in America, 1880–1915*. Ann Arbor: University of Michigan, 1961.

Rudwick, Elliot M. *W.E.B. Du Bois: Propagandist of the Negro Protest*. New York: Atheneum Press, 1978.

Southern, David W. *The Progressive Era and Race: Reform and Reaction, 1900–1917*. Wheeling, WV: Harlan Anderson, 2006.

Ward, Geoffrey C. *Unforgivable Blackness: The Rise and Fall of Jack Johnson*. New York: Vintage Books, 2006.

Wiebe, Robert. *The Search for Order, 1877–1920*. New York: Hill and Wang, 1966.

# CHAPTER 6

# The Roaring Twenties and the Great Depression: 1920 to 1939

**THE AFRICAN-AMERICAN MIGRATION** that had such dynamic effects during the Progressive Era continued unabated during the 1920s and 1930s. A number of factors influenced this huge movement of people away from their previous agricultural existences in the south. The presence of Jim Crow restrictions throughout the south made discrimination an uncomfortable way of life. Segregation created separate and unequal communities. For many blacks guaranteed constitutional rights and liberties were few and far between, and humiliation was often a daily occurrence.

Economic issues also stimulated the movement northward. The agricultural boom of World War I was followed in the 1920s with a steady decline in the number of farms, as well as a rise in farm debt. Agricultural commodity prices collapsed because of overproduction. In addition the boll weevil severely reduced southern cotton production, and this further undermined African-American employment for both laborers and sharecroppers.

Declining agricultural prospects became the push, and expanding industry in the north was the pull that drew increasing numbers to jobs in the cities. The interruption of European immigration by World War I and then the quota system after 1924 meant that other workers had to be found. By the 1920s major northern and Midwestern cities such as Chicago, New York, Boston, Detroit, Philadelphia, Pittsburgh, Washington, D.C., Cincinnati, and others saw their African-American populations double. The relatively better conditions of the north and the increasing presence of large numbers of African Americans carved new communities out of old neighborhoods. The city sections that blacks inherited were often overcrowded. The housing stock was poorly maintained, and often hindered by restrictive residential covenants. Therefore African-American migration and settlement brought with it new dilemmas as the urbanization process accelerated.

## THE 1920s

The 1920s introduced other changes that affected African Americans, such as Prohibition that lasted until 1933, as well as the arrival of women's voting rights, both important and transforming social developments. The Ku Klux Klan also escaped its southern confines by the mid-1920s to become a national racist enterprise with millions of members. This cast a somber prospect for those recently arrived.

Racial hostility and discrimination remained realities to be confronted in the north. The May 31, 1921, race riots in Tulsa, Oklahoma reflected these underlying tensions. Here 60 blacks and 25 whites died in KKK-inspired attacks on black residential areas. Throughout the nation the Ku Klux Klan's influence that stirred hundreds of violent incidents could be seen. A pattern of beating, lynching, and murder as well as burning crosses and other forms of intimidation became frequent occurrences for many blacks.

Efforts were made to combat violent racist incidents, particularly lynching, which was a persistent extralegal feature of the African-American experience. An antilynching bill was first introduced by Missouri Representative L.C. Dyer in 1921, which passed the House in 1922. This measure appeared as a hopeful means to curtail this most obvious violation of basic due process. However southern opposition in the Senate secured the defeat of the Dyer Act on January 26, 1922, leaving lynching a continuing stain on the national conscience for years to come.

*Ku Klux Klan leaders from Texas marching in front of the U.S. Capitol on September 13, 1926.*

# The Scottsboro Boys Trials

The sensational Scottsboro Boys Trials began in 1931 after nine black youths were arrested and charged with the rape of two white women, Victoria Price and Ruby Bates, in Scottsboro, Alabama, following a disturbance on the Chattanooga to Memphis railroad line. On March 25, 1931, police were called to an incident involving a fight between blacks and whites in a freight car. It was subsequently discovered that there were two white women also present. At first these women were not observed—they were dressed in men's overalls. Following a doctor's examination, it was determined that the women had engaged in intercourse and, although they appeared uninjured, the women claimed that they vigorously resisted all advances but were nevertheless raped. The presence of the girls in the rail car was explained by the fact that they were riding the rails in hobo fashion.

Four of the nine youths—Roy and Andy Wright, Eugene Williams, and Heywood Patterson—had been raised in Chattanooga, Tennessee. The others—Ozie Powell, Clarence Norris, Olen Montgomery, Charlie Weems, and William Roberson—came from Georgia. Olen Montgomery was blind in one eye, and Willie Roberson suffered from syphilis and had difficulty walking.

The first trial—by an all-white jury—occurred in April. Six of the youth denied the charges, two confessed apparently under duress, and one blamed all the others. Ultimately all were convicted and sentenced to death except 12-year-old Roy Wright, although the jury wanted the death penalty in his case as well. Following these convictions, the case was appealed and eventually reached the U.S. Supreme Court in 1932 (*Powell v. Alabama*), which found that effective counsel had been denied and ordered new trials.

A second trial was held in 1933, which caused great controversy because of the arrival of northern Jewish lawyers supported by International Labor Defense, a legal arm of the Communist Party. This was viewed as a foreign invasion and highly suspect in the south. Recanted testimony was introduced, as were challenges to the white-only jury system, but again eight of the youths were found guilty and sentenced to death—a sentence that was repeated once more following a third trial that year.

The stage was now set for still more trials and appeals, leading to the 1935 *Norris v. Alabama* decision, which found that blacks could not be systematically denied admission to jury service in criminal cases. After more legal proceedings, charges against five of the defendants were dropped in 1937. The remaining defendants were released on parole over the next few years, which left only Heywood Patterson in custody. In 1948 he escaped from prison and fled to Michigan, which refused to return him to Alabama.

The Scottsboro cases drew national attention and support from different political quarters including the NAACP, the American Communist Party, and New Deal Democrats. The case ultimately embarrassed the south, exposing the region as a backwater of intolerance and ignorance.

As a more positive symbol, in 1922 the Lincoln Memorial was dedicated and quickly became a key Washington historical landmark. The audience viewing the ceremony was segregated by race, clearly underlining the essence of the nation's continuing racial divides.

To combat such serious abuses and discriminations, Marcus Garvey's Universal Negro Improvement Association (UNIA), founded in 1914, grew extremely popular during the 1920s and helped frame the era. UNIA campaigned against the violence and injustices just as the NAACP did; however, the movement had a back-to-Africa nationalist flavor, and promoted black enterprises and independent social development to accomplish its liberationist goals. Garvey initially had great success and drew tens of thousands to his addresses and meetings, which often filled Madison Square Garden. Unfortunately for the movement, Garvey's conviction on mail fraud charges led to his 1925 imprisonment and eventual deportation. Without his dynamic leadership, UNIA fell into steady decline.

The NAACP also continued its growth during the 1920s, gaining 90,000 members nationally. Its energies were consumed with the drive to end lynching and to secure legal due process and full civil rights for African Americans. The pervasiveness of the problem was indicated in its 1925 report revealing that 1889–1925, 90 women had also been lynched.

In 1920 James Weldon Johnson became the first black secretary of the NAACP, a post he held until 1930. Blatant civil rights abuses became paramount causes for elimination. In the area of African-American workers' rights, in 1925 A. Philip Randolph organized the Brotherhood of Sleeping Car Porters. This was a critical undertaking, because many blacks found work as porters on the nation's railroads. In a similar vein and in the same year, African-American attorneys established the National Bar Association to protect their interests in light of a segregated legal profession.

## SOCIAL DEVELOPMENT

During the 1920s there was much positive change within the African-American community, even in the face of persistent discrimination. The National Negro Baseball League was formed in 1920, providing an outlet for talented black ballplayers.

The first professional black team, the New York Renaissance, was started by Robert Douglas and played out of Harlem, New York. In 1924 University of Michigan athlete William D. Hubbard became the first African American to win a gold medal at that year's Paris Summer Olympics when he won the broad jump. In addition the Harlem Globetrotters basketball team was formed in 1927, reflecting basketball's increasing importance as a popular urban sport.

In the early years of this decade, Eva B. Dykes, Sadie T. Mossell, and Georgiana R. Simpson made use of educational opportunities in the north to become the first African-American women to earn doctoral degrees. In 1921 Bessie Coleman earned her international pilot's license when she qualified and met the requirements at France's Federation Aeronautique.

As the first black woman pilot, she gained fame as a stunt aviator; unfortunately a plane crash in 1926 ended her career. In the field of engineering, in

*Bessie Coleman in 1921. She was the first American woman to earn an international pilot's license.*

1923, Garrett Morgan confirmed African-American inventiveness when he received his patent for the traffic light, which he later sold to General Electric for $40,000.

In the field of performing arts, *Shuffle Along* opened on Broadway in 1921 and starred such notables as Eubie Blake, Florence Mills, Noble Sissle, and eventually Paul Robeson and Josephine Baker. Robeson and Baker would in time become international sensations. In 1923 Bessie Smith's Columbia record *Down Hearted Blues* sold over a million copies, making her the most popular blues singer of the period. The year also saw the appearance of another hit all-black show, *Running Wild*, which introduced the Charleston dance to America. This dance craze soon spread around the world, and became a defining Roaring Twenties icon.

In 1924 Florence Mills opened the popular *Dixie to Broadway* at New York's Broadhurst Theater, and Roland Hayes became an opera star and the first African American to perform at Carnegie Hall. In addition the 1924 musical *Chocolate Dandies* became another Broadway hit for Eubie Blake, Noble Sissle, and Josephine Baker. The Savoy Ballroom opened in Harlem on New York's Lennox Avenue in 1926, becoming a favorite venue for innovative African-American dance and music entertainment.

In 1925 Josephine Baker took her performances to Paris, where she created *La Revue Negre* that made her a French star and helped popularize American jazz in Europe.

In the same year, Paul Robeson made his film debut in *Body and Soul*, directed by Oscar Micheaux. In the realm of jazz, Duke Ellington made his debut in Harlem's famous Cotton Club in 1927, which further popularized not only the club, but also his supreme musical talents.

In 1928 Paul Robeson's steady rise to stardom continued with *Showboat*. In this show he sang *Ol' Man River*, a tune for which he would long be remembered. To end the decade, *Hot Chocolates* opened on Broadway at the Hudson Theater. The show starred Fats Waller, one of the

*Josephine Baker in a portrait taken in Paris in 1949 by the writer Carl Van Vechten.*

era's most dynamic stride piano players, and a Victor recording artist whose style influenced many fellow musicians.

## THE HARLEM RENAISSANCE

Besides significant developments in a wide range of American cultural and social arenas, the 1920s were also distinguished by a flowering of African-American intellectual endeavor that came to be known as the Harlem Renaissance. This movement was named after New York's Harlem neighborhood, which hosted many of the artists and writers who gave this era its flair. Blacks had moved into the area in the early 1900s, and large sections were developed after 1910 along 135th St. by African-American real estate entrepreneurs who saw the area's potential. Also known as the New Negro Movement and New Negro Renaissance, this awakening began at the end of World War I and reached its apex in the mid-1920s, only to fade in the mid-1930s, its impact reduced by the harsh conditions of the Depression.

The renaissance brought negro art and literature out of isolation from the cultural mainstream. Black creative efforts now entered the U.S. cultural forefront, where they were given serious consideration by publishers and critics. The renaissance also overlapped with other African-American art forms such as music, theater, and dance to make a broader statement of arrival and purpose. The emergence of the movement at this particular time has been attributed to the steady rise of a black bourgeoisie as a result of the Great Migration northward that had opened doors for greater educational and economic opportunities.

Harlem became home to the aspirations of these upwardly mobile people who increasingly embraced equality and justice as a right. Here the work of the NAACP as well as that of Marcus Garvey's UNIA gave legitimacy to black social development. In addition New York was home to various key magazines that gave voice to different aspects of African-American ambition. The NAACP's *Crisis* was edited by W.E.B. Du Bois in New York, as was Charles S. Johnson's National Urban League publication *Opportunity*. A. Phillip Randolph and Charles Owen's *Messenger* and Garvey's magazine *Negro World* were also published in the city, making Harlem an important crossroads for the exchange of black ideas on many different social issues.

Turn-of-the-century successes in the performing arts had to a degree popularized jazz and blues among the new arrivals, as well as for white performers and audiences. Writers such as Paul Laurence Dunbar and Charles W. Chesnutt had previously received national attention, and demonstrated that there was a market for African-American literature.

By the end of World War I, poet Claude McKay and writer James Weldon Johnson had made significant inroads with their descriptions of black experiences. McKay's *Harlem Shadows* (1922) set the stage after he gained a national publisher, Harcourt, Brace and Company. Jean Toomer's innovative novel

*A photograph of singer Bessie Smith taken by Carl Van Vechten in February 1936.*

*Cane* (1923) took the black experience to new heights stylistically with its documentation of both the southern and northern black experiences.

Jessie Fauset's *There is Confusion* (1924) explored black middle-class life from the woman's perspective. Fauset established herself as one of the most prolific novelists of the period.

The name Harlem Renaissance was generally attributed to Alain Locke's publication *The New Negro,* which appeared in 1925, and had an immediate impact throughout the United States. This publication evolved from a National Urban League dinner held on March 21, 1924. Here emerging black writers were introduced for the first time to the New York literary establishment. What followed from this endeavor was the respected sociological magazine *Survey Graphic*'s March 1925 issue exclusively devoted to Harlem's creative forces.

Locke was featured in this issue, along with other black writers who were shaping an African-American approach to the arts. This became the basis for Locke's expanded and pioneering anthology that gave form to the Renaissance. Harlem life was also given a further boost by the appearance of white writer Carl Van Vechten's *Nigger Heaven* in 1926. Vechten explored Harlem's black milieu in both its low and high dimensions in a manner that attracted New York sophisticates to the splendors of Harlem. The effect was an explosion of interest in African-American literature and arts. The publication of *Fire* magazine in 1926 and the introduction of a number of young black writers such as Langston Hughes, Wallace Thurman, and Zora Hurston provided still another direction for the Harlem Renaissance.

The Renaissance attracted a diverse range of artists, and no single theme dominated development. Many whites were attracted to the movement because of curiosity and its faddish appeal. In addition to a literary thrust that examined black subject matter and exposed it to a larger national audience, these years also saw much experimentation in the performing arts with various examples of jazz and blues music mingling with literary expression to become entertainment focal points.

Jelly Roll Morton, Bessie Smith, Louis Armstrong, and Duke Ellington all became established stars during this era, and their legacies would continue to grow as the 20th century progressed. In the visual arts, painters such as Aaron Douglas gained recognition for his combination of modernism and African primitivism. Pittsburgh-born Henry Ossawa Tanner (1859–1937), who was trained in Philadelphia and France and therefore not a member of the Harlem Renaissance, nevertheless became, during the height of the era, the first African-American artist to achieve full member status and recognition at the National Academy of Design.

The impact of the Harlem Renaissance receded during the 1930s as the economic conditions associated with the Depression worsened social conditions for all. Organizations such as the NAACP and the National Urban League shifted focus, and many key artists relocated to other areas, some outside the United States. However what was unleashed artistically could not be reversed even in tough times, and writers and artists who got their start in these years continued to produce in the decades ahead.

*Louis Armstrong, shown above in 1953, performed as many as 300 concerts a year, and is known as one of the founding fathers of jazz.*

## ALAN LOCKE AND JAMES WELDON JOHNSON

Alain Locke (1885–1954) was born in Philadelphia, Pennsylvania, where he gained his initial education. He advanced to Harvard, where he studied English and philosophy, graduating in 1907. His success as a student led to his nomination as the first African-American Rhodes scholar at Oxford University, which he attended 1907–10. Following Oxford, Locke studied in Germany and France; he eventually returned to Harvard, where he completed his Ph.D. in philosophy in 1918 with a dissertation titled *The Problem of Classification in the Theory of Value.*

After receiving his doctorate, Locke became head of the Philosophy Department at Howard University and remained at this post until his retirement in 1953, although he would hold many visiting appointments in later years. Locke was a convinced promoter of African culture and a keen collector of Africana. He believed in an early version of multiculturalism and demanded racial equality as the basis for a just American society.

Locke became a founding voice in the Harlem Renaissance through his many publications in *Opportunity* magazine and by his important anthology of the new black writing, *The New Negro,* published in 1925. His successful promotion of African-American intellectual contributions was reflected in his 1936 publications *The Negro and His Music* and *Negro Art: Past and Present.* Until his death Locke remained an important voice in African-American intellectual history, an influence that extended beyond the 1920s and 1930s.

James Weldon Johnson (1871–1938) was born in Jacksonville, Florida, the son of a waiter and a local teacher. He graduated from Atlanta University in 1894 and eventually taught and studied law, passing the Florida bar to become the first African American to do so since Reconstruction.

Johnson's many varying skills and accomplishments make him a difficult individual to classify. He was a diplomat, novelist, song writer, poet, and civil rights advocate and professor, teaching at New York and Fisk universities. He impressed President Theodore Roosevelt to the degree that he was appointed U.S. consul to Venezuela 1906–09, and to Nicaragua 1909–13. His advocacy of full civil rights for African Americans took him to the NAACP in 1916, where he advanced to become general secretary in 1920, a post he held until 1930.

His writings include the novel *The Autobiography of an Ex-Colored Man* (1912), poetry such as *Fifty Years and Other Poems* (1917), and an examination of African-American life titled *Black Manhattan* (1930). Johnson was a vigorous promoter of African-American talent during the 1920s, and he wrote extensively on negro spirituals and poetry, which made him a central character in the Harlem Renaissance. In addition he was a significant songwriter in collaboration with his brother J. Rosamond Johnson, and Bob Cole, creating songs for Broadway musical theater. Johnson's *Lift Every Voice and Sing* remains a famous song to this day.

# Carter G. Woodson

Carter G. Woodson (1875–1950) was born in Virginia, the son of slaves, and emerged from poverty through self-reliance and endeavor to become a founding father of black history and a scholar of enormous influence. Woodson received his B.A. from Berea College in Kentucky and advanced to the University of Chicago where he earned an M.A. in 1908; he then went to Harvard, where he received his Ph.D. in 1912 with a dissertation titled *The Disruption of Virginia*.

*The influential scholar Carter G. Woodson, who became known as the father of black history.*

Woodson later took up teaching and administrative posts at Howard University and West Virginia State. His significant commitment to African-American history as a valid means of cultural uplift was apparent in 1915, when he founded the Association for the Study of African American Life and History, which was followed by the *Journal of Negro History* in 1916.

Woodson's promotion of scholarship tied to African-American themes built racial respect and revealed a rich culture with roots submerged by racism. His endeavors supported the ideals of black pride, and he supported many of Marcus Garvey's drives for racial achievement and recognition by publishing in UNIA's *Negro World*.

Of particular importance to the Harlem Renaissance was Woodson's establishment of Associated Publishers in 1920, which opened its doors to African-American writers and African-American themes. He followed with the creation in 1926 of Negro History Week as a means for a general public awareness of African-American contributions to U.S. culture. Woodson's academic work covered many areas, but of particular importance in this period were his *History of the Negro Church* (1927) and *Mis-education of the Negro* (1933).

## THE 1930s AND THE GREAT DEPRESSION

The 1929 Wall Street crash and resulting hard times affected all Americans, but was particularly painful for Africans Americans. By 1932 unemployment affected almost half of African-American workers, and social tensions increased proportionately with whites wanting those blacks with jobs dismissed. Violence increased as well, with lynching, especially in the south, leaving 28 victims in 1933.

During the 1930s there was also a major shift in African-American political allegiance away from the Republican Party, to Franklin D. Roosevelt's Democratic Party and its New Deal policies. However the drive to recruit more black Democrats by Roosevelt's New Dealers created major tensions within the party, particularly in the south where the party's solid Democratic base rested.

Southerners were angered by any appeals to African-American political participation, and they made the racial divide a critical issue. This was witnessed during the House debates over the antilynching bill in 1937. Eventually the House passed the bill, but over the objections of every southern Democratic member but one. This abandonment was transferred to the Senate where southern Democratic Senators filibustered the legislation, leading to the antilynching bill's withdrawal in 1938. Racism was clearly alive in the south. African-American migrations to northern cities saw racist tensions increase there as well, establishing patterns of lasting animosities and suspicions ingrained in the fabric of the nation.

Discrimination was still a force that hampered full black participation in the New Deal job schemes and other social programs, particularly housing. Roosevelt sampled black opinion, and built a base of advisers from the

*Ben Shahn photographed this young girl working in a cotton field in 1935. African Americans suffered even higher levels of unemployment and poverty during the Depression than whites.*

community, sometimes referred to as his black cabinet. After 1933 Mary McLeod Bethune became a prominent member of this group, and in 1935, she established the National Council of Negro Women to boost concerted advancement efforts.

A poster for a WPA Negro Theatre Production in New York City around 1936.

Although New Deal programs did not cure injustices or eliminate discrimination, they offered African Americans greater opportunities than what had come before in terms of economic development. The Federal Music Project and the Federal Writers Project as well as Works Progress Administration (WPA) programs for artists offered some level of support for creative employment. However WPA work schemes, especially in the south, revealed hiring inequalities, often excluding blacks who were expected to work privately for less than the WPA paid. New Deal administrators such as Harry Hopkins tried to eliminate such discrimination in hiring and worked with the NAACP; nevertheless employment difficulties persisted, especially in the south.

Tensions and upheavals also increased throughout the period, with the Harlem Riots of 1935 symbolizing the disquiet felt by many. Rumors spread the false report of a police attack on a teenage shoplifter—this caused a riot to break out, resulting in the deaths of three blacks and over 200 injuries to others, both black and white. There was also the destruction of $2 million worth of property.

Even with the introduction of New Deal projects, wage differentials continued to reflect a divided society. By 1939 the mean income for male African-Americans was $537, compared to $1,234 for whites. For black females, the mean income was $331, compared to $771 for white women. In order to deal with the continued issue of economic discrimination, in June 1941 President Roosevelt issued Executive Order 8802, which banned federal job discrimination based on race, creed, color, or national origin.

## 1930s SOCIAL DEVELOPMENT

In the performing arts, African-American contributions to U.S. culture remained active in the Depression years, even in the face of economic chaos. In 1930 Billie Holiday made her entrance at Pod's and Jerry's Speakeasy, launching an influential singing career that continued until her death in 1959. Sarah Vaughan and Ella Fitzgerald also emerged as singing artists during the 1930s. Duke Ellington's smooth hit *Mood Indigo* in 1931 further established his reputation as a musician of importance. Singer/actress Etta Moten set another precedent in 1933, when she was the first African American to perform at the White House, at the invitation of President Roosevelt.

In 1934 the famed Apollo Theater on 135th St. in Harlem staged its first live shows, and Louise Beavers gained central billing in the film *Imitation of Life*. By 1935 Marian Anderson was regarded as one of the greatest singers of the era. However even she faced discrimination when she was denied a chance to perform at Constitution Hall in Washington, D.C. in 1939 by the Daughters of the American Revolution (DAR), who had a whites-only policy.

Other important steps forward were witnessed. William Grant Still conducted the Los Angeles Symphony in 1936, and Benny Goodman, to some protest, integrated his orchestra in 1938 with the arrival of Teddy Wilson and Lionel Hampton. Actress Hattie McDaniel's outstanding performance in 1939's *Gone With the Wind* established her stardom, and set the stage for her to become the first African American to win an Oscar, in 1940. Singer Lena Horne also made her first film appearance in the *Duke is Tops* in 1939.

Sporting success provided another key outlet for African-American achievement during the 1930s. Josh Gibson, who would become known as the black Babe Ruth, started his impressive career in negro baseball in 1930 with the Pittsburgh Homestead Grays. The all-black New York Rens defeated the Boston Celtics in 1932 to win the World Basketball Championship. In boxing, the Joe Louis phenomenon gained a national following in 1935 with his defeat of Primo Carnera at Yankee Stadium.

This set the stage for Louis's gaining the world heavyweight championship when he defeated Jim Braddock in 1937, as well as former champion Max Baer. In 1938 he revenged his 1936 defeat by the German boxer Max Schmeling with a devastating two-minute-and-four-second first-round victory in Yankee Stadium before a crowd of over 70,000. Louis, known as the Brown Bomber, became a major sporting hero, staging 25 title defenses 1937–49. And in an age of rising levels of racism at the 1936 Berlin Olympics, Jesse Owens won four gold medals in athletics, making a mockery of Nazi racial theories of Aryan supremacy.

## POLITICAL DEVELOPMENTS

Other political developments occurred, such as the founding in Detroit, Michigan, of the black nationalist Nation of Islam by Wallace Fard Muhammad in 1930. In 1935 leadership passed to Elijah Muhammad, who controlled the movement until 1975. The Nation of Islam hoped to raise black separatist aspirations through its home-grown religious program. Although the term *Islam* was used in the movement's name, as were other Islamic

# The Brown Bomber

Joe Louis (Barrow) (1914–81) was born in Alabama, and his life personified the African-American migratory experience. Escaping poverty, he and his family moved to Detroit, Michigan, in search of better economic prospects. It was here that he built his boxing skills, becoming a local Golden Gloves champion before turning professional in 1934.

Louis's talents led him to rise quickly through the ranks, fighting frequently, and on the way convincingly defeating former champions Primo Carnera and Max Baer in 1935. In 1936 he faced the German former heavyweight champion, Max Schmeling, who in a surprising reversal of expectations handed Louis, a 10-to-1 favorite, his first defeat following 27 straight victories, 23 of these by knockout. Some interpreted this as a propaganda victory for Nazi Germany and its theories of Aryan supremacy.

Instead of an immediate rematch with Schmeling, Louis returned to serious training, and went directly for the heavyweight championship held by James J. Braddock. He emerged the champion, defeating Braddock in 1937 with an eighth-round knockout.

The 1938 Schmeling rematch came at a time of heightening fears over Nazi aggression and ambition. In front of a crowd of 70,000 and a radio audience of 70 million, Louis annihilated Schmeling in one round, ending any idea of racial supremacy. Both black and white Americans celebrated Louis's victory.

Between 1940 and 1942, Louis fought almost monthly. With the coming of World War II, he joined the army and served as an army spokesman and as a physical trainer, holding the rank of sergeant. Appearing in a series of exhibition matches, he became a major fundraiser for the war effort.

Louis held the championship for 12 years, until 1949, and had an impressive record of 25 successful defenses of his title. While Louis had faced prejudice, he rose above it through personality and physical prowess, and became a national hero.

JOE LOUIS
HEAVYWEIGHT SENSATION

*A promotional photograph of Joe Louis from early in his career.*

symbols, in conventional Islamic circles the Nation of Islam was viewed as a heretical offshoot.

In the world of mainstream politics, in 1934, Arthur W. Mitchell of Illinois became the first African-American Democratic congressman. Roy Wilkins, who later emerged as a major force in the civil rights movement during the 1950s, became editor of the NAACP's *Crisis* magazine in 1934. Thurgood Marshall also came to the legal forefront with the 1935 *Murray v. Pearson* Supreme Court case, and as special counsel to the NAACP in 1938. William H. Hastie became the first African-American Federal District Court judge in 1937 when President Roosevelt appointed him to the Virgin Islands bench, and, in 1939, Jane Bolin became the first African-American female judge when she joined New York's City's Domestic Court system.

## THE EMERGENCE OF THURGOOD MARSHALL

Thurgood Marshall (1908–93) was born in Baltimore and educated locally until attending Lincoln University in Chester County, Pennsylvania, where he graduated in 1930. Following an early interest in constitutional issues, he progressed to Howard University in Washington, D.C., to study law and graduated in 1933. Early in his legal career, Marshall made an impact with his victory in the *Murray v. Pearson* Supreme Court decision of 1935, which challenged the University of Maryland Law School's exclusion of a fully qualified black applicant solely because of race.

Marshall's reputation brought him to the attention of the NAACP, and he joined the organization in New York, first as assistant counsel, and then advancing to lead counsel by the end of the decade. Marshall's profile in civil rights cases continued into the postwar era, and he further cemented his reputation in the *Brown v. the Board of Education* decision in 1954. During the Kennedy administration, he was appointed a judge on the U.S. Court of Appeals, and in 1965 President Lyndon Johnson appointed him solicitor-general. In 1967 his highest accolade came when he was nominated and confirmed to the U.S. Supreme Court, becoming the first African-American justice.

## BLACK PERFORMERS OF THE 1930s

Marian Anderson (1897–1993) was born in Philadelphia, where her vocal abilities were recognized early; however she faced discrimination in white-dominated schools and choral groups. She nevertheless persevered, and developed her talent in local high schools, church choirs, and with private instructors. Her career advanced through tours and competitions, such as with the Philadelphia Philharmonic Society, finally making her major debut in 1925 with the New York Philharmonic Orchestra, which led to her receiving a contract. By 1928 she was performing at Carnegie Hall, where her reputation as the nation's premiere contralto voice was established.

She followed her American success with European tours during the 1930s, impressing audiences and conductors alike. The famous conductor Arturo Toscanini praised her exceptional voice as a true rarity. In the United States, when she was blocked by the DAR from performing in Constitution Hall in Washington, D.C., First Lady Eleanor Roosevelt resigned from the DAR in protest.

Anderson rebounded from this humiliation by staging an Easter 1939 concert at the Lincoln Memorial, which brought a mixed audience of over 75,000 and was a statement against the absurdity of segregationist Washington. Her success was clear when the DAR reversed its racial policies and invited her to perform at Constitution Hall in 1943.

Anderson's career was one in which talent overcame prejudice. By the 1950s she starred at the New York Metropolitan Opera, and through presidential appointments became an American Goodwill Ambassador and eventually a member of the UN Human Rights Commission. Retiring from performing in 1965, she remained a prominent cultural figure, and was awarded the Medal of Freedom by President Johnson as well as numerous other presidential and congressional accolades. Her Connecticut studio is now a museum. Welcomed openly in hotels and restaurants abroad, Anderson did not allow racism to undermine her achievements; her dignity always saw her through.

Hattie McDaniel (1895–1952) was born in Wichita, Kansas, one of 13 children. Her parents were former slaves who passed on to their children the horrors and legacy of slavery. McDaniel's start in the entertainment business began in minstrel shows. By the 1920s she was singing and performing on radio. McDaniel arrived in Los Angeles in 1931, and soon launched a film career that would include over 300 appearances. Although a skilled performer on stage and radio as well as a singer and songwriter, between entertainment jobs she supported herself by working as a maid and cook.

*Marian Anderson in a Carl Van Vechten photograph from 1940.*

Her work offscreen shaped many of her later film roles, where she was given numerous roles playing the maid. McDaniel was clearly confined by the dominant racial stereotypes of the era, but her attitude was that she would rather be paid well for playing a maid, than paid poorly for being one. Her first film role was in *The Golden West* (1932), and her first major role was in John Ford's *Judge Priest* in 1934, the year she joined the Screen Actors Guild. Her rise to stardom followed her role as Mammy in David O. Selznick's *Gone with the Wind* (1939).

However the film's premiere in Atlanta, Georgia, meant that she was denied inclusion in the program, or even attendance due to the city's segregation policies. Friend and fellow star Clark Gable had to be persuaded not to boycott the Atlanta showing. She was included prominently in the Los Angeles premiere. McDaniel's outstanding performance was recognized at the Academy Awards where she won the Oscar for Best Supporting Actress, making her the first African American to be nominated for, and win, an Oscar.

McDaniel contributed to Hollywood's fundraising war efforts during the 1940s, and was active in legal battles against the restrictive covenant that denied African Americans access to certain Los Angeles properties and neighborhoods. Her last film roles were in *Mickey* and *Family Honeymoon* in 1949. Postwar, she became a radio star with her popular show *Beulah*.

McDaniel became a star during a period of continuing discrimination and intolerance. She left a mark in film, even though by today's standards her characters would be dismissed as insulting. However she perfected what she was given, and asserted her personality into her roles, striking an independent and strong presence that was much respected in the industry.

## LANGSTON HUGHES

Langston Hughes (1902–67) was born in Joplin, Missouri, and experienced a childhood of parental separation. For many years he was raised by his grandmother in Kansas before moving to Illinois and eventually rejoining his mother in Cleveland, Ohio, where he attended Central High School. During these years he developed an early love for writing and books. His childhood was not particularly happy, and his relations with his father were intermittent and strained; however to gain his father's financial support for higher education, Hughes agreed to enter Columbia University to study engineering.

This choice did not suit him, and Hughes left the university and drifted through a series of jobs. In the early 1920s he began his long association with Harlem. His 1921 article *The Negro Speaks of Rivers* was published in *Crisis*, making an important impression. Gaining work on a ship, Hughes expanded his horizons, traveling to Africa and Europe, and for a brief period sampled American 1920s expatriate life in Paris. He returned to the United States in 1924, and settled for a time in Washington, where he worked for historian Carter G. Woodson.

Enthused by black themes and jazz-age culture, Hughes was concerned with African-American progress in the face of so many obstacles. He explored these issues in his 1926 essay *The Negro Artist and the Racial Mountain*, published in *The Nation*. With the help of Carl Van Vechten, in 1926 he published his first volume of poetry, *The Weary Blues*. This volume was well received, and made him an important voice in the Harlem Renaissance. With the support of a scholarship, and now committed to his career as a writer, Hughes returned to education, graduating from Lincoln University in 1929.

Hughes's work as a writer of poetry, plays, novels, and essays was prolific. His first novel, *Not Without Laughter*, was published in 1930, and many volumes followed. His talent was recognized in 1935 by the award of a Guggenheim Fellowship. During the 1930s, Hughes was also drawn into Communist Party circles, a movement that promised both socialism and social justice. He traveled during this period to the Soviet Union, and frequently published in the communist press. He also offered his journalistic support during the Spanish Civil War.

With the outbreak of World War II in 1939, he followed the shifting positions of noninvolvement as reflected in the Communist Party line, that is, until the attack on the Soviet Union in 1941 brought a turnaround. In 1953 his communist relationships brought him to the attention of the McCarthy Senate committee. Called before the committee, he was questioned as a communist sympathizer, and this unnerving experience led him to break with several former left-wing associates.

Hughes remained an active writer to the end of his life, and made New York City and Harlem, in particular, home. He valued African roots and promoted African-American growth and development as a distinctive force within the general culture. Most controversially in the context of this period, Hughes was a homosexual, and many of his poems reflected his sexual orientation. Some see this aspect of his life as a difficult burden that he had bear, given the homosexual prejudices of both the African-American and larger U.S. communities.

## RICHARD WRIGHT

Richard Wright (1908–60) was born in Mississippi, the son of a sharecropper, whose youth was plagued by constant moving, poverty, racism, and a disrupted education that ended before it could actually begin. Wright arrived in Chicago in 1927, and found employment as a postal clerk.

The onset of the Depression and the perceived collapse of capitalism drew him into Chicago's communist political circles, which gave him a vehicle for his writing through journals such as *The New Masses*. He completed his first unpublished novel, *Cesspool,* in 1935 and in 1937 moved to New York City where he became active in left-wing literary groups, eventually becoming an editor of *The Daily Worker*. His book of short stories of life in the south appeared as *Uncle Tom's Children* in 1938, establishing his reputation. He followed this success with *Native Son* in 1940, which became a Book of the Month Club selection, making him the first African-American writer so selected.

Wright confronted racism and reflected black aspirations in his writing, often using a backdrop of violence to shape his fiction. Wright's career began in the 1920s and was firmly established during the 1930s. New Deal programs such as the WPA Writers' Project gave him the financial support to settle in Harlem, where he became a writer of influence and talent.

## CONCLUSION

The 1920s and 1930s represented a period of extreme transition in the African-American experience, as blacks left their rural lives in exchange for urban existences. The pattern of southern migration continued on a steady course with blacks attracted to the expanding industrial job opportunities in the northern cities, particularly after the 1920s curbs on foreign immigration.

However upon arrival in the north and Midwest, discrimination did not disappear, but took new forms and new directions. The coming of the Depression renewed economic hardships that were compounded by still-pressing social concerns involving exclusion and denial of opportunity. The situation was made worse by rising unemployment and poverty. Legal remedies were sought, for instance, in campaigns for an end to lynching, but political obstacles prevented solutions. Black political allegiance also shifted during the New Deal years as the Roosevelt administration's policies drew more African-American support for the Democratic Party.

African-American culture flourished in these new urban environments as never before. Black entertainers, jazz and blues musicians, athletes, sportsmen, and young writers, poets, and intellectuals all flowered during these years, reaching new heights of achievement. Important impressions were made, and for the first time the nation took notice of the wide range of African-American accomplishments. This process of change would slowly undercut past neglect and suppression. The social dynamics and gains of this era would be consolidated and expanded in the post–World War II United States, as progress and social inclusion gradually became more commonplace.

THEODORE W. EVERSOLE
NORTHERN KENTUCKY UNIVERSITY

# Further Reading

Blum, E.J. *W.E.B. Du Bois: American Prophet*. Philadelphia: University of Pennsylvania Press, 2007.

Borshak, Michael. *Swinging the Vernacular: Jazz and African American Modern Literature*. New York: Routledge, 2005.

Brown, Mary Jane. *Eradicating this Evil: Women in the American Anti Lynching Movement, 1892–1940*. New York: Routledge, 2000.

Bunch-Lyons, Bev. *Contested Terrain: African American Women Migrate from the South to Cincinnati*. New York: Routledge, 2002.

Campbell, Mary Schmidt. *Harlem Renaissance: Art of Black America*. New York: Harry N. Abrams, 1994.

Carter, Dan T. *Scottsboro: A Tragedy of the American South*. Baton Rouge: Louisiana State University Press, 1979.

Franklin, J. Hope, and A.A. Moss, Jr. *From Slavery to Freedom*. New York: McGraw-Hill, 2000.

Franklin, V.P. *Black Self-Determination: A Cultural History of African American Resistance*. Brooklyn, NY: Lawrence Hill Books, 1993.

Grossman, James R. *A Chance to Make Good: African Americans, 1900–1929*. New York: Oxford University Press, 1997.

Harley, Sharon. *Timetables of African American History: A Chronology of the Most Important People and Events in African American History*. New York: Touchstones Books, 1996.

Hill, Errol G., and James V. Hatch. *A History of African American Theatre*. New York: Cambridge University Press, 2006.

Hill, Laban C. *Harlem Stomp: A Cultural History of the Harlem Renaissance*. New York: Little, Brown, 2004.

Huggins, Nathan I., and Arnold Rampersad. *Harlem Renaissance*. New York: Oxford University Press, 2007.

Johnson, Eloise. *Rediscovering the Harlem Renaissance: The Politics of Exclusion*. New York: Routledge, 1996.

Kelley, Robin D.G., and Earl Lewis. *To Make Our World Anew: A History of African Americans*. New York: Oxford University Press, 2000.

Kennedy, David M. *Freedom from Fear: The American People in Depression and War*. New York: Oxford University Press, 1999.

Lewis, David. *The Portable Harlem Renaissance Reader*. New York: Penguin, 1995.

Potter, Joan. *African American Firsts: Famous Little Known and Unsung Triumphs of Blacks in America*. New York: Kensington Press, 2002.

Taylor, Clarence. *Black Religious Intellectuals: The Fight for Equality from Jim Crow to the 21st Century*. New York: Routledge, 2001.

Taylor, Henry Louis, and Walker Hill. *Historical Roots of the Urban Crisis: African Americans in the Industrial City, 1900–1950*. New York: Routledge, 2000.

Turner-Sandler, Joanne. *African American History: An Introduction*. New York: Peter Lang, 2006.

Watson, Steven. *The Harlem Renaissance: Hub of African American Culture, 1920–1930*. New York: Pantheon, 1996.

Wiggins, David K., ed. *Out of the Shadows: A Biographical History of African American Athletes*. Fayetteville: University of Arkansas Press, 2006.

Wright, Kai. *The African American Archive: The History of the Black Experience through Documents*. New York: Black Dog and Leventhal, 2001.

# CHAPTER 7

# World War II and the Forties: 1939 to 1949

**THE STEADY STREAM** of black migration north that had distinguished previous eras slowed during the 1930s as the Great Depression ended opportunity. However the coming of World War II and the need for war preparedness stimulated new employment possibilities as industrial production accelerated. Accordingly 1940–50, job prospects drew 1.6 million blacks from the south to the north and west. With already established African-American communities in the major northern cities, this movement was not as daunting as previous moves. With friends and relatives in place, life in the north was not as strange or as risky as during World War I.

Although employment conditions were improving, the jobless rate remained relatively high, and white employers favored hiring whites over blacks until necessity dictated otherwise. However as the war progressed, the need for additional labor became pressing and, in 1941, President Franklin Roosevelt ordered that nondiscriminatory practices apply to war industries. Subsequently the Fair Employment Practices Committee was created to oversee existing policies, and after 1943 enforcement became more serious, dramatically improving opportunities for African Americans.

Changes in labor demand and supply, especially in the blue collar manufacturing industries that produced war materiels, provided not only employment, but also better wages for lower-paid workers. The GI Bill was also passed during the war, creating opportunities for veterans to secure a college education. However because African Americans were among the lesser educated, such changes failed to benefit them as greatly as white soldiers.

Nevertheless access to higher education improved during these years as organizations such as the Negro College Fund, founded in 1943, became active. Success was reflected in the numbers as African-American college attendance rose steadily from 23,000 in 1940 to 114,000 in 1950. Higher educational attainment not only raised income levels, but also brought prestige and more middle-class opportunities. In addition higher education created an educated leadership base that would play a huge role in the civil rights struggles of the 1950s.

Beginning in 1940 the Census Bureau collected income statistics that contained comparative information on black and white earnings. The statistics revealed a substantial improvement in comparative income partially attributed to the move north, where pay was considerably higher than in the south. Blacks also increased their access to better-quality white collar jobs during the war years. In 1939 the mean annual earnings for wage and salary workers over 20 years old showed comparative earnings of $537 for blacks and $1,234 for whites. By 1949 the comparison showed blacks' earnings at $1,761, compared to a white mean of $2,984. The income gap would be further narrowed in the 1950s.

The improvement was such that a third of African Americans became homeowners by the early 1950s. Although during the 1940s the income differential was declining, a large percentage of the black population remained in poverty when compared to the total society. Educational divides also remained, with whites averaging over three years more formal schooling for both males and females. However it appeared that at this particular time the fewer years of completed schooling did not always translate into reduced earnings.

## THE NEW DEAL LEGACY

Conditions during the 1930s drew large numbers of African Americans to the Democratic Party. Most blacks believed the New Deal's social and economic programs offered hope in a time of desperation. Yet in reality, many of the New Deal's reforms fell short of the overall needs of African Americans. Often employment opportunities were denied blacks at a time when food prices were rising. Further attempts to end lynching through legislation were stalemated, and the armed forces remained segregated.

The reason behind this only-partial New Deal progress was found in the Democratic Party's dependence on the support of the solid south, and any attempts to improve the lives of African Americans were a low priority. Proposals to advance social integration or to put an end to discrimination were met with clear threats to the party's governing consensus. Furthermore key con-

*Wartime industrial needs improved employment opportunities and increased income for African Americans. This woman worked at the Douglas Aircraft Company's El Segundo Plant in the 1940s.*

gressional committees, because of the seniority system, rested with southern Democrats who consistently opposed measures to improve the lot of African Americans or reverse racial injustice.

Roosevelt realized this situation, for he knew full well that his legislative agenda depended upon such southern Democrats, so he cooperated in a manner that undercut his own reforming legacy. Major New Deal programs were segregated, including the Civilian Conservation Corps (CCC) and the Works Progress Administration (WPA), as were other areas of federal employment. In many ways the Roosevelt White House was closed to African Americans, and access generally had to go through the more receptive First Lady Eleanor Roosevelt. One key example of this practice was the exclusion of African-American reporters from press conferences. This situation began in 1933 and continued for the next 11 years. In the White House there was an overriding fear that southern party functionaries and congressional bodies might be offended.

There were some prominent New Deal liberal cabinet members who opposed FDR's accommodation with racism, such as Frances Perkins, Harold Ickes, Harry Hopkins, Aubrey Williams, his black adviser Mary McLeod

The influential educator Dr. Mary McLeod Bethune around 1938. Dr. Bethune founded the historically black Bethune-Cookman University in Daytona Beach, Florida.

Bethune, and Eleanor Roosevelt, but as influential as these people were, they failed at this stage to achieve much change. The coming of World War II shifted the political climate to a degree that allowed FDR to improve the situation in ways that were not possible during the 1930s.

Roosevelt's New Deal did not have a comprehensive program in regard to a range of discrimination issues. To make matters worse, craft union membership was often denied to blacks, and this meant lower wages and fewer employment possibilities. In addition the white primary system in certain states, as well as the use of poll taxes, denied African Americans their citizenship rights. Yet even in the face of these restrictive practices, the Democratic Party benefited from changes in black voting patterns.

At the ballot box, African Americans rewarded even the limited New Deal progress. The failure of the main craft unions, affiliated with the AFL, to include black workers was regrettable, and reflected among other factors the lack of specific training in the black community. Nevertheless after 1935, the rise of the large industrial unions attached to the CIO did open the door to African-American recruitment. By 1940 about 600,000 blacks belonged to industrial unions, and by 1945 the number had risen to 1.25 million. During the 1940s these unions helped raise wages, deliver equal pay for equal work, and expanded the notion of equal rights for all members of the union, regardless of race.

# The Formation and Expansion of the Nation of Islam

Salesman Wallace Dodd Fard, who became known as Wali Fard Muhammad, founded the Nation of Islam (N.O.I.) in Detroit, Michigan, in 1930. Members are also known as black Muslims. Fard preached that blacks were the chosen people, and that Islam was their natural religion. He also believed that an evil scientist named Yakub had created their persecutors, the white race, but that the white reign would soon come to an end. Nation of Islam principles included knowledge of Islam and Allah, racial pride, discipline, a moral life-style, economic self-sufficiency, and black nationalism, the belief that African Americans should establish a separate nation within the United States. The Nation of Islam attracted African Americans in the urban north suffering from social, political, and economic discrimination.

When Fard Muhammad disappeared in 1934, disciple Elijah Muhammad (born Elijah Poole) became the new leader of the Nation of Islam. Fard had sent Elijah to Chicago to establish a second mosque in 1933. Elijah Muhammad proclaimed Fard Muhammad to have been the prophet and maintained his religious teachings, while adding new business interests and a paramilitary force. Elijah Muhammad began traveling to cities across the country in order to recruit new N.O.I. members. The Nation of Islam grew throughout the 1930s, but remained small, with its membership primarily concentrated in Detroit and Chicago. After U.S. entry into World War II, Elijah Muhammad and the Nation of Islam began encouraging members to avoid the military draft.

The federal government imprisoned Elijah Muhammad 1942–46 for violating the Selective Service Act that implemented the draft. Elijah claimed he had refused, not avoided the draft because his Muslim beliefs should give him status as a conscientious objector, his belief that the United States was on the side of white oppression, and he was 45 at the time, one year above the 44 year old limit of the draft. Other male members were also jailed for draft evasion. Elijah Muhammad and others recruited new members while incarcerated, establishing many prison-based ministries that became important recruit centers. Nation of Islam membership would later surge during the mid to late 1960s as the civil rights movement split, and black separatist leaders like Malcolm X rose to prominence.

Elijah Muhammad, shown above in the early 1960s, led the Nation of Islam beginning in 1934.

## WORLD WAR II

During the 1940 presidential campaign, Roosevelt added a civil rights plank to the party platform and gained the admittance of black delegates to the convention. Nevertheless the party's national committee maintained a colored division that seemingly contradicted the steps toward more integration. With the coming of the military draft, F.D.R secured equal pay for African Americans. This was clearly a step forward, given the earlier discriminatory employment practices of the New Deal.

Roosevelt's most important civil rights decision was Executive Order 8802, issued in June 1941, which ordered an end to employment discrimination and established the Fair Employment Practices Committee to oversee equality in the workplace. For many black leaders, American involvement in the war made the integration of the armed services a pressing issue. In the early days of the war, F.D.R was encouraged by Walter White of the NAACP, T. Arnold Hill of the Urban League, and union activists such as A. Philip Randolph to integrate the armed services. However Roosevelt equivocated due to resistance, particularly from the U.S. Marines and the navy. There was a fear of rebellion by southern white soldiers that could undercut military efforts during a time of conflict. Although Roosevelt promised an integrated military, actual change had to wait for Roosevelt's successor, Harry Truman.

The creation in 1940 of the wartime draft saw over 2.5 million African Americans registering for service. Before this there were but 4,000 African Americans in the military, many of them performing domestic duties. The goal was to have the numbers rise so that those in service reflected the total African-American percentage of the U.S. population. As had occurred in World War I, a considerable numbers of blacks wanted to fight for their country and looked for opportunities within the services. In the end over one million African Americans served the cause, and of these, 700,000 were attached to the army.

However just as in the past, African Americans looking to serve faced continued discrimination and often exclusion from actual combat assignments. Many times combat-ready troops, once in theater, were assigned to labor battalions. Racism remained a powerful component in the grand scheme of military thinking, reflecting the assumptions of many with-

Doris "Dorie" Miller became a hero at Pearl Harbor when he manned antiaircraft guns during the attack on Pearl Harbor, despite having been assigned as a mess attendant.

*A mortar company from the 92nd Infantry Division targets German troops near Massa, Italy, in November 1944.*

# 92nd Infantry Division

The 92nd Infantry division was reactivated in 1942. First organized in 1917, the segregated division was known as the Buffalo Soldiers and was composed of the 365th, 370th, and 371st regiments. During World War II the division was assigned to the Mediterranean battlefront as part of the Fifth Army. The division was made up of 12,000 officers and men, including 200 white and 600 black officers.

The first combat group arrived in Italy in August 1944. This unit was the 370th Regimental Combat Team, which was attached to the 1st Armored Division. They engaged in battle in the Arno River area, attacking the Gothic Line in a drive on Massa. Through October and December 1944, they fought up the coast of Italy, where they met heavy resistance by both Italian fascist and German troops. As German and Italian resistance weakened, the 370th advanced up the Ligurian coastal sector, taking over Serchio, and entered La Spezia and Genoa on April 27, 1945. The 370th continued fighting until the formal surrender of German forces on May 2, 1945.

From August 1944 to May 1945, the unit suffered over 3,000 casualties and was continuously in the front line, often fighting without relief for two months at a time. These losses translated into a quarter of the division being wounded, and included over 330 killed in combat. Recognition of the division's bravery was evident in the award of over 12,000 decorations. The medals included two Distinguished Service Crosses, 95 Silver Stars, 723 Bronze Stars, and 1,891 Purple Hearts.

*African-American troops of the 92nd Infantry on the trail of retreating German troops in the Po Valley in Italy in the spring of 1945.*

in government, as well as society as a whole. It was even argued by Secretary of War Henry L. Stimson and other officials that blacks lacked the educational abilities to effectively use modern weapons. These views insulted and alienated many blacks who were already serving, and on the home front, such assumptions humiliated African-American communities.

Initially black recruitment was underplayed, as was the quality of combat training after recruitment. For those admitted to the military services, prejudice was commonplace, and racial incidents occurred with a degree of frequency that reduced a black soldier's self-worth. The fact that only one percent of black recruits became commissioned officers, compared to 11 percent of white soldiers, indicated the level of discrimination faced by those trying to serve. Discrimination even affected the women's service corps. The WAVES

# The Tuskegee Airmen

In July 1941 the first class of African-American pilots known as the Tuskegee Airmen, or the 332nd Fighter Group, began in Tuskegee, Alabama. They completed training in March 1942. The five who completed the class received commissions as second lieutenants and their silver pilot wings. This began a training program that produced 994 graduate pilots in 1941–46. Other black aircraft crews composed of navigators, bombardiers, and gunners were trained at bases throughout the United States.

Many of the pilots went overseas as part of the 99th Pursuit Squadron, later named the 99th Fighter Squadron. These pilots saw combat in North Africa, Sicily, and Italy, flying P-40 aircraft until July 1944, when they became part of the 332nd Fighter Group along with three other black squadrons, the 100th, the 301st, and the 302nd, all of which were aligned with the 15th Air Force. The pilots flew a variety of aircraft including P-39s and P-47s, and later they gained fame flying the P-51 Mustangs, the Cadillac of the Skies.

Flying as bomber escorts over Nazi-occupied Europe, the 332nd, also known as the Red Tails, struck at the heart of the Luftwaffe. They saved the lives of many bomber crews, enabling them to drop their bomb loads and to return safely to base. The unit's success even in the face of ongoing discrimination within the military was seen in the award of 150 Distinguished Flying Crosses, eight Purple Hearts, 14 Bronze Stars, and 774 Air Medals. In addition, for the integrated postwar air force, the Tuskegee experience produced three future generals: Daniel James (the first African-American four-star general), Benjamin O. Davis, Jr., and Lucius Theus.

*Three Tuskegee Airmen in Ramitelli, Italy, in March 1945*

(Navy) and SPARS (Coast Guard) excluded black women until protests reversed the policy in 1944, just before the presidential election. The army's WACS did accept black women, but assigned them to menial work, with only one WAC unit being sent overseas. The U.S. Marines' Marinettes never accepted black membership during the war.

A particular illustration of wartime segregationist practices was the Red Cross's decision to separate blood supplies on the basis of race. This decision seemed even more ridiculous because it was an African-American doctor, Dr. Charles Drew, who had invented the blood preservation processes that had made blood banks possible.

The military willingly perpetuated the Jim Crow world of the south, meaning that regardless of commitment, loyalty, and bravery, discrimination and segregation dominated service. This resulted in poor training and equipment, as well as being commanded by a white officer corps who sometimes failed to promote the interests of their black units. To improve upon the situation, the War Department called for the organization of four segregated army divisions, but in the end only three were created: the 2nd Cavalry and the 92nd and 93rd Divisions.

The 2nd served in North Africa; the 93rd served in the Pacific in the Bougainville region as well as the Treasury Islands, Moratai Island, and the Philippines; and the 92nd engaged in the Italian campaign. In addition after the Normandy invasion in June 1944, African-American drivers, working around the clock, delivered vital supplies as part of the Red Ball Express. The 161st Chemical Smoke Screen Generator Company was another black unit that performed well in the European theater. One key example of their service occurred in the vital December 1944 winter campaign when they flooded the Saar Valley with fog to cover the movement of the 90th Division.

## FIGHTING WARTIME DISCRIMINATION

By 1943 there was increased evidence of mounting rage over these segregationist and racist attitudes that directly contributed to unrest both overseas and at home. Fights erupted at military bases in Britain, Australia, and the Pacific. It was a clear ideological contradiction to be fighting Nazi racism in Europe, while at the same time perpetuating it within branches of the U.S. military. Some historians have linked race riots in the United States during 1943 to the resentment felt over the poor treatment of African Americans in the military. The Detroit race riot of 1943 proved to be the most serious of these outbreaks, resulting in the deaths of 23 blacks and nine whites. There were also riots in Harlem, Texas, and Los Angeles that exposed accumulated resentments.

Some African-American soldiers felt that they were fighting their own two-front wars: at home against their inferior treatment, and abroad against the common Axis foes. This second-rate status was seen in the awarding

*A police escort accompanies moving vans belonging to black families relocating to the Sojourner Truth homes, a new federal housing project, during rioting in Detroit in 1942.*

of medals, the Medal of Honor a case in point. During World War II, not one African-American soldier received the award, even though there was an abundance of brave acts. (Belatedly, in 1997, seven black soldiers were awared the Medal of Honor.) Many other military actions received little acknowledgment, such as the building of the Ledo Road in South Asia to bring vital supplies to anti-Japanese forces. Of the 15,000 men involved in this dangerous project, 60 percent were black. The reversal of this inequality did not finally occur until President Truman ordered the integration of all branches of the military in 1948.

## DOMESTIC PROGRESS DURING THE 1940s

The wartime battles against discrimination, particularly in the context of a war against Nazi racism in its most supremacist forms, launched major reevaluations of U.S. racial attitudes, and the effect these experiences had on African Americans. The intellectual climate was helped by the publication of works such as Gunnar Myrdal's *An American Dilemma* in 1944, which acknowledged American racism as a failure of the majority culture to deliver on its values and ideals. Other important sociological works were published in the 1940s that challenged prevailing racial viewpoints, such as Carey McWilliams' 1942 *Brothers Under the Skin*. These publications reflected a changing intellectual framework that was increasingly being embraced by whites who saw discrimination and racism as blight on the country's reputation and standing at home and abroad.

On another equally important level during the 1940s, the first steps toward the integration of professional sports provided a symbolic gesture of future hope and progress. No one symbolized this change more than Jackie Robinson, who in 1947 was brought to the major leagues by Branch Rickey, general manager of the Brooklyn Dodgers. The National Football League had been integrated the previous season, in 1946. Both moves set the stage for the emergence in the 1950s of black stars in all mainstream U.S. sports.

Another sign of changing attitudes was the creation of human relations commissions in many cities. These commissions attempted to reduce the more obvious discriminatory practices that held back black progress. Religious groups both black and white, as well as the NAACP, worked throughout the era to end lynching. This was an embarrassing moral gap left by Congress' failure to legislate.

In response to such worthwhile efforts, NAACP membership increased from 51,000 in 1940 to over 350,000 in 1945, which meant that there were more resources available to combat civil rights issues. Other civil rights organizations appeared, such as CORE (Congress of Racial Equality), formed in 1942, which was dedicated to the pursuit of equality and the end to racial abuse. One indication of the success of the antilynching campaign was the fact that finally, in 1952, there was no recorded lynching. This was the first such occasion since the beginning of records in the 1880s.

## LEGAL ACTION

The willingness to use the courts proved another useful tactic in the battle against discrimination. Small victories sometimes resulted, for example, the 1946 *Morgan v. Virginia* Supreme Court decision that banned segregated seating on interstate buses. Along with this victory, additional positive changes came about through legal pressures, including the ending of the poll tax in southern states. In addition the Supreme Court's 1944 *Smith v. Allright* decision that ended the exclusion of black voters from Democratic primaries was seen as another triumph in the drive for equality. This case followed earlier decisions (*Patterson v. Alabama*, 1935) that called for the inclusion of African Americans on southern juries. The immediate effect of the Patterson decision was a review of African Americans' convictions in southern courts where all-white juries had delivered the verdicts.

These positive actions had their greatest impact in the upper south, where Jim Crow discriminatory practices still existed; however the Deep South proved more resistant. Nevertheless the numbers of black voters increased from only about five percent in 1940, to about 20 percent in 1950. In certain northern cities such as New York City, Chicago, and Detroit, this would translate into more black representatives in Congress. During the 1940s, besides increased voting on state and city issues, many communities insisted on locally based fair employment legislation as well. This had a direct effect on previously exclusive professional associations, which began to open their membership to African Americans. At least 18 states, primarily in the north and west, by the end of the decade had ended the more obvious vestiges of segregation in transport, education, hotels, and restaurants.

## THE TRUMAN ADMINISTRATION: 1945–52

Although African-American concerns and reservations over racial discrimination remained paramount, there was hope for significant civil rights advancement during Truman's years in office. Truman was receptive to a permanent fair employment practices law, and he gave his support to antilynching legislation, which Roosevelt had failed to do. Further Truman addressed the NAACP convention in 1947 and formed a Committee on Civil Rights to set an agenda for change; this led to a 1947 report, *To Secure These Rights.* Many historians have seen this report as the formal launch of the civil rights movement in the United States that would dominate domestic politics in the 1950s and 1960s.

During the 1948 election, however, Truman faced challenges within his own party. These challenges included the Progressive Party element led by Henry Wallace, who endorsed a full civil rights platform, and the southern segregationist Democrats who had been so influential in combating change during the Roosevelt presidency. The party's civil rights proposals caused splits within the party, leading southern delegates to walk out of the convention. A staged rebellion was led by Senator Strom Thurmond of South Carolina, and ultimately Thurmond ran against Truman and won four southern states and 38 Electoral College votes.

Truman accepted these divides and moved ahead with antidiscrimination proposals in his 1948 State of the Union message. More dramatically, Truman issued Executive Order 9980, which ended discrimination in federal employment; and Executive Order 9981, which called for equality in the military services—meaning integration. However the existing party splits did not doom Truman's election chances. His pro-civil rights position helped secure 70 percent of the black vote, which contributed to his narrow election victory over Republican Thomas Dewey of New York.

Following his election, Truman moved forward with his agenda. One of his earliest acts was his October 1949 appointment of William H. Hastie to the Third Circuit Court of Appeals, the most prestigious judgeship ever held by an African American. The administration also backed NAACP positions in many other legal areas. There were legal moves against restrictive property covenants such as that seen in the *Shelley v. Kraemer* decision, and in other decisions overturning state restrictions on travel and higher education. The early campaigns against state school segregation set the course for later developments leading

William H. Hastie, left, consulting with U.S. Under Secretary of War Robert Patterson in his capacity as the civilian aide to the secretary of war in 1942. Hastie gained the judgeship of the Third Circuit Court of Appeals in 1949.

to the famous *Brown v. the Board of Education* decision in 1954. Truman made other important appointments outside the federal court system such as the selection of Ambrose Caliver as assistant commissioner in the Office of Education. He also appointed Robert P. Barnes to the National Science Foundation, and made Edith Sampson a UN delegate.

Although the Truman administration attempted to set a new policy framework, at almost every turn it found itself stymied by a Congress unwilling to act. Part of this problem can be blamed on the fundamental contradictions found within the Democratic Party, which increasingly found itself internally divided between liberals and southern conservatives. The same dilemma characterized the party in the Roosevelt years and prevented substantive change. Congress refused to act on most issues, including a permanent Fair Employment Practices Commission, the abolishment of poll taxes, segregation in terminals, housing discrimination, and home rule for Washington, D.C., as well as legislation making lynching a federal crime. During these years southern senators gained a reputation for filibustering, successfully frustrating any full Senate votes on civil rights matters. In the final analysis, Truman's civil rights gains were relatively modest and often only provided lip service to change. Yet the issues that emerged would not go away, and the administration clearly let the racial genie out of the bottle. The significance of this would not materialize fully until the 1950s and 1960s, when the major drives against racial discrimination and injustice occurred.

## ANNA MURRAY

Anna (Pauli) Murray (1910–85) was born in Baltimore to parents who died during her childhood, so she and her children were raised by relatives. After a successful high school education, she moved to New York City, where she attended Hunter College and supported herself through various jobs. The stock market crash temporarily ended her formal education, and she was forced to find work in the 1930s with the WPA. She also pursued various writing projects and became an early civil rights activist. In 1938 with support from the NAACP, Murray campaigned for admission to the segregated University of North Carolina—this brought her national notoriety. Her actions also drew the attention of Eleanor Roosevelt, who became her lifelong friend.

In the 1940s Murray's civil rights campaigning drew her to issues involving segregated transport, and introduced her to the idea of using civil disobedience as a tactic. In Virginia she was arrested and imprisoned for refusing to sit at the back of a bus, applying her new ideas of resistance. Her drive for change took her to Howard University in 1941, and in 1942, she became instrumental, along with Bayard Rustin, James Farmer, and George Houser, in the formation of the Congress of Racial Equality (CORE). She also continued to study the passive resistance strategies that had proven so effective for Mahatma Gandhi in India.

Following graduation from Howard in 1944, she initially hoped to attend Harvard Law School, but was denied admission due to gender. This led her to enroll in the University of California, from which she took her law degree. She returned to New York City and in 1951 published the influential *States' Laws on Race and Color*. Murray proved to be one of the most noteworthy predecessors to those civil rights activists who followed in the 1950s and 1960s. During the coming years, and under McCarthy-era pressures to desist with her more radical inclinations, she continued to be a vocal and commanding presence. Murray returned to favor during the 1960s, and was appointed to the Committee on Civil and Political Rights by President John F. Kennedy. Her religious leanings during the 1970s led her to become the first African-American woman admitted to the Episcopal priesthood.

## BAYARD RUSTIN

Bayard Rustin (1912–87) was born into a large family in West Chester, Pennsylvania, and was raised by his grandparents. Heavily influenced by the Quaker faith, Rustin emerged in the 1940s as one of the central civil rights figures of that era, and would later become a significant voice in the civil rights movement during the 1950s and 1960s. Some historians have suggested that his relative lack of historical appreciation today could be attributed to his homo-sexuality and his communist affiliations, which made him seem undesirable on two counts.

From 1932 to 1936 Rustin attended Wilberforce University and Cheyney State Teachers College, a black institution in Pennsylvania. In 1937 he moved to New York City, which became his permanent base. While attend-ing the City College of New York, he became involved in Communist Party activities, impressed by the party's civil rights policies, its commitment to equality, and its support for the legal plight of the Scottsboro Boys in the south. He remained active in the Communist Party until the German inva-sion of the Soviet Union in 1941 forced the Soviet Union to join the war effort. Rustin's pacifism made it impossible for him to become involved in war of any kind. This conviction would in time draw him to the work of the War Resisters League.

In 1942 Rustin became a founding member of CORE, an organization devoted to the end of all discriminatory practices. He had earlier worked with A. Philip Randolph as part of the Fellowship of Reconciliation, which protested unfairness in employment and segregation in the armed forces. In 1944 his commitment to pacifism brought him into conflict with the Se-lective Service Act and resulted in a three-year federal jail sentence. Upon release he again became active in the Fellowship of Reconciliation. This as-sociation allowed him to travel to India and Ghana to study those countries' nonviolent protest strategies.

In 1947 he undertook a "journey of reconstruction" to test the supposed end of segregation on interstate transport as ordered by the Supreme Court. In this instance, Rustin found Jim Crow still alive and well in North Carolina, and as a consequence ended up in jail. What he learned from this experience would later be applied to the civil rights struggles of the 1950s and 1960s. Rus-tin subsequently became an adviser to Martin Luther King on civil disobedi-ence tactics, and joined with him to found the Southern Christian Leadership Conference (SCLC).

Rustin's 1953 arrest in California for public indecency brought the issue of his homosexuality into the open—at the time, homosexuality was a crimi-nal offense. His sexual proclivities unfortunately obscured his record of resis-tance. From the 1940s until his death, Bayard Rustin stood at the forefront of the African-American pursuit of full equality.

## ADAM CLAYTON POWELL, JR.

Adam Clayton Powell, Jr. (1908–72), was born in New Haven, Connecticut, the son of an influential Baptist minister who was for many years pastor of Harlem's large and influential Abyssinian Baptist Church. In 1930 Powell graduated from Colgate University and, in 1932, he received a master's degree in religious education from Columbia University. He also studied divinity at

Shaw University in North Carolina, graduating in 1934. During the 1930s, as his father neared retirement, Powell became an assistant pastor, and later the pastor at Abyssinian Baptist Church, where he built a reputation as an advocate for jobs and housing reform during the height of the Depression.

In 1941 he was elected to the New York City Council, where he worked for the improvement of civil rights and greater economic opportunities for the city's African Americans. Charismatic and a gifted orator, Powell became a force to be reckoned with in New York politics. During the war his economic skills were further sharpened with service in the Office of Price Administration in 1942–45.

In 1945 Powell entered the national stage when he became the first African American elected to Congress from New York State. From 1945 until 1967 he served continuously as the Democratic congressman from Harlem's 18th District. In Congress, he combated the segregationist attitudes and practices that he encountered both within and outside the halls of government. His challenges often led to conflict with southern members from his own party. Because of these Democratic Party segregationist elements, he supported Republican Dwight D. Eisenhower's 1956 reelection bid.

In 1961 Powell became chairman of the influential Education and Labor Committee, giving him the power to shape much of the social legislation of the era. In 1967 Powell's colorful life outside Congress, as well as budget and tax irregularities caught up with him. He ran afoul of congressional rules, which led to his eventual censure and exclusion. His exile proved only temporary, for he won reelection to his seat in 1968, and gained the satisfaction of a Supreme Court review that found that Congress had acted inappropriately in banning him. However dissatisfaction grew in his district, and his popularity diminished to the point that he lost the 1970 Democratic primary and subsequently left Congress. Thereafter he escaped the limelight by withdrawing to Bimini Island in the Bahamas.

Powell was a highly visible and popular African-American voice of the 1940s who, after 1945, became a prominent national figure. Although his notoriety and views often courted controversy, he was steadfast in his opposition to discrimination and segregation. Yet his own prejudices existed and were revealed in his threat to use his congressional office to expose Bayard Rustin's homosexuality; this led directly to Rustin's 1960 resignation from the SCLC.

## PAUL ROBESON

Paul Robeson (1898–1976) was born in Princeton, New Jersey, the son of a minister. As a young man, Robeson made a substantial impression as a star athlete and student at Rutgers University, where he was a two-time All-American in football (in 1917 and 1918). After Rutgers, he attended Columbia Law School, graduating in 1923. He abandoned a legal career when he discovered that

*Paul Robeson starring opposite Uta Hagen in* Othello *in the Theatre Guild Production on Broadway in 1943, which drew large audiences.*

his artistic talents offered even greater opportunities as both an actor and a singer, given the existing racial climate. By the 1920s and 1930s he was famous on stage and screen in both Great Britain and the United States. He starred in shows such as *Porgy and Bess* and *Showboat*, and his rendition of *Old Man River* established a classic.

Although spending much time in Great Britain, he returned to the New York stage and appeared as *Othello* 1943–45, eventually performing before an estimated audience of over half a million. In 1945 the quality of this performance, as well as his many previous contributions to African-American advancement, was acknowledged by the NAACP, which awarded him the prestigious Spingard Medal.

Robeson's politics were sharpened by the discrimination and denial of civil rights that he encountered in the United States and these pressing issues, along with the economic catastrophe brought about by the Depression, drew him into the orbit of the Communist Party. This was a similar course to that taken by other civil rights activists of the era. However his associations became more suspect as the 1940s unfolded, and suspicions against communist intentions grew with the rising tide of the cold war.

Robeson was also instrumental in launching the 1946 American Campaign Against Lynching, which strove to finally end the horrific practice. Also in

1946, he vigorously campaigned for famine relief in South Africa. He later gave his support to Henry Wallace's 1948 Progressive Party campaign for the presidency, and headlined the 1949 Civil Rights Congress Benefit Concert that resulted in the Peekskill riots. Furthermore from 1937 he was active in the Council on African Affairs, which promoted a liberationist postcolonial future for the continent.

Robeson was a welcome visitor to the Soviet Union, and he deflected any criticism of Stalin's regime, preferring to denounce U.S. actions instead through organizations such as the World Peace Congress. In 1943 he even recorded an English version of the Soviet anthem. His actions brought him to the attention of the House Committee on Un-American Activities and the Federal Bureau of Investigation, although during the 1940s he actually denied being a Communist Party member.

In 1950 his passport was revoked by the State Department because of his vocal anti-Americanism. This was at a time when U.S. troops were dying in Korea fighting communist aggression, and cold war fears were rising around the world. His passport was not restored until 1958 after a number of legal challenges. To make the case against him worse, he was awarded the Lenin Peace Prize in 1952, which signified his importance as a Communist Fellow Traveler. In 1988 Robeson's secret Communist Party affiliation was confirmed in a publication by the American Communist Party.

Robeson's strident criticisms of the United States, while at the same time underplaying communism's horrendous crimes, caused him in the 1950s to steadily lose support with many African-American civil rights activists. Given the political climate, it was more advantageous when seeking liberal support to disassociate civil rights organizations from such a controversial, though talented figure. In his later years, due to both ill health and his political choices, Robeson drifted into obscurity. However in recent decades his Stalinism has been forgotten, and he has been rehabilitated as a legitimate African-American hero.

## JACKIE ROBINSON

Jackie Robinson (1919–72) was born in Georgia and raised in humble circumstances in California by a single mother. Robinson emerged as a multisport athlete of superior talents, which took him to Pasadena Junior College and later the University of California, Los Angeles (UCLA) where he played baseball, basketball, football, and track. He played in the 1940 Rose Bowl against the University of Southern California (USC).

The coming of World War II saw Robinson drafted into the army; there he faced the many issues and compromises associated with a segregated and discriminatory system. Robinson's college background eventually enabled him to train as an officer, and he was initially assigned to the 761st Tank Battalion. However conflicts developed that led to transfers and charges of

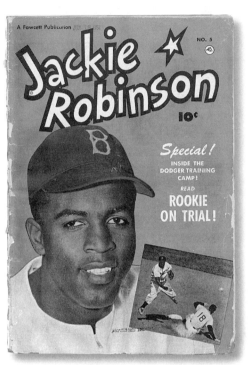

*Jackie Robinson was Rookie of the Year in 1947, and league Most Valuable Player in 1949.*

insubordination, principally involving his failure to submit to the racial climate of the times. In due course, Robinson was cleared and in 1944 he was honorably discharged.

In 1945 Robinson joined the Kansas City Monarchs in the Negro National League, and his outstanding play brought him to the notice of Branch Rickey, general manager of the Brooklyn Dodgers. Rickey saw the talent and signed Robinson, sending him to play for the Montreal Royals, the Dodgers' AAA minor league affiliate. By the 1947 season, his abilities demonstrated that he was ready for the major leagues, and he joined the then Brooklyn Dodgers. Robinson became the first African American to play in the majors, breaking the color line that had previously segregated professional baseball.

Robinson's transition to the majors meant that he had to endure a stream of racial abuse from some players, and from a number of hostile fans. His character saw him through the torment, but it was his all-around ability as a player that really won the day and silenced his critics. He was Rookie of the Year in 1947, and by 1949 was league Most Valuable Player. Over the next few years pressure on him lessened as more and more black players came to the majors. Given his late age upon entering the professional ranks, Robinson's career, although impressive, lasted but 10 seasons; he retired in 1957.

Robinson's life after baseball saw him become a corporate executive with coffee company Chock Full O' Nuts. He was also involved in New York Republican politics, and was instrumental in launching the Freedom Bank in Harlem, an African-American owned and operated bank. In 1962 he was elected to the Baseball Hall of Fame, the first African American so honored. Jackie Robinson's career set the stage for change, not only in American sports, but in society as a whole. By breaking this most prominent color line, the beginning of the end of segregation was at hand. Robinson's abilities, courage, and determination led the way, and for this reason he is celebrated today.

## CONCLUSION

The African-American experience during World War II and the 1940s was one of consolidation and maturation following the upheavals associated with the northern migration that characterized the earlier decades of the 20th century. Communities not only expanded, but also became more independent and socially adept as the increased population helped support a rising black middle class. In addition, electoral influence expanded as more blacks gained and used the vote. This would eventually translate into more elected black politicians and officeholders.

Racism and discrimination persisted in this era, and took new forms different from the more blatant Jim Crow conditions found in the south. Reform was slow and haphazard, but there were signs of change. The Democratic Party that dominated 1940s politics was fragmented in regard to race but efforts, particularly during the Truman administration, were being made to break from the past. World War II brought issues to the forefront as African Americans demanded that a fight against racism abroad should also apply at home. These demands would lead to the end of segregation in the military and the introduction—at least at the federal level—of fairer employment practices in hiring and pay.

During the 1940s there was also a growing and highly visible African-American presence in all walks of U.S. cultural life. The writings of Ralph Ellison, Langston Hughes, Richard Wright, Dorothy West, and a young James Baldwin, whose writing career was launched in 1943, were making a sizable impact in American literature. In music, African-American contributions were enormous and extremely varied, with Duke Ellington, Lionel Hampton, Charlie Parker, Dizzy Gillespie, Louis Armstrong, and singers Sarah Vaughan, Billie Holiday, and Ella Fitzgerald emerging as major performers. Jazz was constantly evolving and becoming an intricate and unconventional American art form, particularly as Bebop jazz and rhythm and blues found wider audiences.

The 1940s also gave a start to future stars such as Nat King Cole, who had a major hit with *Nature Boy* in 1948. Harry Belafonte started to gain notice as both an actor and a singer during this era as well. Lena Horne's successes in the 1930s continued unabated as she emerged as an important star in films such as *Stormy Weather* (1943), which also became the title of her hit song from the film. Canada Lee increased his acting credits during the 1940s on both stage and screen. In 1941 he starred in Orson Welles's New York production of *Native Son*, and in 1944, he appeared in Alfred Hitchcock's important *Life Boat*. For those coming of age during the 1940s, the seeds for future action leading to full civil rights and an equal place in American society were being planted.

THEODORE W. EVERSOLE
NORTHERN KENTUCKY UNIVERSITY

# Further Reading

Berman, William C. *The Politics of Civil Rights in the Truman Administration.* Columbus, OH: Ohio State University Press, 1970.

Brandt, Nat. *Harlem at War: The Black Experience in World War II.* Syracuse, NY: Syracuse University Press, 1996.

Buchanon, A. Russell. *Black America in World War II.* Santa Barbara, CA: CLIO Books, 1979.

Collins, William J. "Race, Roosevelt, and Wartime Production: Fair Employment in World War II Labor Markets." *American Economic Review* (v.91/1, 2001).

Duberman, Martin. *Paul Robeson.* New York: The New Press, 2005.

Horne, Gerald. *Communist Front? The Civil Rights Congress, 1945–1956.* Teaneck, NJ: Fairleigh-Dickinson University Press, 1988.

Hornsby, Alton. J., ed. *A Companion to African American History.* Hoboken, NJ: Wiley-Blackwell, 2005.

Kelley, Robin D.G., and Earl Lewis. *To Make Our World Anew: A History of African Americans.* New York: Oxford University Press, 2001.

Kryder, David. *Divided Arsenal: Race and the American State during World War II.* New York: Cambridge University Press, 2001.

Lusane, Clarence. *Hitler's Black Victims: The Historical Experiences of European Blacks, Africans and African Americans during the Nazi Era.* New York: Routledge, 2001.

McClendon, William H. *Straight Ahead: Essays on the Struggle of Blacks in America, 1934–1994.* Oakland, CA: Black Scholar Press, 1995.

Moon, Henry L. *Balance of Power: The Negro Vote.* Greenwood, CT: Greenwood Press, 1977;

Savage, Barbara D. *Broadcasting Freedom: Radio, War and the Politics of Race, 1938–1948.* Chapel Hill: University of North Carolina Press, 1999.

Sitkoff, Harvard. *A New Deal for Blacks, The Emergence of Civil Rights as a National Issue: The Depression Decade.* New York: Oxford University Press, 1978.

Southern, Eileen. *The Music of Black America: A History.* New York: W.W. Norton, 1997.

Sundstrom, William A. "Last Hired, First Fired? Unemployment and Urban Black Workers During the Great Depression." *Journal of Economic History* (v.52/2, 1992).

Takaki, Ronald. *Double Victory: A Multicultural History of America in World War II.* New York: Back Bay Books, 2001.

Trotter, Joe William. *From a Raw Deal to a New Deal? African Americans, 1929–1945.* New York: Oxford University Press, 1995.

Tushnet, Mark V. *NAACP's Legal Strategy against Segregated Education, 1925–1950.* Chapel Hill: University of North Carolina Press, 2005.

# CHAPTER 8

# The Civil Rights Era: 1950 to 1969

**AT THE BEGINNING** of the 1950s, segregation was a way of life for African Americans who lived in southern and border states where the "separate but equal" doctrine had been mandated since the end of the Civil War. This doctrine allowed state governments to pass Jim Crow laws, which created an environment in which African Americans were treated as second-class citizens, despite the guarantee of citizenship provided for in the Fourteenth Amendment, ratified in 1868. Under Jim Crow laws, African Americans in many areas were required to sit in the back of the bus, yielding their seats to white passengers when ordered to do so. Blacks were also relegated to assigned sections at train stations and bus depots. Separate waiting rooms were provided in doctors' and dentists' offices. Water fountains were often labeled "Whites Only." Outside southern and border states, discrimination was also present, but it tended to be less overt.

Among African Americans, attitudes toward accepting Jim Crow laws and the denial of constitutional rights had begun to change by the early 1950s, particularly among African-American males who had fought in World War II. Many black veterans were taking advantage of the GI Bill to attend institutions of higher learning, where they were opening their minds while learning how to provide greater financial opportunities for themselves and their families. Unquestioning acceptance of second-class citizenship was

*A sign indicating a separate waiting room in a bus station in Durham, North Carolina, in the 1940s. In the early 1950s, Jim Crow laws still imposed segregated public facilities in 17 states.*

also changing in response to the prominence of African Americans who had become successful in their respective fields. These celebrities included diplomat and Nobel Peace Prize–winner Ralph Bunche; singers Nat "King" Cole, Mahalia Jackson, and Sarah Vaughan; jazz musician Miles Davis; athletes Muhammad Ali and Willie Mays; and writers Ralph Ellison (*Invisible Man*, 1952) and Lorraine Hansberry (*A Raisin in the Sun*, 1959).

Great strides had been made in the 1950s after the U.S. Supreme Court handed down *Brown v. Board of Education of Topeka* (1954), which began to chip away at all forms of legal discrimination by holding that the "separate but equal" doctrine was unconstitutional. Then, in the early 1960s, more than 200 U.S. cities launched efforts to integrate public accommodations, and desegregation of the public schools continued to be a major focus of change.

Throughout the 1960s, the country underwent major social upheaval that redefined what it meant to be an American. For African Americans, the 1960s provided legal remedies for social and political exclusion that had been put in place in southern and border states after Reconstruction was abruptly halted in 1876. Civil rights strategies during the first half of the 1960s were chiefly a continuation of the previous decade, but the years after 1965 were marked by increasing urgency and militancy. Under the leadership of Malcolm X, a black Muslim minister, the new creed became "If ballots won't work, bullets will." Between 1964 and 1968, 300 race riots occurred in the United States.

During the 1960s a number of African Americans gained widespread acceptance in ways that bridged the gap between black and white. Actor Sidney Poitier became a top box office draw at the movies. Supreme Court Justice Thurgood Marshall became an advocate for all Americans who lacked a political voice. Writer James Baldwin created an unrelenting portrait of what life was like for African Americans, thereby opening the eyes of many white Americans who had distanced themselves from the civil rights struggle. On the other hand, many whites felt alienated from the movement by the actions of militants such as the Black Panthers, who made it clear that even sympathetic white Americans were perceived as enemies.

## BEGINNINGS

President Harry Truman began the federal process of desegregation by integrating the military, a feat that was accomplished with little incident, in part because of military discipline. In the early 1950s, segregation of blacks and whites was mandated by the laws of 17 states. In four others, individual districts were given the choice to accept or reject segregation. Because of the "separate but equal" doctrine, states were able to meet the letter of federal laws by providing separate schools for black children. In truth these schools were far from equal. African-American students sometimes attended brand new schools that had no heat in the winter. Textbooks were secondhand and were often out of date and in poor condition. Many African-American teachers had received inferior educations themselves, and lacked the knowledge needed to provide equal education for black students.

Inside the African-American community, the initial focus for change was concentrated on using the federal court system to force desegregation of public schools. In 1950 in *Sweatt v. Painter*, the Supreme Court held that segregated African-American schools did not provide an equal education to that of white students attending the University of Texas. The court case involved an African-American student who had been forced to attend a separate law school where he was taught by part-time faculty, and had no interaction with white law students. In *McLaurin v. Oklahoma State Regents*, a companion case to *Sweatt*, the Court determined that isolating black students within white schools prevented them from engaging in the interaction with other students that was an integral part of a university education. In class, McLaurin, a 68-year-old African-American teacher and doctoral student at the University of Oklahoma, was forced to sit behind a railing in an area designated as "reserved for coloreds." In the library, McLaurin was assigned to an isolated table, and he could eat in the dining hall only when no white students were present.

As the momentum for integration built, segregationist politicians became determined to block all efforts at integrating public schools. On December 22, 1952, Georgia governor Herman Talmadge, who later enjoyed a long tenure in the U.S. Senate, announced, "As long as I am governor, Negroes will not be admitted to white schools." A rejuvenated Ku Klux Klan joined the fray. Grand Dragon Bill Hendrix proclaimed that abolishing segregation would result in the Confederate Army marching in "armed rebellion." South Carolina governor Jimmy Byrnes pledged to close the state's public schools rather than allow integration.

Although not an overt racist, President Dwight Eisenhower believed he lacked a mandate to promote a civil rights agenda. Eisenhower maintained that racial problems should be solved in the course of time through local and state actions. From a political standpoint, it might be argued that Eisenhower had no obligation to the African-American community, since 73 percent of blacks had voted for his Democratic opponent, Adlai Stevenson, in 1952. Whatever his shortcomings on civil rights, Eisenhower did believe he had a responsibility to keep America safe. When violence erupted in the south, he did not hesitate to use the U.S. military to restore peace.

## SCHOOL INTEGRATION: 1954

The National Association for the Advancement of Colored People (NAACP), the leading civil rights organization in the 1950s, created a special Legal Defense Fund, and charged it with promoting integration of U.S. society. The legal defense team was made up of some of the best legal minds in the African-American community, including Charles Hamilton Houston, who had turned the law school of Howard University into a respected legal program, and his protégé Thurgood Marshall, who later became the first African American to serve on the Supreme Court. Since the 1930s Houston had traveled around the United States, filming schools, students, teachers, buildings, and buses in an effort to document the condition of African-American students in segregated schools. Later Marshall joined him on these sojourns. Once they decided on a case, Houston and Marshall honed their argument by holding mock trials before Howard law students.

In 1954 the Supreme Court agreed to hear school desegregation cases from South Carolina, Delaware, Virginia, Kansas, and Washington, D.C. As chief counsel for the Legal Defense Fund, Thurgood Marshall served as the major spokesperson for African-American students and their families. Before his death in 1950, Charles Hamilton Houston had brought James Nabrit onto the legal defense team. Nabrit developed the strategy of pressuring the Supreme Court to reject the "separate but equal" doctrine of *Plessy v. Ferguson* (1896) outright by declaring it unconstitutional.

The Supreme Court announced that the Kansas case, *Brown v. Board of Education of Topeka*, would serve as an umbrella for companion cases that included *Briggs v. Elliott*, *Davis v. Prince Edward County*, and *Gebhart v. Belton*. The cases were chosen because they represented distinct problems inherent in segregated school systems, and because they came from four separate states. Since Washington, D.C., is not a state, *Bolling v. Sharpe* was handled separately. This case concerned a suit in which the Consolidated Parents Group was attempting to force the integration of the recently built John Phillip Sousa Junior High School.

In mainly black Clarendon, South Carolina (*Briggs v. Elliott*), the suit was brought by African-American parents who where outraged that the state spent only $43 per pupil on black students, compared to $179 per pupil on white students. After 20 sets of parents signed the suit, they were immediately faced with intimidation and threats. Some lost their jobs because they refused to drop the suit. The *Brown* case involved seven-year-old Linda Brown, the daughter of a local African-American minister, who was forced to cross dangerous

Thurgood Marshall, who became the first African American to serve on the Supreme Court when he was appointed in 1967.

railroad tracks to reach the spot where she was required to wait for a rattletrap bus to carry her to a black school in Topeka, Kansas, even though there was a white school nearby that Linda Brown could have safely attended. The first plaintiff in the Prince Edward County case was Dorothy Davis, 14, one of 117 students from Moton High School who petitioned the courts to force the state of Virginia to abolish segregation in public education. In Newcastle, Delaware (*Gebhart v. Belton*), parents of high school and elementary students sued to end laws that enforced segregation and denied them equal access to education.

On May 17, 1954, the Supreme Court was scheduled to announce the *Brown* decision. The courtroom was packed, and hundreds of people waited outside, unable to enter. At 12:52 P.M. Chief Justice Earl Warren began reading the unanimous decision, which ultimately became one of the greatest victories of the civil rights movement, and changed life in the United States forever. Many of those in the courtroom were stunned when Warren proclaimed, "in the field of public education 'separate but equal' has no place" because "even [when] physical facilities [are] equal . . . intangible factors" prevent "separate from being equal." This finding was based on the conclusion that segregation of public schools violated the due process clause of the Fourteenth Amendment. School segregation was also abolished in *Bolling*, but findings were based on the guarantee of liberty inherent in the due process clause of the Fifth Amendment.

Partly as a concession to Justice Stanley Reed of Kentucky, the lone southerner on the bench, and partly due to the realization that instituting such sweeping changes would take time and be met with extensive resistance, and because of the realization that a plethora of cases would soon be crowding the dockets of federal courts, the justices decided to rehear arguments on

# Emmett Till

In August 1955 14-year-old Emmett Till, a Chicago youth known to his friends as "Bobo," arrived in Money, Mississippi, to spend the summer with his uncle, Moses Wright. Till was scheduled to enter the eighth grade in the fall. His mother warned him that blacks in the segregated south were expected to refrain from calling attention to themselves, but he was not used to acting subservient. Till bragged to his relatives that he had white friends in Chicago. On a dare, Till whistled at a white woman in a local grocery. Wiser in the ways of life in Jim Crow states, the other boys hastened him from the scene.

Three days later, Roy Bryant, the husband of the woman Till had flirted with, and his half-brother J.W. Milam, kidnapped Till from his uncle's home at gunpoint. Three days after the kidnapping, fishermen found Till's body in the Tallahatchie River. The wheel of an iron cotton mill gin fan had been tied to his neck with barbed wire. He had been shot above his left ear, and his left eye was gouged out. His body was swollen almost beyond recognition. When it arrived in Chicago, his mother, Mamie Till Mobley, collapsed. She later asked reporters, "Have you ever sent a loved son on vacation and had him returned to you in a pine box, so horribly battered and water-logged that someone needs to tell you this sickening sight is your son—lynched." Some 600,000 mourners filed by Till's body to pay their respects.

Despite nationwide outrage from both black and white Americans, an all-white jury found Till's murderers "not guilty" during a trial that had the atmosphere of a public picnic. Bryant and Milam were later paid $4,000 to tell their story, and admitted that they had committed the murder because they could not let Till go after he claimed to have a white girlfriend. Those who knew Till doubted the validity of this claim. In 1991 Chicago honored Till by naming a downtown street after him. His mother said she felt on that day as if she had "the voice of 10,000 angels" around her. Early in the 21st century, a grand jury refused to indict other defendants in the case, citing "insufficient evidence."

The impact of Till's murder has continued to resonate across the decades, motivating noted African Americans such as Rosa Parks, Muhammad Ali, James Baldwin, and Toni Morrison. In 2005 the state of Mississippi recognized Till's contribution to the civil rights movement by renaming Highway 49E Emmett Till Memorial Highway, a stretch of road that traverses an area enclosing the place where his body was found, as well the site where the trial of his killers took place.

*Brown* the following year. At that time they planned to consider methods of ending segregation in public schools. When Warren finished reading, reporters rushed out of the courtroom to spread the news. Throughout the country, radio stations broke into regular programming, and newspapers stopped the presses to announce the landmark decision. The *Washington Post* declared that *Brown* had ushered in a "new birth of freedom."

White supremacists began holding strategy sessions. On July 11 the first white Citizens' Council met in Mississippi and began devising plans to block the implementation of *Brown*. Within two years, Citizens' Council membership had grown to 250,000, and the group became adept at organizing reprisals against those who dared to challenge the status quo. In 1959 Ross Barnett, who had been elected governor of Mississippi on a segregationist platform, began channeling state funds to the Citizens' Council through the Mississippi State Sovereignty Commission.

## MONTGOMERY BOYCOTT: 1955

On December 1, Rosa Parks, a member of the local NAACP who had been trained in peaceful resistance, refused to give up her seat on a Montgomery bus to a white passenger. Local African-American businessman E.D. Nixon and Jo Ann Robinson, a black English professor at Alabama State College, immediately began organizing a boycott of the Montgomery bus system. African-American ministers banded together to found the Montgomery Improvement Council (MIA) to promote the boycott, and to seek changes in the way African Americans were treated on buses in the city.

By December 5, Martin Luther King Jr. the pastor of Dexter Baptist Church and a doctoral candidate at Boston University, had agreed to spearhead the boycott, which was so successful that it was extended until December 21, 1956. During this time, MIA filed suit in federal district court, arguing that Jim Crow laws were inherently unconstitutional. In retaliation, homes were bombed and MIA members were arrested on a variety of trumped-up charges. The most common charges were violating state laws banning boycotts, and interfering with a company's ability to conduct normal business.

Since African Americans made up 75 percent of all bus passengers in Montgomery, the boycott plunged the bus company into financial ruin and forced city officials to the negotiating table. African-American demands were simple: seating passengers on a first-come-first-served basis regardless of race, eliminating the practice of forcing blacks to vacate seats for white passengers, requiring drivers to be courteous to black passengers, and employing African-American drivers for routes that traversed predominately black communities.

Initially agreeing only to require greater driver courtesy, bus companies tried to recoup losses by raising fares from five to eight cents and eliminating free transfers. Undaunted, African Americans continued to avoid buses

# Rosa Parks

Rosa Parks, *The Mother of the Civil Rights Movement*, in 1964.

As 1955 drew to a close, African-American seamstress Rosa Parks (1913–2005) was growing steadily tired of how her people were treated in the highly segregated city of Montgomery, Alabama. At the age of 10, Parks had been thrown off a city bus for refusing to enter through the back door. The driver had driven off without refunding her fare. At the age of 43, Parks was wiser than she had been at 10. She had been trained in nonviolent resistance, and believed that it was time for African Americans to demand their right to be treated fairly. On December 1, Parks refused to yield her seat to a white man. "No, I'm not [moving]," she told driver James Blake, who had forced her off the bus as a child. Parks was also treated as a second-class citizen at the police station, where she was prohibited from quenching her thirst at a water fountain designated "for whites only." Rosa Parks's courage proved a catalyst, and local NAACP leaders quickly launched a bus boycott.

After becoming known as the Mother of the Civil Rights Movement, Rosa Parks became one of the most respected women in the United States. She left Montgomery for Chicago two years after the boycott, and worked on the staff of Congressman John Conyers. Her contributions to civil rights have been recognized through an annual award bestowed by the Southern Christian Leadership Council, the success of the Rosa and Raymond Parks Institute for Self-Development, and her receipt of the Presidential Medal of Freedom in 1999. Asked if she was happy after she retired, Parks answered, "I do the very best I can to look upon life with optimism and hope." When she died at the age of 92 in 2005, Parks was further honored when her body lay in state in the congressional rotunda for two days.

and set up carpools to ferry blacks around the city. One African-American minister told of asking an elderly woman he had picked up if she was tired. She responded, "My soul has been tired for a long time. Now my feet are tired, and my soul is resting." City officials began arresting African-American drivers of carpools and charging them with preventing bus company owners from conducting daily business. Martin Luther King Jr. was found guilty and ordered to pay a $500 fine and another $500 in court costs. Despite all efforts by Montgomery segregationists, the Supreme Court determined that segregation in all forms of public transportation was illegal. On November 25, 1955, the Interstate Commerce Commission officially banned segregation in interstate travel.

## "ALL DELIBERATE SPEED:" 1955

Across the south, political officials reacted to the Supreme Court's overthrow of "separate but equal" by attempting to ignore *Brown,* or by devising plans to circumvent federal mandates. One method involved the use of placement tests, which ostensibly used nonracial criteria to access qualifications of both new and transfer students. In reality the tests were used to restrict African-American students to all-black schools. On May 31, 1955, the Supreme Court announced in *Brown II* that integration of public schools must proceed with "all deliberate speed." Judges were given a good deal of discretion in how desegregation was carried out, and federal courts began by ordering integration of public colleges and universities. In the south, most judges were white, and many were covert segregationists. Nevertheless there was a core group of white judges who used their positions to force compliance with federal integration laws, including John Minor Wisdom, John R. Brown, Elbert Tuttle, and Richard Rivers of the Fifth Circuit, Frank Johnson of Alabama, and Skelly Wright of Louisiana.

In 1952 before the Supreme Court ordered an end to "separate but equal," Autherine Lucy had been accepted at the University of Alabama. When it was discovered that she was an African American, she was told she was ineligible to enroll. Her situation changed with the *Brown* decision, and Lucy was slated to become the first African American to attend the University of Alabama. Classes were scheduled to begin on February 20, 1956, but segregationists around the state were determined that she would never be allowed to "taint their sacred halls."

Autherine Lucy arrived at Smith Hall for her first class in a black Cadillac driven by Henry Nathaniel Guinn, the African-American owner of a Birmingham finance company. She discovered that 300 people had gathered outside the building. As the car pulled up, onlookers began chanting, "Hey, hey, ho, ho. Autherine must go!" At the end of class, Lucy was escorted out a back door by Dean of Women Sarah L. Healy. The mob had already regrouped, however, and began throwing eggs and stones. After Lucy attended a children's literature class at Bibb Graves Hall, the crowd focused their attention on her escort, Jefferson Bennett, shouting "Kill him! Kill him!" School officials ordered Lucy to remain inside after her next class. She was later escorted back to Birmingham by state police, and subsequently received a telegram announcing that she was suspended from school until further notice for "safety"

*Autherine Lucy leaving the federal courthouse in Birmingham, Alabama, on February 29, 1956, accompanied by Thurgood Marshall (center) and Arthur Shores, who served as her lawyers.*

reasons. On March 12, 1956, Alabama attempted to outlaw the National Association for the Advancement of Colored People (NAACP) within state borders. Two months later, the Montgomery home of Dr. Martin Luther King Jr. was bombed, but the family escaped harm.

## CENTRAL HIGH SCHOOL: 1957

At the high school level, the most publicized event of the 1950s took place in Little Rock, Arkansas, when nine students had been admitted to Central High School by court order in 1957. Governor Orval Faubus claimed that he was not a segregationist, but was simply committed to carrying out the wishes of 85 percent of Arkansans who had expressed disapproval of integration. When eight of the students arrived accompanied by adults, they were met by a group of 100 people that included reporters and other pupils, and by a cadre of National Guardsmen 250 strong. The eight students turned back when ordered to do so, but 15-year-old Elizabeth Eckford had failed to rendezvous with the other eight students. Instead she arrived at the school alone to face National Guardsmen armed with rifles, determined to prevent her from entering the school.

A militia officer shielded Elizabeth Eckford from the crowd, and escorted her to a bus stop where she could catch a bus to take her home. After arriving at the bus stop, the officer left her to face the hostile crowd alone. Someone in the crowd yelled, "Go home, you burr head." Grace Lorch, the wife of a teacher at the school, was in the crowd as an interested observer. Horrified at the hatred directed at Eckford, Lorch sat down beside her and placed her arm around the young woman's shoulders. She shouted at the crowd, "This is just a little girl . . . Next week you'll all be ashamed of yourselves." Lorch remained with Eckford until the bus arrived 35 minutes later. As the white-haired lady escorted the terrified student to the bus, she ordered the crowd not to touch them and threatened, "I'm just aching to punch somebody in the nose."

After a judge ordered the National Guard removed, the nine students returned to school. This time the students saw police officers with swinging billy clubs determined to prevent them from entering Central High. After they were secretly hustled inside, four African-American journalists approached the crowd from the rear. The crowd began chasing them, believing they were the Arkansas Nine. The threatening mob quickly grew from 300 to 500 to 900. A crowd member shouted out, suggesting one student should be hanged to provide an example to others. On September 30 President Eisenhower dispatched the Screaming Eagles of the 101st Airborne to Little Rock. Subsequently paratroopers with orders to protect the students and maintain peace stood at the ready with drawn bayonets.

Under the protection of the federal government, the African-American students were escorted to Central High School in an army station wagon positioned between two army jeeps. When asked by reporters how they were treated, they responded that they were treated well. The truth was shared only with leaders of the civil rights movement, who knew that the Little Rock Nine faced daily threats and intimidation. In a Gallup poll conducted in December 1958, Governor Faubus was named one of the 10 most admired men in America. Even though 80 students left the school to avoid integration, the rest remained in the public school system. Faubus closed Arkansas public schools the following year, and half the student population enrolled in private schools. Another third enrolled in schools outside the state, but 643 Arkansan students attended no school at all in the 1958–59 school year. The Supreme Court forced Faubus to reopen the schools, finding his actions unconstitutional. Public schools in Arkansas reopened in August 1959.

## INTENSIFYING RESISTANCE

Violent responses to "uppity blacks" had been considered a way of life in the American south since the post–Civil War years. That violence increased as the pace of integration accelerated. As early as 1955, three prominent African-American leaders had been murdered in Mississippi. The murder of

Lemar Smith had brazenly taken place in broad daylight at the Pike County Courthouse. Segregationists in Birmingham became so incensed in 1957 over desegregation efforts that an African-American male was savagely beaten and castrated. This action was a direct result of segregationist propaganda that integration of schools would lead to sexual intercourse between black men and white women, and the ingrained myth that all black men were potential rapists of white women.

The Southern Christian Leadership Council (SCLC) was founded January 10–11, 1957, as a way to bring local African-American leaders together to advance civil rights within individual cities and communities. Later that same month, South Carolina Republican senator Strom Thurmond engaged in what became the longest filibuster in the history of the Senate. Thurmond talked for 25 hours and 18 minutes, reading election laws from various states to maintain the floor. His attempt to block passage of the Civil Rights Act of 1957 failed, and the weak voting rights measure passed.

The Supreme Court handed down *Cooper v. Aaron* on September 20, 1958, with the intention of speeding up the process of enforcing *Brown*. In reality *Cooper* left individual states with a good deal of leeway in how they complied with federal mandates. In Virginia, Prince Edward County abandoned its public school system on June 26, 1959, in an unsuccessful attempt to avoid integration.

*This group continued to try to protest the integration of Central High School in Little Rock, Arkansas, in August 1959 by holding a rally at the state capitol.*

After the crisis at Central High, Arkansas state officials became determined to force the NAACP out of existence, because they believed its absence would cut down on "outside agitators" determined to promote civil rights. Daisy Bates, who had been involved in protecting the Arkansas Nine, was the head of the Arkansas branch of the NAACP at the time. Officials demanded that Bates turn over lists of NAACP members, but she refused to comply with their demands. On Halloween night in 1957, while the 101st Airborne continued to patrol the downtown streets, council members decided to issue arrest warrants for Daisy Bates and J.C. Crenchaw, a local minister. The ordinance that Bates and Crenchaw were accused of flaunting had been drafted by state attorney general Bruce Bennett for the express purpose of forcing the NAACP out of Arkansas, and was patterned after a similar law in Alabama.

The two civil rights activists faced criminal prosecution, and a $100,000 fine. After Bates returned from a speaking engagement in New York, she and Crenchaw followed the advice of Thurgood Marshall and surrendered to authorities. Charges were dismissed against Crenchaw, but Bates was scheduled for trial on December 3, 1957. She was found guilty and ordered to pay a $100 fine. Because her case had been decided by a municipal court judge, Bates was eligible by state law to request a new trial. The new trial opened on February 11 the following year. Bates stated in court that the Arkansas NAACP had lost between 100 and 150 donors the previous year because of the publicity and fear of reprisals.

Bates appealed her guilty verdict in the second trial, and her case reached the U.S. Supreme Court in November 1959. In the interim, her house had been bombed, and her newspaper had been forced out of business in response to an advertising boycott. All nine members of the Court agreed that the civil liberties of Bates and other NAACP members had been denied. Justice Potter Stewart wrote the unanimous opinion, which declared that Little Rock's ordinance had violated the due process clause of the Fourteenth Amendment by interfering with freedom of association.

On October 13, 1958, the Supreme Court refused to accept an attempt to delay integration of public schools for an additional two and a half years. Some states continued to resist, however. In Virginia, Governor J. Lindsay Almond closed three schools, rather than integrate them.

## THE 1960s

As the 1950s gave way to the 1960s, many African Americans had few tangible results to show as a result of the civil rights movement. Although it had been six years since the Supreme Court had ordered that public schools be integrated, white supremacists in the Deep South continued to block federal desegregation efforts. Jim Crow laws continued to flourish. The pace of the movement picked up drastically on February 1, 1960, when four black students in Greensboro, North Carolina, decided they had waited long enough.

College students Ezell Blair, Jr., Franklin McCain, Joseph McNeil, and David Richmond sat down at a lunch counter at the local Woolworth's, insisting they would not leave unless they were served. Although the four young men left at closing time, they returned the next morning with 25 cohorts. Within two weeks, 14 sit-ins had been staged in five different southern states. In Orangeburg, South Carolina, 600 African-American students marched, carrying placards that announced, "We want liberty." One white and one black protestor were arrested. In Nashville, Tennessee, 500 protesters marched on stores and bus stations to demand an end to segregation in public places. Sit-ins subsequently became a popular tool among various groups of activists.

## FREEDOM RIDES: 1961

The Student Non-Violent Coordinating Committee (SNCC) was founded on April 17, 1960, by students dedicated to the concept of change through peaceful resistance. The success of this student group gave new life to the Congress for Racial Equality (CORE), which had been founded in 1942 as a biracial student group concerned with changing racial attitudes. Under CORE's sponsorship, an integrated group of civil rights activists set out from Washington, D.C., on May 4, 1961, with the goal of challenging the Interstate Commerce Commission's mandate to integrate all transportation facilities involved in interstate travel. The group included seven African-American activists and six whites, including two college professors. White passengers planned to sit in the back of the bus, while their black cohorts agreed to sit in the front and refuse to move if ordered to do so. The schedule included stops in Virginia, North Carolina, and South Carolina, as well as the highly segregated states of Alabama and Mississippi. The Freedom Riders planned to arrive in New Orleans on May 17, the anniversary of the *Brown* decision.

The first sign of serious trouble came on May 14 when the Freedom Riders separated, with one group destined for Atlanta and the other for Birmingham. Upon arrival in Anniston, Alabama, a crowd of 200 segregationists attacked the Greyhound bus carrying the Freedom Riders. Several riders were beaten, and William Barbee was paralyzed for life. The bus driver fled the scene, driving some 60 miles before feeling safe enough to fix the tires that had been damaged in the attack. During the emergency stop, someone threw a firebomb into the bus, which burst into flames. Birmingham chief of police Bull Connor continued to refuse to assign police officers to protect the Freedom Riders.

Despite the savage attack, the Freedom Riders remained committed to challenging segregation. A second group arrived in Montgomery, Alabama, on May 20 after being assured of protection. That protection melted away when an airplane pilot and patrol officers fled the scene. The crowd attacked the Freedom Riders with baseball bats, pipes, and other objects at hand, as well as with their fists. One of those injured was presidential aide John Seigenthal, who was beaten into unconsciousness. Floyd Mann, the head of the

*Freedom Riders, who were working with the Congress of Racial Equality, watch as their Greyhound bus burns in Anniston, Alabama, in May 1961.*

Alabama State Police, ended the riot by holding a gun to the head of an attacker. The governor declared martial law in Montgomery.

President John F. Kennedy responded to the crisis by sending 600 federal marshals to Alabama's Maxwell Air Force Base to protect the Freedom Riders and to maintain peace. Another 200 were dispatched to Birmingham, where the injured had been transported. Dr. Martin Luther King Jr. arrived in Montgomery to conduct a mass meeting at a local church. Despite the protection of federal marshals, a mob of several thousand gathered outside the church. The marshals were forced to use tear gas against the mob, who pelted them with bottles. King contacted Attorney General Bobby Kennedy, who called Governor John Patterson. The governor extended martial law to the entire state, and dispatched state police and the National Guard to help restore order.

On May 24 the Freedom Riders left Montgomery. At the Mississippi state line, they met a cadre of armed National Guardsmen. Bobby Kennedy had worked with Senator James O. Eastland to ensure that the Freedom Riders encountered no other mobs. Instead the Freedom Riders were arrested and charged with violating state laws. The original Freedom Riders opted to fly to New Orleans. Undaunted, others arrived in Jackson, Mississippi, to carry on the battle. By summer's end, more than 300 civil rights activists had journeyed to the Deep South.

Georgia managed to avoid much of the racial strife that divided the other southern states. Atlanta, the state capital, called itself "the city too busy to hate." The environment in rural areas was less progressive, and Dr. Martin Luther King Jr., a Georgia native and the de facto leader of the civil rights movement, targeted Albany for a major voting rights battle. Located in southwestern Georgia, Albany was chiefly a farming area. It also had its share of liquor stores, pool halls, taxi companies, and beauty salons, some of which were owned by African Americans. Albany State College, an all-black institution, offered educational opportunities that African Americans lacked in many other southern states. Nevertheless the city was still segregated in many respects, and the percentage of registered African-American voters was low.

SNCC arrived in Albany in the summer of 1961 to begin organizing protests. However Albany blacks were not receptive. They refused to join in voting rights drives, and were not interested in forcing integration of public terminals. Despite his best efforts to transform Albany into a more integrated city, the Albany Movement became one of Dr. King's few failures. Athens, Georgia also became a focus of civil rights activity when rioting broke out after two African-American students were admitted to the University of Georgia. The following September, rioting broke out at the University of Mississippi, and President Kennedy federalized the Mississippi National Guard. Before the riots ended, 160 marshals had been injured, 28 people had been shot, two had died, and 200 people had been arrested.

## DEATH AND RHETORIC: 1963

President Kennedy won the support of the black community during the 1960 campaign, carrying 68 percent of the African-American vote. Despite this support, Kennedy originally lacked a strong commitment to civil rights. During his presidency, Kennedy slowly began to understand the importance of ending segregation. On February 28, 1963, he addressed the nation in what became known as a "special civil rights message." Two months later protests in Alabama became violent, and the president, along with other Americans, watched in horror as television cameras captured peace officers attacking innocent black children with water hoses and police dogs. Along with his brother, Attorney General Robert Kennedy, the president became more actively involved in the civil rights movement. On June 12 he spoke again to the nation on the issue.

Several hours after listening to Kennedy's message, Medgar Evers, a field representative for the NAACP, arrived in his own driveway. Throughout 1963 Evers had spent most of his days traveling the state of Mississippi, attempting to register black Mississippians to vote. Well aware of the segregationist potential to commit violence, Evers had told supporters, "If I die, it will be in a good cause. I've been fighting for American justice as much as the soldiers in Vietnam." As Evers stepped out of his car, he was carrying T-shirts that

# Dr. King's Dream

From 1955 to 1968, Dr. Martin Luther King Jr. led the civil rights movement in the direction of nonviolence. He experienced both successes and failures as the movement gained momentum. On August 28, 1963, at the March on Washington, which brought some 200,000 protesters to the nation's capital, King gave a speech that has stood as a lasting legacy to his work and to the civil rights movement as a whole. After recognizing that "the Negro is still not free" due to being "sadly crippled by the manacles of segregation and the manacles of discrimination," King laid out his hope of a more equitable America, a country that adhered to the principle "that all men are created equal."

*Martin Luther King Jr. speaking to reporters at the U.S. Capitol on March 26, 1964.*

King's vision included the ability of "the sons of former slaves and the sons of former slaveowners" to come together to the "table of brotherhood." King expressed the hope that Mississippi, which many saw as the cradle of segregationist hatred, could be "transformed into an oasis of freedom and justice." In Alabama, where governors had led the battle to prevent integrated schools, King saw the potential for "little black boys and black girls . . . to join hands with little white boys and girls and walk together as sisters and brothers." King's vision encompassed the entire nation, predicting that when freedom rang throughout the country, "all God's children . . . will be able to join hands and sing, 'Free at last: Free at last: Thank God Almighty, we are free at last!'"

Although Martin Luther King Jr. did not live to see the full realization of his dream, he would say that it did not matter. On April 3, 1968, in Memphis, Tennessee, where he had come to support striking sanitation workers, King told listeners that no matter what happened next, "it really doesn't matter with me now because I've been to the mountaintop."

Admitting that he hoped for a long life, King said God "has allowed me [to see] the Promised Land." He closed his speech by assuring supporters that he was happy and "not worried about anything" and was "not fearing any man" because he had seen "the glory of the coming of the Lord." At 7:00 the next night, King was assassinated when he stepped onto the balcony of the Lorraine Hotel.

read "Jim Crow must go." Shots rang out, and his horrified wife and children rushed to his side. It was not until 1994 that white segregationist Byron de la Beckwith was sent to prison for murdering Evers. A few weeks after Evers's death, the Department of Justice announced that integration was proceeding well, and that public facilities in 143 cities had been desegregated in a three-week period. On June 19, Kennedy sent a more comprehensive civil rights bill to Congress. The new legislation was designed to guarantee African Americans access to places of public accommodation, and to allow the federal government to file discrimination suits and cut off funds for failure to comply with federal civil rights statutes. Congressman Emanuel Celler (D-NY) worked with members of the House Judiciary Sub-Committee to produce an even stronger civil rights bill.

On August 28, 200,000 civil rights protestors arrived in Washington, D.C. to begin their trek to the Lincoln Memorial. That same day King gave his "I Have a Dream" speech, which has become the most quoted speech of the civil rights movement. King maintained that economically most African Americans lived "on a lonely island of poverty in the vast ocean of material prosperity," finding himself "an exile in his own land." John Lewis, a member of SNCC and a future congressman from Georgia, pulled no punches in his address.

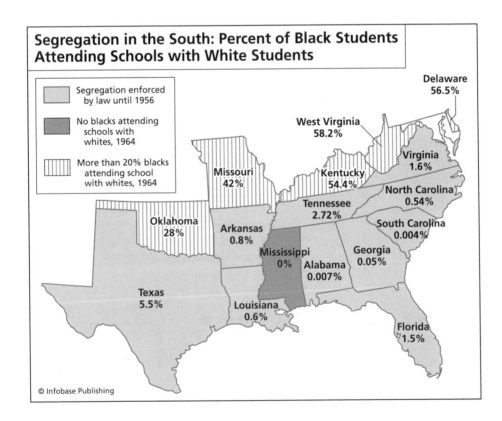

**Segregation in the South: Percent of Black Students Attending Schools with White Students**

Segregation enforced by law until 1956

No blacks attending schools with whites, 1964

More than 20% blacks attending school with whites, 1964

Delaware 56.5%

West Virginia 58.2%

Virginia 1.6%

Missouri 42%

Kentucky 54.4%

North Carolina 0.54%

Tennessee 2.72%

Oklahoma 28%

Arkansas 0.8%

South Carolina 0.004%

Mississippi 0%

Alabama 0.007%

Georgia 0.05%

Texas 5.5%

Louisiana 0.6%

Florida 1.5%

© Infobase Publishing

Lewis insisted that the "revolution is at hand, and we must free ourselves of the chains of political and economic slavery."

The following month, innocent children became the target of racial hatred just as they had in 1954 when segregationists murdered Emmett Till, a Chicago youth visiting southern relatives. On September 15, 1963, Denise McNair, 11, and three 14-year-olds, Cynthia Wesley, Carole Robertson, and Addie Mae Collins, were killed when members of the Ku Klux Kan detonated a bomb during a Sunday school meeting. By the end of October, the House Judiciary Committee had approved a new bipartisan civil rights bill with full presidential support. The bill was reported out on November 20. Two days later, President Kennedy was assassinated in Dallas, Texas.

## THE CIVIL RIGHTS ACT: 1964

Reconstruction ended in 1876 without completely bringing African Americans into the mainstream of life in southern and border states. Many Jim Crow lawssuch as poll taxes, were designed to keep African Americans from exercising their right to vote. Poll taxes were banned in all national elections by ratification of the Twenty-fourth Amendment on January 23, 1964, but it was not until 1966 that the Supreme Court banned poll taxes in all elections in *Harper v. Virginia Board of Elections*, forcing Virginia, Alabama, Mississippi, and Texas to remove this last legal barrier to exercising the right to vote.

Even though significant gains were made, individual African Americans paid a heavy price for their activism. On June 16 Fannie Lou Hamer appeared before a congressional committee testifying about the violence directed at her when she tried to register African-American voters in Mississippi. "After I was beaten by the first Negro," she said, "the state highway patrolman ordered the other Negro to take the blackjack [to me]."

Increasing public pressure and the assassination of President Kennedy enabled President Lyndon Johnson to guide the Civil Rights Act of 1964 through Congress. Johnson labeled the landmark legislation a "memorial" to Kennedy. This comprehensive civil rights measure was sent to the floor of the Senate after 71 senators voted to force an end to debate on the bill. This was the first time cloture had been used to break a civil rights filibuster. The purpose of a filibuster is to talk a bill to death to keep it from coming to a vote, and southern senators had used the tactic to block all civil rights legislation from the end of Reconstruction to 1957. Senate majority leader Mike Mansfield (D-MT) attempted to ensure that the new bill was left unchanged by requesting that it be sent to the Senate Judiciary Committee with instructions to report it back to the floor without amendment within seven days. Although the tactic failed, it encouraged senators to work out compromises on controversial issues. On the floor of the Senate, 50 separate amendments were voted down. The Civil Rights Act of 1964 passed the Senate by a vote of 98–0, and the House of Representatives approved it by a vote of 290–130. In a surprise move, "sex" was added to race, color, religion, and national origin in Title VII, thereby protecting women from employment discrimination for the first time.

The bill became Public Law 88-352 when it was signed by President Johnson in July 1963. It ushered in a period of sweeping changes in U.S. politics and soci-

# Watts Riots

In August 1965 the predominantly black Los Angeles neighborhood of Watts was on the verge of destruction, both physically and socially. Nearly 95 percent of homes in Watts had been built before 1939. These dwellings were in poor repair, providing only minimal amenities. Two-thirds of residents had less than a high school education, and one-eighth classified as technically illiterate. Most residents were unemployed. They were poor and often hungry. Crime, ranging from simple thefts and assaults to murders and rapes, was considered a part of daily life. Widespread anger and alienation were rampant, and the atmosphere was volatile.

Around 7:45 P.M. in the evening of August 11, police officers spotted Watts resident Marquette Frye, 21, who was intoxicated and driving erratically. At the end of a six-block chase, Frye was apprehended in front of 25 witnesses. Accounts vary as to specific details of what happened, but locals responded to what they believed was police brutality by launching a riot that raged for six days and spread 150 blocks. Whites passing through the area were pelted with Molotov cocktails, bottles, rocks, concrete, and other handy objects. Stores were looted for rifles, shotguns, pistols, and machetes to provide more sophisticated weapons. Looters also stole televisions, radios, clothing, and anything else they could carry away. Objects that could not be easily removed were destroyed. After stores were stripped, they were burned to the ground. Thirty-four people were killed, 1,032 injured, and 3,952 arrested before the riots ended on August 16. Property damage was estimated at $100 million. The effects of the riots resonated around the country, as evidenced in the lyrics of *Loaded Gun* by American Steel: "I didn't see Watts burn but I felt the embers."

The McCone Commission, headed by industrialist John McCone, issued its final report on the Watts riots in December 1967, announcing that although 17,900 Watts residents had become employed through job training programs, the "unemployment rate among Negroes [in Watts] has not been substantially reduced." The report stated that 36,000 residents—nearly the entire population of the area—were receiving welfare payments. The chief recommendation was that government officials launch a "massive, expansive assault on the problem of illiteracy." Many African Americans insisted that the report lacked substance and failed to go far enough in offering suggestions for change.

ety. The Civil Rights Act of 1964 was identified as an act "to enforce the constitutional right to vote, to confer jurisdiction upon the district courts of the United States to provide injunctive relief against discrimination in public accommodations, to authorize the Attorney General to institute suits to protect constitutional rights in public facilities and public education, to extend the Commission on Civil Rights, to prevent discrimination in federally assisted programs, to establish a Commission on Equal Opportunity, and for other purposes." The bill was divided into separate titles to ensure that African Americans were able to claim all rights they had been granted in the Thirteenth, Fourteenth, and Fifteenth Amendments, and by a plethora of federal laws and court decisions.

The most important provisions were found in Title I, which protected the right to vote; Title III, which banned discrimination in places of public accommodation; Title IV, which banned all segregation in public education; and Title VII, which prohibited discrimination in employment. By providing injunctive relief, withholding federal funds in cases of persistent discrimination, and giving the attorney general of the United States, the Civil Rights Commission, and the Equal Employment Opportunity Commission broad investigatory powers, the federal government effectively ended legal discrimination throughout the United States. On the other hand, social and private discrimination proved much more difficult to eradicate.

## RESPONSES AND RETALIATION

Although the passage of the Civil Rights Act was welcomed by most Americans, it served as a catalyst for rioting in major cities, including New York, New Jersey, Chicago, and Philadelphia. In some cases, the perpetrators of violence were African Americans who directed their anger at people of their own race. On February 21, 1964, noted civil rights leader Malcolm X was assassinated while giving a speech at the Audubon Ballroom in Washington Heights. Formerly a black Muslim minister, Malcolm X had left the organization in 1964. His assassins were black Muslims who were enraged at Malcolm X's rejection of their principles and goals.

On July 31, 1964, the Congress for Racial Equality (CORE) held a protest march in Harlem in New York. On the way to present their demands at a local station house, rioting broke out as perpetrators threw bricks, bottles, and the lids of garbage cans at passing whites. Rioters broke the doors and windows of Jewish-owned shops. After tearing down iron gates and protective screens, looters swarmed in, carrying away television sets, appliances, canned goods, and clothing. The police fired so many shots that they ran out of ammunition. Many civil rights workers spent the summer of 1964 more peacefully. They went to Mississippi, where they educated more than 2,600 African Americans about the rights of citizenship through courses designed to promote racial pride and domestic harmony. Civil rights workers also taught summer classes in social studies, black history, drama, art, and nonviolent protest.

*Police beating a man on the sidewalk at 133rd Street and Seventh Avenue during a 1964 riot in Harlem in New York.*

In August, in 101-degree weather, FBI agents found the decomposed bodies of Michael Schwerner, Andrew Goodman, and James Chaney, the three civil rights workers who had received national attention after their disappearance on June 21. The young men were found buried in a 25-foot levee located on Olen Burrage's Old Jolly Farm in Philadelphia, Mississippi. Although 21 segregationists were arrested, including a deputy sheriff, it took more than four decades for Edgar Ray Killen to be sentenced to 60 years in prison for the murder, which was depicted in the 1988 movie *Mississippi Burning*. Although original criminal charges had been dropped against all defendants, six of the men served time in federal prison for violating the civil rights of the slain activists.

On October 23, 1964, Dr. Martin Luther King Jr. was awarded the Nobel Peace Prize. He was the second African American to win the prize. At 35, King was the youngest recipient in Nobel history. The $54,000 prize money was donated to the civil rights movement. For King, this prestigious acknowledgement of his efforts signaled a more active stage in the movement, and he announced plans for a voting rights march from Selma, Alabama, where only one percent of all eligible black voters were registered, to the state capital in Montgomery. During the first march in January 1965, protestors were turned back at the Edmund Pettus Bridge by armed police.

The second attempt on March 6 proved to be one of the most violent events in civil rights history, becoming known as Bloody Sunday. Hosea Williams led the biracial group of marchers as they started out. Under official orders to prevent their progress, police officers began attacking protestors indiscriminately as television cameras rolled. Jim Reeb, a white Unitarian minister, was beaten so badly that he died five days later. Treatment for Reeb, who had been struck in the head, was delayed because he had to be transported 65 miles to Birmingham before being treated, and the ambulance that transported him had a flat tire. Sheriff's deputies refused to provide a protective escort for the ambulance.

Thousands of Americans staged protests around the country; and in Toronto, 2,000 Canadians gathered to express their support for the American civil rights movement. On March 21, with protection by 2,000 federal military police, 1,900 nationalized Alabama National Guardsmen, and platoons of U.S. marshals and FBI agents, 3,400 civil rights marchers led by King and fellow African-American Nobel Peace Prize–winner Ralph Bunche finally succeeded in reaching Montgomery. However Governor George Wallace reneged on his promise to meet with them.

## VOTING RIGHTS ACT: 1965

In 1870 African Americans had been given the right to vote in the Fifteenth Amendment, and blacks gained a political voice for the first time in American history. However in the contested election of 1876, Republican presidential candidate Rutherford B. Hayes agreed to end Reconstruction in exchange for southern support of his right to the presidency over Samuel Tilden, who had won the popular vote. This move cleared the way for the passage of Jim Crow laws that prevented African Americans from exercising their right to vote through such measures as primaries in which only whites were eligible to vote, grandfather clauses in which eligibility was based on whether or not one's grandfather had voted before the Civil War, poll taxes that required a small payment for voting, literacy tests that were given only to African Americans, and tests in which African Americans were required to explain complicated passages from the U.S. Constitution. In addition to these legal measures designed to disenfranchise African Americans, white supremacists engaged in campaigns of intimidation, interference, and violence. Blacks who tried to register to vote faced loss of jobs, eviction from their homes, and bans on obtaining credit at local establishments.

The violence in Selma served as a catalyst for restoring the right of African Americans to participate in the political process, clearing the way for the passage of the Voting Rights Act of 1965. This act allowed the federal government to take an active role in registering black voters in states with past records of discrimination, to oversee the electoral process, and to monitor the number of African Americans casting ballots in various elections. Almost immediately, the number of African-American voters began to rise. The Supreme Court upheld the act in 1966 in *South Carolina v. Katzenbach.*

## ATTITUDES AND REALITIES

In the summer of 1963, *Newsweek* magazine sponsored an in-depth poll of social attitudes on the civil rights movement, canvassing 1,000 African Americans and 1,200 whites. The poll was conducted by Louis Harris and Associates, one of the most highly respected polling companies in the United States. On July 29 *Newsweek* published the results of the African-American poll, concluding that most blacks saw the civil rights movement as a "revolution" that was designed to allow them an equal role in society. Even though most responders endorsed nonviolence, they acknowledged that an undercurrent of unrest was always present.

In 1966 *Newsweek* repeated the study, polling 1,059 African Americans and 1,088 whites. A separate poll was conducted among African-American leaders who ranged from civil rights leader Dr. Martin Luther King Jr. to

An African-American woman casts her vote on November 3, 1964, in Washington, D.C. The Voting Rights Act of 1965 soon increased the number of African-American voters substantially.

entertainer Sammy Davis, Jr. On August 22 the cover story of *Newsweek* was devoted to the new study. The overall conclusion was that the revolution had reached "full tide" between 1963 and 1966. White sympathy had been aroused by the violence against peaceful demonstrators shown on national television. That sympathy reached its peak with the incidents in Selma in 1964. Responders believed that as the civil rights movement turned violent, internal disagreements had created fissures within the African-American community, alienated sympathetic whites, and provided ammunition to segregationists.

White social attitudes had changed considerably in the three years between the two studies. There were substantially fewer objections to integration in transportation and housing, and to intermarriage. Nevertheless many whites felt threatened by accelerating militancy. The most tolerant group of white responders was middle and upper class. Blacks had also become more tolerant of whites during the same period, but they were less optimistic about the chance of ultimate success. Among African Americans, 58 percent believed that education among blacks was better, compared to only 39 percent in 1963. Some 53 percent of black responders were pleased with gains in voting rights, and 54 percent believed employment opportunities were greater than three years before.

While educational opportunities had improved for African Americans, a number of states closed public schools to avoid integration. In cases such as *Griffin v. Prince Edward County* (1964), the Supreme Court made it clear that such actions were unconstitutional. Because of obstacles to integration, in 1966, only 12.5 percent of 2.9 million African-American students living in former Confederate states attended integrated schools. In Alabama, only one in 42 black students attended integrated schools, one in 28 in Louisiana, and one in three in Mississippi. Running out of patience, President Johnson ordered the Department of Health, Education, and Welfare to suspend all federal funds to segregated school districts.

## UNEQUAL AND MILITANT

President Kennedy had devised the idea of appointing a commission to analyze the status of African Americans in U.S. society. In July 1967 his successor Lyndon Johnson created the 11-member National Advisory Commission on Civil Disorders, popularly known as the Kerner Commission. In 1968 the commission issued its final report, concluding that "Our nation is moving toward two societies, one black, one white—separate and unequal." Recommendations for reversing this trend included education, job training, and expanding job opportunities.

The entrenched alienation of many African Americans provided a fertile ground for violence, and even rumors could set off days of rioting. In 1967 in Newark, New Jersey, a rumor spread that a white police officer had killed a popular trumpet-playing taxi driver. Even though 4,000 police officers were dispatched to the scene, 21 people died, 1,000 were injured, and 1,600 individuals were arrested. Property damage was estimated in the millions. August proved to be a particularly violent month, with riots breaking out in black ghettos in Albany, New York; Albion, Michigan; Waterbury, Connecticut; and Waukegan, Illinois. These riots left 45 people dead, thousands of others injured, and more than $1 billion in property damage.

When Dr. Martin Luther King Jr. was assassinated in Memphis on April 12 during a strike by sanitation workers, riots erupted around the country. Witnesses noted that Washington, D.C. looked like a city that had been bombed. In Chicago, rioting spread over eight city blocks, and National Guardsmen patrolled the streets to enforce the designated curfew. Much of the militancy of the civil rights movement in the late 1960s was a response to *Politics of Liberation in America* (1969) by Stokely Carmichael and Charles Hamilton. Carmichael used his position as chair of SNCC to promote the concept of "black power." The Black Panther Party for Self-Defense, which had been founded in 1966, was also a major force for militancy in the late 1960s. Party leaders Huey P. Newton and Bobby Seale were considered by many, including FBI director J. Edgar Hoover, to be the most dangerous men in America. Hoover was determined to eliminate the Black Panthers as a threat to American peace, and by the beginning of the 1970s, the party had lost most of its influence.

## CONCLUSION

Despite increasing violence, there were major gains among African Americans during the late 1960s. In Gary, Indiana, long considered the northern bastion of the Ku Klux Klan, African-American Richard Hatcher was elected mayor, with white voters supplying the winning margin. In 1969 in *Alexander v. Holmes County Board of Education*, the Supreme Court determined that the policy of integrating public schools through "all deliberate speed" should be replaced with ending segregation at once. Although effectively forcing desegregation, this decision set the stage for heated controversy during the following decade over the issue of busing students to meet racial quotas. African Americans had been leaving the south since the 19th century for what they believed were greater opportunities for economic success and more equitable treatment in other areas of the United States. By the late 1960s, this trend accelerated as African Americans fled the violence of the civil rights movement. By the next decade, however, that trend was reversed, and many African Americans returned to a transformed south.

ELIZABETH R. PURDY
INDEPENDENT SCHOLAR

# Further Reading

Academy of Achievement. "Rosa Parks." Available online, URL: http://www.achievement.org/autodoc/page/par0bio-1. Accessed July 2008.

Belknap, Michael R. *Securing the Enactment of Civil Rights Legislation: Civil Rights Act of 1964*. New York: Garland, 1991.

Brink, William, and Louis Harris. *Black and White: A Study of United States Racial Attitudes Today*. New York: Simon and Schuster, 1966.

Cashman, Sean Dennis. *African Americans and the Quest for Civil Rights, 1900–1990*. New York: New York University Press, 1991.

"Chicago's 71st Street Renamed for Emmett Till." *Jet* (August 12, 1991).

"Civil Rights Act," 1964. Available online, URL: http://www.ourdocuments. gov/doc.php?flash=true&doc=97&page=transcript. Accessed July 2008.

Davis, Michael D., and Hunter R. Clark. *Thurgood Marshall: Warrior at the Bar, Rebel on the Bench*. New York: Birch Lane, 1992.

Estes, Steve. *I Am A Man: Race, Manhood, and the Civil Rights Movement*. Chapel Hill: University of North Carolina, 2005.

Gates, Henry Louis, Jr., and Cornel West. *The African American Century: How Black Americans Have Shaped Our Century*. New York: Free Press, 2000.

Grossman, Joel B., and Richard S. Wells. *Constitutional Law and Judicial Policy Making*. New York: Longman, 1988.

Hamby, Alonzo. *Outline of United States History*. New York: Nova Science, 2007.

Hampton, Henry, and Steve Fayer. *Voices of Freedom: An Oral History of the Civil Rights Movement from the 1950s through the 1980s*. New York: Bantam, 1990.

Houck, Davis W., and Matthew A. Grindy. *Emmett Till and the Mississippi Press*. Jackson: University of Mississippi Press, 2008.

Irons, Peter. *The Courage of Their Convictions: Sixteen Americans Who Fought Their Way to the Supreme Court*. New York: Penguin, 1988.

King, Martin Luther, Jr. "I See The Promised Land." In *A Testament of Hope: The Essential Writings of Martin Luther King, Jr.* Ed. by James Melvin Washington. San Francisco, CA: Harper and Row, 1986.

King, Martin Luther, Jr. "The March on Washington Address." In *The American Reader: Words That Moved a Nation*, edited by Diane Ravitch. New York: HarperCollins, 1990.

Kirk, John A., ed. *An Epitaph for Little Rock: A Fiftieth Anniversary Retrospective on the Central High Crisis*. Fayetteville: University of Arkansas Press, 2008.

Lawson, Steven F. *Running for Freedom: Civil Rights in America since 1941*. New York: McGraw-Hill, 1991.

Loevy, Robert D., ed. *Civil Rights Act of 1964: The Passage of the Law That Ended Segregation*. New York: New York State University, 1997.

Long, Michael G., ed. *First Class Citizenship: The Civil Rights Letters of Jackie Robinson*. New York: New York Times Books, 2007.

Miyares, Ines M., and Christopher A. Airriess, eds. *Contemporary Ethnic Geographies in America*. Lanham, MD: Rowman and Littlefied, 2007.

"Nation Horrified by Murder of Chicago Youth." *Jet* (reprinted September 15, 1991).

Nieman, Donald G. *Promises to Keep: African Americans and the Constitutional Order, 1776 to the Present*. New York: Oxford, 1991.

O'Brien, David M. *Constitutional Law and Politics, Vol. 2: Civil Rights and Civil Liberties*. New York: Norton, 1991.

Street, Joe. *The Culture War in the Civil Rights Movement*. Gainesville: University Press of Florida, 2007.

Sundquist, James L. *Politics and Policy: The Eisenhower, Kennedy, and Johnson Years*. Washington, D.C.: Brookings, 1968.

Towns, W. Stuart. *"We Want Our Freedom" Rhetoric of the Civil Rights Movement*. Westport, CT: Praeger, 2002.

"Trigger of Hate." *Time* (August 20, 1965; 1987).

Walton, Hanes, Jr., and Robert C. Smith. *American Politics and the African American Quest for Universal Freedom*. New York: Pearson Longman, 2008.

"Watts Panel Issues Its Final Report." *New York Times*. (August 27, 1967).

Weisbrot, Robert. *Freedom Bound: A History of America's Civil Rights Movement*. New York: Norton, 1990.

Williams, Juan. *Eyes on the Prize: America's Civil Rights Years, 1954–1965*. New York: Penguin, 1987.

Witt, Elder. *The Supreme Court and Individual Rights*. Washington, D.C.: Congressional Quarterly Press, 1988.

# CHAPTER 9

# A Changing Community: 1970 to 1989

**IN 1970** the African-American population of the United States was 22.6 million, or about 11 percent of the total population. During the next decade the black population increased by over 17 percent. By 1980 African Americans numbered approximately 26.5 million, or 12 percent of the population. One major black population trend that had characterized much of the earlier 20th century appeared to end—and began to reverse itself—during the 1970s. Throughout the previous seven decades, though most notably 1910–30 and 1940–60, large numbers of African Americans left the rural south for urban centers, many of them in the north and the west. From 1975 to 1980, almost twice as many African Americans moved to the south as moved away from it. A majority of African Americans—53 percent—lived in the south in 1980, and the same held true in 1990.

The African-American population of the United States in the 1970s was mostly, though not exclusively, urban. In 1970 60 percent of African Americans lived in central-city environments, 20 percent lived in cities but outside the central city, and 20 percent lived in nonmetropolitan places. By 1980 85.3 percent of African Americans lived in cities (compared to 71.3 percent for whites). That year, New York had the highest number of African Americans, with 1.78 million black residents. Chicago had 1.19 million African-American residents. In terms of percentage of the total population,

East St. Louis, Illinois, had the highest percentage of African-American residents at 96 percent.

Broadly speaking, the gains of the civil rights generation, particularly in regard to education and employment, continued in the early part of the 1970s. By the middle of the decade, a furious backlash against civil rights combined with sour economic times for the United States to stall progress toward meaningful black equality. By the 1980s, a robust African-American middle class had come into being, and it was flexing its political muscle in some quarters. Unfortunately many more African Americans were mired in generational poverty in declining urban industrial centers.

## TWILIGHT OF CIVIL RIGHTS AND BLACK POWER

By the early 1970s, the civil rights movement, never a truly unified or monolithic force, had fractured along several different lines. The most widely known fissure developed between more moderate activists, and advocates of Black Power (encompassing any number of competing philosophies as well). Black Power was born from the dissatisfaction of younger activists with the slow pace of change, and the realization that racism was pervasive in the United States and deeply entrenched in American society and institutions.

*Eldridge Cleaver of the Black Panthers at American University on October 18, 1968.*

The federal government, and especially the Federal Bureau of Investigation under J. Edgar Hoover, had long been suspicious of civil rights activists and had clandestinely monitored the activities of such luminaries as Martin Luther King Jr. and Malcolm X. The response to Black Power was even more aggressive. The Counter Intelligence Project (COINTELPRO), which lasted from the 1950s until 1971, infiltrated Black Power groups and other activist entities in an effort to bring them down from the inside. Groups like the Black Panthers may have splintered on their own in the early 1970s, but President Richard Nixon's administration made crushing radical political groups, and especially the Black Panthers, a top priority. By the 1970s, law enforcement officials had killed nearly 30 Black Panthers and imprisoned hundreds more. Among those incarcerated at various times were Huey Newton, Eldridge Cleaver, and Angela Davis.

Davis, in particular, had been active in campaigns on behalf of prisoners' rights. She was charged with murder after a violent incident at a Marin County, California, courthouse in which a young man, Jonathon Jackson, attempted to seize hostages to exchange for Black Power activists in prison, including his older brother, George Jackson, author of *Soledad Brother*. The elder Jackson was killed in August 1971 during what guards described as an escape attempt. Jackson's death sparked prison uprisings, most famously at New York State's Attica prison. The September 1971 uprising at Attica resulted in nearly 40 deaths, and scores of gunshot wounds.

## VIETNAM

While struggles over prisoners' rights, Black Power, and the legacy of the civil rights movement continued to flare at home in the early 1970s, U.S. foreign policy experts were concerned with affairs overseas. Specifically, how the United States would extract itself with some dignity intact from the Vietnam War. Vietnam affected black America in a profound way. African Americans

On September 1, 1975, Air Force Colonel Daniel "Chappie" James, shown here meeting with officials in the Pentagon, became the first African-American four-star general in American history.

# "I Was Sworn into the Army in Manacles": A Vietnam Memoir

Robert E. Holcomb of New York served in Vietnam as an armorer for most of 1970, first with the 4th Infantry Division at Pleiku and An Khe, and later with the 101st Airborne Division at Camp Eagle. His story is one of the 20 collected by Wallace Terry for his oral history of black experiences in Vietnam, published in 1984 as *Bloods*.

*I was sworn into the Army in manacles . . . I had evaded the draft for more than a year, but my antiwar views were shaped long before, while I was a student at Tennessee State University . . . Tennessee State was a hotbed of social and political unrest in the mid-sixties . . . We thought the government was going to be more and more oppressive, especially to black and other minority people . . . We wanted the war in Vietnam to cease and desist. We felt that it was an attack on minority people, minority people were being used to fight each other.*

*. . . I landed at Cam Ranh Bay in January 1970. It was just a big sand bowl. There was nothing there . . . It could have been anywhere . . . After two days I told my commanding officer to send me to the field immediately. I was bored. And I wanted to be somewhere where I could get involved more with the Vietnamese people, but not necessarily fighting against them.*

*. . . During the Cambodian incursion, we went in about 2 miles deep to secure the roads for the 101st Airborne. In the sense that we uncovered an awful lot of munitions, I think that operation was a victory. But it was also a defeat because we pushed the VC more into Cambodia, involving them more with the Cambodian people. And that helped lead to the overthrow of the Cambodian government by the Khmer Rouge, who then destroyed 2 million of their own people.*

*. . . We made some contact. It wasn't the sporadic pop, pop, pop you would hear when there are maybe just a small group of people fighting. Just an absolute wall of noise.*

*. . . When I turned around forward, everybody was gone . . . Your adrenaline is pumping so hard it seems like your chest is going to burst. I just had a terrible sinking feeling that—that I was just gonna be left there.*

*I was the only one there.*

*I got down as low as I could . . . I crawled into some bushes, but I still didn't see anyone. Five minutes. Ten minutes . . . Always there was the fear of getting killed by your own troops as you get closer and closer, because they don't know who you are.*

*Finally, I saw one of the tracks off the trail, and some people hiding beside it. I was scared to wave at 'em. I was scared to do anything.*

*Then I heard somebody yell, "All clear."*

*African-American soldiers served in the Vietnam War in large numbers. This group of Air Force security policemen were patrolling the perimeter of an air base in Vietnam.*

enlisted in the U.S. armed forces to demonstrate their patriotism, to get benefits that were unavailable to many working-class people, and because they were drafted. The draft had a disproportionate effect on poor communities because of a deferment system that made many college students, at both graduate and undergraduate levels, ineligible for the draft. African-American soldiers were acutely aware of this fact, and racial tensions simmered, even among troops in the field.

Protests against the war at home served as another example of the lingering presence of racism. When four white students were shot and killed at Kent State University in Ohio during an antiwar protest in 1970, the reaction was immediate and nationwide. A few days later, two black students at Mississippi's Jackson State University were killed while protesting the war, and the reaction was much more subdued.

## STRUGGLES OVER BUSING

Beyond the struggles over radical politics in the immediate post–civil rights era, a remarkable change had occurred in U.S. education. As federal courts slowly but surely began to enforce the 1954 antisegregation decision in *Brown v. Board of Education*, southern school systems grudgingly complied with desegregation orders. The result was that by the early 1970s, the most segregated schools in the United States were in the north. The situation was the result of residential segregation, rather than the legally mandated segregation of Jim Crow, but the effect on black education was much the same.

The decade began with a Supreme Court decision in favor of the busing plan adopted by the schools in Mecklenburg County, North Carolina, home to Charlotte, a burgeoning New South metropolis. In its ruling on *Swann v. Charlotte-Mecklenburg Board of Education* (1971), the Court noted that busing was an acceptable remedy to assure integration. For many years, Charlotte was perceived as a success story of school desegregation. In the 1980s and 1990s, however, Charlotte scaled back and finally terminated the program. This trend is in keeping with larger national trends away from race-based remedies.

The busing crisis in Boston, Massachusetts, captured national media attention in the mid-1970s. A federal court found that Boston's school board had essentially maintained two separate and unequal public school systems: an inferior one for black students, and a superior one for white students. The remedy to the situation was an ambitious busing plan drawn up in 1974 by Judge W. Arthur Garrity. Students from predominately black schools (like those in Roxbury) and those from predominately white schools (like those in South Boston's Irish-American neighborhood) would be bused to schools in the other neighborhood. On the designated day, the few white students who were bused to previously black schools were welcomed by parents and community leaders and given tours of the facilities. The black students who were bused to previously white schools were met by seething mobs chanting racial epithets and throwing stones at their buses. Though the violence reached its peak in the first few weeks of the 1974 school year, serious incidents continued to occur, and the violence was seared into the national consciousness when a young white student assaulted black attorney Theodore Landsmark outside Boston's City Hall, beating the attorney savagely with an American flag. The resulting image, *The Soiling of Old Glory*, won a Pulitzer Prize for photography.

## 1970s POLITICS

The 1970s witnessed an increase in African-American participation in politics, and increasing representation for African Americans on the local, the state, and even the national level. A signal moment for black politics occurred in Gary, Indiana, in 1972. Over 8,000 people, including labor activists, politicians, intellectuals, and veterans of the civil rights movement and Black Power struggles came together in Gary for the National Black Political Convention. The convention's theme, "Unity Without Uniformity," stressed the diversity of black political thought in post-civil-rights-era America. It was cochaired by Charles Diggs, Richard Hatcher, and Amiri Baraka (formerly LeRoi Jones).

One of the stars of the convention was Jesse Jackson, a complex figure who embodied and embraced many different philosophies of African-American activism and politics. By the time of the Gary Convention, Jackson had a large afro, and had recognized the rhetorical power of black nationalism—as exemplified by his repeated rallying cry: "What Time Is It?" to which enthusiastic crowds responded: "Nation Time!" He was a liberal integrationist, and a follower of Martin Luther King Jr. (he was present in 1968 when King was assassinated in Memphis), but he was also intrigued by Black Power and relished the possibility of creating a political party that would work outside the two-party system to enhance black visibility and treatment of black issues on the national political scene. The Gary Convention did not create such a party. Many of its delegates were frustrated with their subordinate status within the Democratic Party, but they saw the difficulty of working outside the two-party system.

The National Black Political Assembly, part of the convention, came out against busing to achieve integration, and in support of a Palestinian homeland. Both measures were controversial, and press reports invariably focused on these two issues. More important, the Gary Convention pointed the way toward a different kind of future, one that embraced "protest *and* politics," in the words of Peniel Joseph, its ablest chronicler. According to Joseph, "Gary illustrated the new political understanding that revolution, far from being the hundred-yard dash that many had predicted during the late 1960s, was in fact a marathon that required a community of long-distance runners."

It was not a coincidence that the convention was held in Gary, Indiana. In the late 1960s, inspired by the Voting Rights Act and Black Power, African Americans went to the polls in increasing numbers in both the north and the south. Elected in the late 1960s, Mayor Richard Hatcher of Gary was one of a handful of black elected officials (others included Carl Stokes of Cleveland, Coleman Young of Detroit, Maynard Jackson of Atlanta, and Tom Bradley of Los Angeles). In fact the rapid rise in the number of black officeholders was one of the most promising trends of the 1970s and 1980s. In 1972 there were 2,427 black elected officials,

*Shirley Chisholm on the day she announced her candidacy in January 1972.*

most of whom served outside the south. Two decades later, there were over 8,100 black elected officials. One reason for increased black representation in government was a 1975 amendment to the 1965 Voting Rights Act. The amendment allowed court challenges to "at-large" voting, which often had the effect of diluting black voting power. As a result of the amendment, districts and precincts were redrawn with an eye toward increasing black political clout.

Shirley Chisholm of New York conducted a remarkable presidential campaign in 1972. Chisholm had served since the 1950s in the New York State legislature. When she was elected to the U.S. House of Representatives from New York's 12th District in 1968, she became the first African-American woman elected to that legislative body. As a congresswoman, she fought fiercely to improve life in America's inner cities, striving to increase access to healthcare, education, and child care. In 1972 she announced her candidacy for president, entering several Democratic Party primaries. Chisholm faced an uphill battle against a wide array of forces, but she confronted challenges with courage and wit, and managed to win over 400,000 votes in Democratic primaries, including wins in New Jersey, Mississippi, and Louisiana, and 28 convention delegates. She ended up with over 150 convention delegates when Hubert Humphrey released his black delegates to vote for her in a symbolic gesture. Her delegate total put her in fourth place; Alabama governor and segregationist George Wallace finished third. George McGovern won the nomination.

## AFRICAN AMERICANS IN THE CARTER ADMINISTRATION

1976 was a watershed year for black political participation. Not since 1964—before the Voting Rights Act—had the majority of African Americans voted for the winning candidate in a presidential election. Nine out of 10 African-American voters chose Jimmy Carter over Gerald Ford in the 1976 election. The connection between Jimmy Carter and black Americans was more than just a matter of simple party affiliation, however. Many African Americans were drawn personally to Carter, and Carter exhibited an affinity for them and an awareness of the issues facing them.

African Americans played leading roles in Jimmy Carter's administration. While it may be possible to see this as a form of political payback to thank black men and women for their electoral support, this is too simple. Carter appointed African Americans to positions where they wielded real power. Patricia Harris became secretary of housing and urban development, making her the first black woman to occupy a cabinet-level post. Harris joined Carter on a tour of depressed areas in the South Bronx in 1977. Other prominent African Americans in the Carter administration included Andrew Young, who served as ambassador to the United Nations; Eleanor Holmes Norton, who ran the Equal Employment Opportunity Commission; Ernest

# Shirley Chisholm Announces Her Candidacy

Shirley Chisholm announced her candidacy for president on January 25, 1972, in Brooklyn, New York. The following is transcribed from video footage of the event. By June, Chisholm recognized that she would not win, but she persisted nonetheless.

*I stand before you today as a candidate for the Democratic nomination for the Presidency of the United States of America.*

*I am not the candidate of black America, although I am black and proud. I am not the candidate of the women's movement of this country, although I am a woman, and I am equally proud of that.*

*I am not the candidate of any political bosses or fat cats or special interests.*

*I stand here now without endorsements from many big name politicians or celebrities or any other kind of prop. I do not intend to offer to you the tired and glib clichés, which for too long have been an accepted part of our political life. I am the candidate of the people of America. And my presence before you now symbolizes a new era in American political history.*

*I have always earnestly believed in the great potential of America. Our constitutional democracy will soon celebrate its 200th anniversary, effective testimony, to the longevity to our cherished constitution and its unique bill of rights, which continues to give to the world an inspirational message of freedom and liberty.*

*. . . I have faith in the American people. I believe that we are smart enough to correct our mistakes. I believe that we are intelligent enough to recognize the talent, energy, and dedication, which all Americans including women and minorities have to offer. I know from my travels to the cities and small towns of America that we have a vast potential, which can and must be put to constructive use in getting this great nation together. I know that millions of Americans, from all walks of life agree with me that leadership does not mean putting the ear to the ground, to follow public opinion, but to have the vision of what is necessary and the courage to make it possible, building a strong and just society, which in its diversity and is noble in its quality of life.*

*I stand before you today, to repudiate the ridiculous notion that the American people will not vote for qualified candidates, simply because he is not white or because she is not a male. I do not believe that in 1972, the great majority of Americans will continue to harbor such narrow and petty prejudice . . .*

Green, assistant secretary of labor; Wade McCree, solicitor general; Mary Frances Berry, assistant secretary of education; and Drew Days, assistant attorney general for civil rights.

Despite all this, Carter's efforts on behalf of African Americans were a mixed bag. The Carter presidency was hampered at every turn by foreign policy troubles and domestic economic crises. The economic crises of the 1970s affected Americans of all races, but its effects were amplified in communities that already suffered from concentrated, generational poverty and faced additional burdens of racial discrimination in employment and housing. Carter could not pass a universal healthcare bill, and his efforts to cut government spending sucked resources out of school lunch and financial aid programs that had been vital to many African-American communities. All of this did little to weaken overall black support for Carter, and the Republican selection of Ronald Reagan, a staunch conservative, ensured that once again in 1980, about 90 percent of African-American voters chose Carter. It did not matter, as the public in general had lost confidence in Carter's abilities, and Reagan won in a landslide.

## ECONOMIC HARD TIMES AND AFRICAN AMERICANS

The 1970s are remembered as a time when economic crises dominated the national consciousness. The kinds of economic changes taking place in the 1970s, especially the decline of the manufacturing sector of the United States' economy, affected African Americans at a disproportionate rate. Statistics back up the sobering assessment that even as African Americans made great strides in politics, the arts, and other areas, economic parity with white people was as far away in 1980 as it had been in 1970.

Over the course of the 1970s, median black family income dropped. While married-couple black families reported a 6.9 percent gain in real income 1970–81, this group represented a smaller portion of black families overall. The percentage of black families headed by women leaped from 28 to 41 percent over the course of the decade. Inflation and a stagnant economy conspired to increase the number of African Americans living in poverty during the 1970s. The U.S. government noted in the early 1980s that the African-American poverty rate ($9,287 for a family of four) was more than three times that of white families. As it did during other periods of economic duress, the African-American unemployment rate hovered around twice the white unemployment rate for much of the 1970s.

One innovative response to the economic situation of the 1970s was Jesse Jackson's Operation PUSH (first named People United to Save Humanity, then People United to Serve Humanity). Headquartered in Chicago's predominately black South Side, Operation PUSH combined politics with social action to improve neighborhoods. PUSH worked to keep young black men and women away from the streets and drugs, while at the same time encouraging black capitalism and entrepreneurship. Jackson was especially adept at leaning on major U.S. corporations to hire larger numbers of African Americans and to promote them to management positions. By 1977 there were 231,200 black-owned businesses in the United States. Most well known were black insurance companies like North Carolina Mutual and Atlanta Life Insurance. As much larger corporations became aware of the buying habits of black consumers, they could tailor their marketing campaigns, and limited the ability of generally smaller black-owned businesses to compete.

## WORK, EDUCATION, AND HEALTH IN THE 1970s

Part of the reason that the economic downturns of the 1970s affected African-American families more severely than white families is that African Americans were overrepresented in areas of the economy that were adversely affected by the downturns. African Americans made up 10 percent of the U.S. labor force at the end of the decade, but 14 percent of laborers, operators, and fabricators were black, and 18 percent of all service workers were black. African Americans were underrepresented in sectors of the economy that were unlikely to suffer as much during the downturns. Blacks represented about six percent of managers and professionals, and eight percent of technical, sales, and administrative support workers. Broken down a little further, the disparity was even more stark. African Americans comprised 54 percent of those working in private households as cleaners or servants. They also accounted for disproportionately small numbers in the specialized professions of medicine and the law. African-American home ownership rose dramatically during the 1970s, up 45 percent to 3.7 million units. White homeownership rose only 26 percent during the same period, though the overall number of white homeowners dwarfed the same figure for African Americans, with 46.7 million units.

Looking at the overall educational statistics for the 1970s, there is reason for optimism. But a closer examination reveals a troubling trend. Most of the increase in college enrollment, and in high school graduation rates, occurred in the first half of the 1970s. Finally, although black health had improved dramatically since the early 20th century (at which point white life expectancies far outstripped those of blacks), African Americans could expect to live about four years shorter than white men and women. Though the homicide rate for African Americans dropped during the 1970s, blacks were still substantially more likely to die violently than white people.

## ARTS IN THE 1970s

Black Power made substantial contributions to the U.S. arts scene, and the black arts scene made substantial contributions to Black Power and racial awareness during the 1970s. The beginning of the Black Arts movement can be traced to the Black Arts Repertory Theater, founded by LeRoi Jones (later Amiri Baraka) in 1965. Early proponents noted the explicit connection between black arts, Black Power, and black communities in general. The Black

*Alice Walker reading from her work in November 1989. Walker published poetry, short stories, and two novels in the 1970s before her bestselling novel* The Color Purple *came out in 1982.*

Arts movement was not without its critics, who pointed out its tendencies toward male chauvinism and homophobia.

The Black Arts movement made its presence widely known in poetry and theater. Maya Angelou's *I Know Why the Caged Bird Sings*, published in 1970 as the first of four volumes of autobiography, was greeted with wide acclaim (it was nominated for a National Book Award in 1970 and was a best seller for many weeks). *I Know Why the Caged Bird Sings* traces the story of young Maya as she grows up in Stamps, Arkansas. The writers Toni Morrison and Alice Walker also came into their own as powerful black female voices in the 1970s.

Motown Records, established in the late 1950s and early 1960s by Berry Gordy, had avoided explicitly political music in its earliest years. Reflecting shifts in U.S. culture, black identity, and Gordy's own philosophy, Motown artists were recording biting political songs by the late 1960s and into the 1970s. Gordy contributed handsome sums to black candidates for elected office, and gave generously to other black causes as well. Motown artists like Stevie Wonder and Marvin Gaye continued to make phenomenal music, while at the same time penning thoughtful lyrics that addressed the social troubles that tormented black America in the 1970s. Wonder's 1973 masterpiece *Living for the City* traced a young man's journey from rural Mississippi to inner-city New York. Wonder's lyrics condemned both the racism of the New York City police, and the brutality of life on the streets. Marvin Gaye did some of the finest work of his career in the 1970s, scoring hits with songs like *What's Going On* and *Inner City Blues*. Gaye connected black ghetto struggles with worldwide struggles for peace and human rights (and the war in Vietnam, thanks to correspondence between Gaye and his brother stationed in that country) in a unique way. One of the most interesting confluences between art and politics involved one of Motown's main competitors, however.

Stax Records (the name is a blend of the names of Jim Stewart and Estelle Axton, the siblings who founded it) operated out of Memphis. By the 1970s, Stax had lost its greatest artist, Otis Redding, to a tragic plane crash, and had also lost its distribution deal with Atlantic Records. Stax continued as an independent label, with such legends as Isaac Hayes producing hit music. In 1972 Stax, Schlitz Brewing, and Jesse Jackson's Operation PUSH (People Uniting to Save Humanity) came together in Watts, the site of one of the most violent ghetto uprisings of the previous decade, to stage a massive concert called Wattstax. Schlitz's sponsorship gave the 90,000 attendees a chance to see some legendary artists for only $1. Schlitz had previously been targeted by civil rights activists for antiblack bias in hiring and promotion, so the concert provided a shot at redemption for the corporation. Stax got exposure for its artists, and hoped that a documentary film made of the concert would increase that exposure. Jesse Jackson got a chance to fulfill his goal of building a bridge between the civil rights and the Black Power generations. As he opened the festival, sporting what one historian calls a "formidable afro" and wearing a dashiki, Jackson reveled: "This is a beautiful day. It is a new day. It is a day of black awareness. It is a day of black people taking care of black people's business. It is beautiful that the Stax record company has come out [of the] south to talk about liberation through music and lyrics."

## AFRICAN AMERICANS IN FILM

The 1970s witnessed a whole genre of American film starring black actors and actresses for primarily black audiences. The genre was "blaxploitation," a blend of "black" and "exploitation," which in this context means the films "exploit" shocking subject matter. One of the most popular films of this nature was 1971's *Shaft*, starring Richard Roundtree as a black detective and featuring a funky soundtrack by Isaac Hayes. Prominent stars of the genre included Pam Grier and Jim Brown (the football legend). These films demonstrate the increasing prominence of African Americans in the film industry, while depicting life in America's big cities as shockingly violent and drug-ridden.

In 1977 Alex Haley's fictionalized family history *Roots* became an epic television miniseries. *Roots* featured some of television's most popular black and white actors as it followed the story of Kunta Kinte from his capture in Africa, through the Middle Passage, to his sale in the plantation south. *Roots* followed Kunta Kinte's descendants until they finally achieved their freedom in the last days of the Civil War. Scholars disputed Haley's portrayal of Africa, and the author settled a plagiarism case out of court, but these strikes against the work matter less than the fact that *Roots* brought black history into the homes of millions of Americans of all races. It was estimated that approximately one-half of all the families in the United States watched at least some of the miniseries.

In 1978 William J. Wilson, a sociologist at the University of Chicago, published *The Declining Significance of Race*. In this book he argued that well-educated young black men and women who were entering the job market in the post–civil rights era were not experiencing the same kind of obstacles faced by their forbears. Wilson noted that a widening gulf separated the black middle class from the black poor.

## AFRICAN AMERICANS IN THE 1980s

In spite of all the gains in politics, and the increasing prominence of black artists, the 1970s ended with the same kind of uncertainty with which they began. Though some African Americans had managed to join the middle class, many more did not, and some, especially in depressed inner cities, seemed farther away than ever. For most African Americans, the 1980s continued the depressing trends of the late 1970s. The struggle for racial equality seemed to slip even further from the national consciousness as the fight against affirmative action gained steam. Apart from a small African-American upper class and moderately sized middle class, the majority of black families were hit hard by the increasing economic disparity that characterized the 1980s. As in the 1970s, African Americans continued to play leading roles in U.S. cinema, music, and literature, and black political power continued to increase during the 1980s, though its influence was limited by the conservative ascendancy that characterized the era. On the whole, though, in part because of continuing deindustrialization and in part due to policy decisions at the national level, prospects for African-American equality did not brighten significantly during the 1980s.

## THE FATE OF AFFIRMATIVE ACTION AND THE BACKLASH

The idea of taking positive steps (or affirmative action) to counter the lingering effects of racism has deep roots in 20th-century America. On a national level, Democratic presidents from Truman forward tended to favor such measures, though the modern understanding of race-based affirmative action is usually traced to a speech Lyndon Johnson made at Howard University in 1965. Johnson's administration, and even Richard Nixon's for a time, instituted policies designed to foster equality of opportunity for people of all races. As part of a wider backlash against the civil rights movement and Black Power, increasing numbers of white Americans began to see race-based remedies as discriminatory against white people. This attitude combined with a hard turn to the right in national politics, signaling the beginning of the end for affirmative action.

The rollback began in the 1970s, when the U.S. Supreme Court determined that Allen Bakke, a white applicant to the University of California, Davis medical school had been denied admission because of the color of his skin. UC-Davis had reserved, or set aside, 16 of its 100 spots for applicants who were racial minorities. In a rather confusing, but influential ruling, 1978's *Regents of the University of California v. Bakke*, the Court ruled that Bakke's civil rights had been violated. The court allowed that race could be a factor in determining admission to educational institutions, but that the way UC-Davis had used race was unacceptable. This opened the door to the dismantling of race-based affirmative action, though the immediate effects were muted. In the early 1980s, the Carter-era Public Works Employment Act remained in effect, setting aside 10 percent of its grants for minority enterprises (including those owned by white women). The Surface Transportation Act of 1982 mandated that 10 percent of federal highway spending be directed to businesses owned by minorities. Along the same lines, a 1987 defense bill set a goal for minority contracts at five percent.

The coalition that had supported the Democratic Party since the days of FDR, consisting of African Americans, northern liberals, and working-class white ethnics, weakened considerably in the late 1970s. Though a number of factors can be cited, including the sour economy of the 1970s, a couple of trends deserve closer attention. One was the increasing unwillingness of white ethnics to align themselves with inner-city blacks. This voting bloc instead broke for Reagan in 1980. African Americans, especially those left of center, were faced with a disappointing choice in the presidential campaign. They could continue to support Carter, whose lofty promises remained largely unfulfilled in black communities, most notably in urban settings. Or they

Coretta Scott King, the widow of Martin Luther King Jr., appearing in support of the Democrats at their national convention in 1976.

could choose a candidate who had already stated his opposition to affirmative action, promoted busing as a remedy for residential segregation, and supported a host of other programs designed to lift African Americans out of generational poverty. The choice was a fairly obvious one for most African Americans. As in the 1976 election, approximately 90 percent of African Americans chose Jimmy Carter. In the popular vote count, Reagan dominated Carter, winning more than eight million more votes. The Electoral College victory was even more lopsided, with Ronald Reagan and George H.W. Bush racking up a 489–44 win.

## REAGAN AND AFRICAN AMERICANS

In various stops on the 1980 campaign trail, Reagan had signaled his hostility to the urban poor—who were disproportionately black. Reagan perceived this class of people too unworthy of federal assistance, and even dangerous. His speech at the 1980 Neshoba County Fair, not too far from the site of the gruesome 1964 murders of civil rights workers James Chaney, Andrew Goodman, and Michael Schwerner, featured lines praising states' rights and noting that the reason many people were on welfare was that the federal bureaucracy had trapped them there. In a 1976 speech, Reagan had raised the specter of a "welfare queen," a woman who had cheated a too-generous welfare system with the intention of never returning to work. Depending on which version of the story he told, the woman had as many as 80 false names, 30 different addresses, and an astonishing $150,000 annual income, tax free. Occasionally Reagan added driving a white Cadillac to her list of offenses. The tale appears to have grown from the true story of a Chicago woman who had used four false names to cheat the welfare system out of about $8,000. Though false, shot through with longstanding white notions about black poverty, malfeasance, and an extremely biased view of black women in particular, the image was a popular one and stuck in many people's minds, despite the fact that the majority of recipients of public aid were not black.

Reagan's first term in office featured some ominous steps backward in terms of the relationship between the federal government and African Americans. Reagan appointed fewer than one-third the number of black people to high-level jobs than his predecessor had. Those that he did select often shared his conservative views. Clarence Thomas replaced Eleanor Holmes Norton at the Equal Employment Opportunity Commission, for instance. African-American political philosophy was not monolithic, but voting records indicate that the vast majority of African Americans were not conservatives during the 1980s. Reagan's administration cut enforcement powers at the Office of Federal Contract Compliance and the Equal Employment Opportunity Commission. In the Department of Justice, Reagan's civil rights attorneys filed remarkably fewer civil rights violation cases than their predecessors under Nixon and Carter. One of Reagan's most memorable run-ins with civil rights activists occurred over his 1983 decision to fire three liberal members of the Commission on Civil Rights and replace them with people more in line with his philosophy. One of those fired was commission chair Arthur Flemming, who was white, replaced by Clarence Pendleton, a black Republican. Mary Frances Berry, an outspoken advocate for black equality and a vocal critic of Reagan's civil rights record, was fired as well. She fought her dismissal in court. Though she remained on the commission, the commission declined in influence.

On a more positive note, during Ronald Reagan's first term the birthday of Martin Luther King Jr. became a national holiday. Reagan had initially favored a recognition of the day that would not rise to the level of a national holiday (like Lincoln's Birthday or comparable observances), and threatened to veto a national holiday bill, but black civil rights activists and their white allies prevailed upon him, and when the bill passed Congress with a veto-proof majority, Reagan agreed to sign it. The legislation was enacted in 1983, and the first national King holiday observances took place in January 1986.

## THE CONTINUING STRUGGLE FOR ECONOMIC EQUALITY

Due to a variety of factors, such as disproportionate representation in industrial labor and hiring discrimination, African-American unemployment is historically much higher than white unemployment. Following this pattern, in the recession of the early 1980s, African-American unemployment jumped to over 20 percent. Even in the recovery of the mid-1980s, black unemployment remained twice as high as white unemployment. By 1988, at the end of Reagan's term in office, 14 states still had black unemployment rates of 15 percent or higher. Young African Americans, often isolated in inner cities far from growing sectors of the economy and the jobs they produced, were hit particularly hard.

Not all African Americans lived in inner-city poverty. The black middle class had been growing since World War II. In the 1980s, though, even the black middle class was vulnerable to shifts in the economy (it was also far more likely to require two paychecks to stay in the middle class). Relative to their white peers, black college graduates also tended to earn less. The gap between the earnings of black women and white women was closing much faster than that between black and white men.

## RACIST VIOLENCE IN THE 1980s

Several shocking incidents of antiblack violence occurred in the 1980s. In 1983 Michael Stewart was arrested by transit police for spray-painting a train in New York City's East Village. A half-hour after he was arrested, his wrists and ankles were tied together, and he was unconscious, and unable to breathe. Stewart lingered for 13 days before he finally died from injuries sustained in police custody. Despite evidence that Stewart was choked and had received several vicious blows to the head, New York's chief medical examiner determined that

*The Reverend Al Sharpton (fourth from right) leads a protest march through Bensonhurst, Brooklyn, in 1989 after the killing of Yusuf Hawkins.*

his death was the result of a heart attack. In 1982 a record number of complaints of police misconduct had been filed in the city. A congressional inquiry into the matter discovered that a disproportionate number of complaints involved white officers using excessive force against people of color, and that many of these had resulted in death. In the Michael Stewart case, three of the 11 officers involved in his arrest were eventually brought up on charges. These charges were dropped because of fears that the grand jury had been tainted (one of its members, convinced that the problem was more wide-reaching, had been doing his own investigation). In 1985 the district attorney indicted six officers on the charge of "criminally negligent homicide"—a fairly risky legal gambit. An all-white jury acquitted the officers, despite clearly contradictory testimony from the medical examiner and the officers.

Other incidents of racial violence that capture the essence of urban life in the 1980s include the subway shootings by Bernard Goetz, and the murders of Michael Griffith and Yusuf Hawkins. Bernard Goetz was riding the subway when four young black men approached him. One asked him for $5. Goetz responded by shooting all four—two of them in the back—and leaving one of them, 19-year-old Derrell Caby, paralyzed. To some, Goetz was a hero who had stood up for a silent majority against rising crime rates. To others, he had overreacted violently to a situation that may or may not have been dangerous. In any event, the public response and the trial were illuminating. Many of Goetz's supporters sent him money to pay his bail and fund his defense. A majority-white jury acquitted Goetz of all serious charges, but convicted him of illegal possession of a handgun.

Elsewhere in New York, black men continued to be the targets of white violence. In late 1986, a 23-year-old Trinidadian American named Michael Griffith was run over by a car and killed in Howard Beach. He and his friends had gone to get help after their car had broken down. They were accosted by a drunken white mob wielding baseball bats. After receiving a savage beating, Griffith fled through a tunnel and onto a nearby highway, where he was run over and killed. Protest marches ensued, and three of the perpetrators were eventually convicted of manslaughter. In a similar case in 1989, Yusuf Hawkins went to Brooklyn to look at a used car. He and his friends were confronted by a mob waving golf clubs and bats. After a brief confrontation, one of the members of the mob stepped forward and shot Yusuf Hawkins four times in the chest. The killing sparked another round of protest marches led by Al Sharpton. Though the killer, Joey Fama, was convicted of second-degree murder, racial tensions remained high in America's largest city throughout the 1980s.

## LOCAL POLITICS AND ANTI-APARTHEID ACTIVISM

African Americans continued to make significant strides in big-city politics, building on the successes of the 1970s. In Philadelphia, a majority-white metropolis, Wilson Goode became the city's first black mayor in 1983. Goode played down the subject of race and stressed his reformist strategies. In Chicago, Harold Washington won the 1983 mayoral election with a large majority of the black vote, and just enough votes from white reformers tired of machine politics. The increasing visibility of African Americans in positions of power was a good thing in the 1980s. However the policies of black mayors in the 1980s did not differ substantially from those of their white predecessors. They advocated bringing development back to blighted inner cities, but focused on high-rise office buildings, convention centers, and other commercially attractive politics, sometimes to the chagrin of those who had elected them. Big city mayors, regardless of race, faced a dismal situation in the 1980s. The federal government continued to slash aid to big cities, leaving them to fend for themselves in a brutal economic transition.

## PRESIDENTIAL POLITICS IN THE 1980s

The presidential campaigns of Jesse Jackson deserve close examination. Jackson performed the way he did during these two crucial campaigns for a variety of reasons. He was a highly skilled and talented politician with credentials in both the civil rights movement and the political wing of Black Power. He also arrived on the national political scene when the gains of the civil rights generation seemed to be in danger of evaporating. Though Jackson did not

*Frequent presidential candidate and civil rights activist Jesse Jackson on July 1, 1983.*

secure the Democratic nomination in either 1984 or 1988, he did demonstrate the power of black political activism at the grassroots level, and the people who participated in his campaign demonstrated an increasing desire, and ability, to participate in national-level political discussions and policy formation. Ronald W. Walters, a scholar who has examined the campaigns in detail, notes that they "enhanced the role of blacks as citizens."

In 1984 Jackson faced a field of candidates thick with party luminaries—well-known personalities and career politicians, including Walter Mondale, Gary Hart, George McGovern, and John Glenn. There were more, but three candidates withdrew after poor showings in the New Hampshire primary. One of the keys to Jackson's strategy was to register voters, and the 1984 campaign registered two million of them. Jackson built what he referred to as a Rainbow Coalition, consisting of blacks, progressive whites, Latinos and Latinas, feminists, and environmentalists. His plan, Rebuilding America, called for tax reform and a national industrial policy that would work with labor, capital, and government. It was in some sense a revival of 1960s-style Great Society liberalism, but in the mid-1980s, such ideas placed Jackson in the progressive wing of the Democratic Party. Jackson failed to win the nomination, finishing third behind Walter Mondale and Gary Hart, but his candidacy made history nonetheless.

In 1988 Jackson again sought the Democratic Party's presidential nomination. He managed to win 15 presidential primaries and caucuses, totaling nearly seven million votes (just under 30 percent of those cast). His strongest showing was in the Deep South states. Unfortunately for Jackson's presidential ambition, his support was not strong enough outside the African-American community. The only group of white voters that broke overwhelmingly for Jackson was comprised of those living in college towns and other well-educated whites. The winning nominee, Michael Dukakis of Massachusetts, went on to lose the 1988 election to George H.W. Bush.

In terms of its effects on African Americans, the George H.W. Bush administration picked up more or less where Reagan's had left off. Bush repeatedly vetoed legislation that he perceived to favor disadvantaged Americans, regardless of skin color. In June 1989, for instance, Bush vetoed a bill that would have raised the minimum wage from $3.35 an hour (unchanged since 1977) to $4.55. A compromise rate of $4.25 was eventually agreed upon. He also vetoed a civil rights bill in 1990, dismissing it as a "quotas bill." Bush did nominate General Colin Powell to head the Joint Chiefs of Staff, and in 1989, Powell became both the youngest chairman of the Joint Chiefs of Staff, and the first African American to serve in that office. On the other side of the aisle, Democrats elected Ron Brown the first African American to lead a major political party in the United States in 1988. Brown would later be instrumental in the 1992 election of Bill Clinton, and would serve as Clinton's secretary of commerce before his untimely death in a plane crash while on a trade mission to Croatia in 1996.

## ARTS IN THE 1980s

African Americans continued to make significant contributions to American culture. In the 1980s, black entertainers rose to new heights of wealth and celebrity. Innovators such as Michael Jackson, Oprah Winfrey, Bill Cosby, and Spike Lee are but a few of the influential African-American entertainers of the 1980s. The advent of Robert Johnson's Black Entertainment Television in 1980 only increased the number of available outlets for black entertainers in the decade.

Michael Jackson began his musical career as the lead singer of the Jackson Five, comprised of five brothers from Gary, Indiana. Jackson's solo career began in the 1970s and reached its zenith in the 1980s as the King of Pop released *Thriller* and *Bad* in 1982 and 1987, respectively. Jackson's celebrity stretched far beyond the borders of the United States, and his concert tours in this country and beyond were some of the most spectacular musical events of the 1980s.

Oprah Winfrey launched her television show in 1985. At that point, the show mainly reached the Chicago television market. Just a year later, *The Oprah Winfrey Show* could be seen throughout the United States. The genius of Winfrey's show rested on her ability to relate to her guests, and to anticipate the preferences of her large, diverse audience. Winfrey parlayed her television career into a multimedia empire that made her one of the wealthiest people in the United States, with a fortune of over $2.5 billion. She also used her wealth to bring attention and financial support to various causes around the world.

Bill Cosby, whose career as a stand-up comedian was well established by the 1980s, was the mastermind behind two of the most popular sitcoms of the decade, *The Cosby Show* and its spinoff *A Different World*. Both shows

## Spike Lee

Spike Lee's feature-film career began in the 1980s with a string of inde-pendently produced movies, including *She's Gotta Have It, School Daze,* and *Do the Right Thing. Do the Right Thing* shined a light on one of the most distressing problems facing the United States in the 1980s, interracial ten-sion and violence in the inner city. In the climactic scene of the film, Mookie (Spike Lee) throws a garbage can through the window of a pizzeria owned by an Italian American, Sal (Danny Aiello) in a rage over the death of Radio Raheem (Bill Nunn) at the hands of the police. The incident sparks a riot. The Public Enemy song *Fight the Power* plays at various points throughout the film. The film caused controversy when some early reviews suggested that it might incite young black men to violence. In an essay taking stock of his career in the early 1990s, Lee penned a summary of the controversy:

"Some of these critics were more concerned about Sal's Pizzeria burning down than they were with a human life—a black human life. But then again, maybe they didn't consider Radio Raheem human but had neatly relegated him to subhuman, a wilding animal—exactly like all young black males are. Radio Raheem is the same as those kids Bernard Goetz shot and maimed. Radio Raheem is the same as those black bastards who raped that white woman in Central Park. Radio Raheem is the same as all these animals who drop out of high school, rob, steal, murder, father unwanted babies, and use and sell crack. So, of course, the racist critics would be more concerned about the destruction of private property, Sal's Pizzeria, in that ghetto, Bed-ford-Stuyvesant. Radio Raheem isn't human; he's an animal with a ghetto blaster, polluting the environment with that rap noise *Fight the Power.*"

followed the struggles and triumphs of a family of African-American profes-sionals and their children.

### HIP-HOP CULTURE AND RAP MUSIC
One of the most significant developments of the 1980s was the rise of hip-hop culture and rap music. From relatively humble origins in the South Bronx, rap music became a commercial gold mine for rappers and producers as it hit MTV, and was eagerly adopted by a whole generation of young people of all races. Apart from its commercial viability, demonstrated by the career of Run DMC, among others, rap music could also showcase black politics and aware-ness of the racial issues of the 1980s. Though many groups included politically driven lyrics, the best known of the late 1980s was Public Enemy. Their 1980s releases include *Yo! Bum Rush the Show* and *It Takes a Nation of Millions to Hold Us Back.*

## CONCLUSION

African Americans looked to the 1990s hopefully. Though the hardest economic times of the 1970s and 1980s seemed over, their effects would continue to wreak havoc on America's disproportionately black inner cities. Deindustrialization continued to sweep jobs away from urban centers to suburbs or outside the United States entirely. By the end of the 1980s, the black middle class was well established, but it would remain more fragile than its white counterpart. Also by the end of 1980s, approximately 30 percent of African Americans earned more than $35,000, another third earned between $13,000 and $35,000, while still about one-third were stuck in poverty. In fact more than half of black children were raised in this lowest income group. In some areas, notably entertainment, politics, and sports, African Americans continued to have a dramatic influence on American life more broadly.

MATTHEW JENNINGS
MACON STATE COLLEGE

# Further Reading

Allen, Robert L. *Black Awakening in Capitalist America: An Analytic History*. Trenton, NJ: Africa World Press, 1990.

Bloom, Jack M. *Class, Race, and the Civil Rights Movement*. Bloomington, IN: Indiana University Press, 1987.

Brown, Michael K. *Race, Money, and the American Welfare State*. Ithaca, NY: Cornell University Press, 1999.

Carnoy, Martin. *Faded Dreams: The Politics and Economics of Race in America*. Cambridge: Cambridge University Press, 1995.

Chang, Jeff. *Can't Stop Won't Stop: A History of the Hip-Hop Generation*. New York: St. Martin's Press, 2005.

Dawson, Michael C. *Behind the Mule: Race and Class in African American Politics*. Princeton, NJ: Princeton University Press, 1994.

Drake, W. Avon, and Robert D. Holsworth. *Affirmative Action and the Stalled Quest for Black Progress*. Urbana: University of Illinois Press, 1996.

Exum, William H. *Paradoxes of Protest: Black Student Activism in a White University*. Philadelphia, PA: Temple University Press, 1985.

Franklin, John Hope, and Alfred A. Moss, Jr. *From Slavery to Freedom: A History of African Americans*. New York: McGraw-Hill, 1994.

Gaillard, Frye. *The Dream Long Deferred: The Landmark Struggle for Desegregation in Charlotte, North Carolina*. Columbia: University of South Carolina Press, 2006.

Hine, Darlene Clark, et al. *The African-American Odyssey*. Upper Saddle River, NJ: Pearson, 2008.

Joseph, Peniel. *Waiting 'Til the Midnight Hour: A Narrative History of Black Power in America*. New York: Henry Holt, 2006.

Kaufman, Burton I., and Scott Kaufman. *The Presidency of James Earl Carter, Jr.* Lawrence: University Press of Kansas, 2006.

Landry, Bart. *The New Black Middle Class*. Berkeley: University of California Press, 1987.

Lawson, Steven F. *In Pursuit of Power: Southern Blacks and Electoral Politics, 1965–1982*. New York: Columbia University Press, 1985.

Lee, Spike, et al. *Five for Five: The Films of Spike Lee*. New York: Stewart, Tabori & Chang, 1991.

Lukas, J. Anthony. *Common Ground: A Turbulent Decade in the Lives of Three American Families*. New York: Vintage Books, 1986.

Massey, Douglas S., and Nancy A. Denton. *American Apartheid: Segregation and the Making of the Underclass*. Cambridge, MA: Harvard University Press, 1993.

Matney, William C., and Dwight L. Johnson. *America's Black Population, 1970 to 1982: A Statistical View*. Washington, D.C.: Bureau of the Census, Government Printing Office, 1983. Special Publication PIO/POP-83-1. Available online, URL: http://www.eric.ed.gov/ERICDocs/data/ericdocs2sql/content_storage_01/0000019b/80/34/7c/de.pdf. Accessed August 2009.

Simpson, Andrea Y. *The Tie That Binds: Identity and Political Attitudes in the Post–Civil Rights Generation*. New York: New York University Press, 1998.

Sitkoff, Harvard. *The Struggle for Black Equality, 1954–1992*, Rev. ed. New York: Hill and Wang, 1993.

Sugrue, Thomas J. *Sweet Land of Liberty: The Forgotten Struggle for Civil Rights in the North*. New York: Random House, 2008.

Terry, Wallace. *Bloods: An Oral History of the Vietnam War by Black Veterans*. New York: Ballantine Books, 1984.

Trotter, Joe William, Jr. *The African American Experience*. Boston, MA: Houghton Mifflin, 2001.

Walters, Ronald W. *Freedom Is Not Enough: Black Voters, Black Candidates, and American Presidential Politics*. Lanham, MD: Rowman and Littlefield, 2005.

Ward, Brian. *Just My Soul Responding: Rhythm and Blues, Black Consciousness and Race Relations*. London: University College London Press, 1998.

# CHAPTER 10

# Black America Today: 1990 to the Present

**IN 1990, THE** African-American population of the United States was just under 30 million, representing approximately 12 percent of the total U.S. population. In *Black Americans: A Profile,* the Census Bureau gives a basic statistical overview of the African-American population. The data reveal some modest gains for African Americans in income and education over the prior decades, but also some stark differences between African Americans and whites. Over the course of the 1980s, for instance, the total of young black men and women with high school diplomas jumped from 75 to 82 percent, while the number of young white people graduating held steady at 87 percent. Overall since the 1960s, black families' income increased 12 percent—approximately the same rate as white families'—but black median income rose from $19,080 to $21,420 while white median income rose from $32,220 to $36,920. Poverty remained dire for many African Americans in 1990: 29 percent of black families lived in poverty, compared to eight percent of white families. Even in the 2000s, the poverty rate for African Americans remained approximately twice as high as that of the population as a whole. As significant and troubling as these statistics are, they should be weighed against the fact that many millions of African Americans were of middle-class status, and African Americans had achieved prominence in every conceivable field of endeavor in the 1990s and 2000s, from the arts to politics, business, and education.

Two major events in the history of American race relations bookend the most recent period in African-American history. The 1990s began with the discovery of the African Burial Ground in New York City and the shock of the Los Angeles riots, and the period concluded with the election of Barack Obama as the first African-American president of the United States in November 2008. It remains to be seen whether the 2008 election marks a significant turning point in African-American history.

## BLACK POLITICS IN THE LATE 1980s AND EARLY 1990s
The backlash against the civil rights movement continued apace in the late 1980s and early 1990s, and one of the most effective tactics relied upon by the Reagan and Bush administrations was to appoint prominent conservative African Americans to direct government offices. Clarence Thomas, an opponent of affirmative action, served as head of the Equal Employment Opportunity Commission (EEOC), for example. Thomas was one of a number of black conservatives who rose to prominence in the late 1980s and early 1990s. Others included Thomas Sowell, Ward Connerly, Walter Williams, and Armstrong Williams. Many more African Americans supported the Democratic Party, attained powerful positions within that party, and were essential to any success that the Democratic Party might have on the national level. Jesse Jackson, who ran twice for president in the 1980s, has remained extremely influential in the Democratic Party.

In 1991 George H.W. Bush nominated Clarence Thomas to replace the retiring Thurgood Marshall on the Supreme Court. The resulting confirmation hearings pitted Anita Hill (a conservative law professor, also African American, who had worked with Thomas at the EEOC) against her former boss on national television. Hill claimed to have been sexually harassed by Thomas during their tenure at the EEOC. Thomas vehemently denied the charges, and added a layer of racial intrigue to the mix when he claimed to have suffered a "high-tech lynching" at the hands of his detractors. The hearings captivated America, and split many black communities between supporters of Hill and supporters of Thomas. Clarence Thomas was confirmed by a narrow vote, and has maintained steadfastly conservative views.

One of the major ongoing debates of the past two decades has been over affirmative action, or the use of race-based remedies to lessen inequality in education and hiring practices. Opponents of affirmative action, mostly though not entirely white (Ward Connerly of California is but one prominent anti–affirmative action African American), argue that affirmative action can lead to negative stereotyping, and that it is not terribly effective. Supporters of affirmative action argue that it is a temporary, imperfect, and necessary way to lessen the stigma of nonwhite status in the United States. The U.S. Supreme Court has been of little assistance, ruling repeatedly

## Police Brutality and the Los Angeles Riots

The 1990s and 2000s witnessed despicable acts of police brutality against African Americans, from the nightstick sodomizing of Abner Louima, and the killing of Amadou Diallo and Sean Bell in New York City, to the savage beating of Rodney King in Los Angeles. King's case deserves special attention because of its role in sparking a wave of riots. In 1991 Rodney King was beaten by Los Angeles police after a high-speed chase. The beating, caught on video, was replayed constantly on television news broadcasts. The footage showed King lying on the ground, encircled by police officers beating him savagely with clubs and kicking him in the head.

At their trial in April 1992, the officers were acquitted of nearly all the charges, and mayhem ensued as thousands of enraged African Americans and Latinos took to the streets. Arson, looting, and violence ripped Los Angeles apart, causing $500 million in property damage during several days of rioting. More than 50 people lost their lives. One of the iconic images of the rioting was of Reginald Denny, a white truck driver pulled from his rig and beaten senseless while young rioters watched and celebrated. Most news coverage failed to mention that the people who rescued Denny, and other victims of violence, were black. The Los Angeles riots exposed deep rifts in U.S. society.

that race may be used as a determining factor but rarely indicating how it should be properly applied. In a 2007 case, *Parents Involved in Community Schools v. Seattle School District No. 1,* the Court ruled that race could not be used as a factor in assigning students to high schools. It is unclear what long-term effects this ruling may have, or how the decision will affect higher education or employers.

### INCOME AND EDUCATION

By most measures, the gap between African Americans and white Americans in income, education, and wealth narrowed 1990–2008. Many African Americans rose to the top of their chosen fields, and accumulated wealth and prestige that made them some of the richest and most recognizable Americans. Their names and faces became well known in the United States and around the world: Oprah Winfrey, Michael Jordan, Tiger Woods, Michael Jackson. Winfrey, Jordan, and Woods parlayed their success in entertainment and sports to lucrative endorsements and the kind of wealth that very few people of any race can match.

Perhaps less widely known, but also tremendously successful were entrepreneurs like Robert Johnson, the founder of Black Entertainment Television

*By 2005 48.6 percent of African-American families owned their own homes, but this still lagged far behind the 70.7 percent homeownership rate for white families.*

(BET) and owner of the Charlotte Bobcats of the NBA. Reginald Lewis, whose life was cut short by brain cancer in 1993, oversaw two major corporate buyouts and had a net worth of $400 million in 1992. His autobiography was titled *Why Should White Guys Have All the Fun?*

Most African Americans during this time did not make nearly as much money as these few superrich. Yet the gap in median income between white and black households narrowed significantly in the 1990s and 2000s. Between 1992 and 2005, black households' median income rose from $23,190 to $30,000, an increase of 33 percent. In the same time period, white households' median income rose by 22 percent. Still the median income for white families in 2005 was $48,554, while that of black families lagged behind at $30,858.

Many scholars attribute the long, slow rise in income to the changes unleashed by the civil rights movement and affirmative action. By 2000, 35 percent of black men and 62 percent of black women worked in the white-collar sector, holding jobs that would have excluded their parents and grandparents.

The gap between white and African-American income persists in an era devoid of the blatant discrimination of Jim Crow laws, partly because of the long-term effects of wealth and poverty in the United States. Many white families benefit from the kind of capital in real estate and other investment

# Maxine Waters on the L.A. Riots

Maxine Waters was elected to Congress to represent California's 35th District in 1990, and has served that district, west of downtown Los Angeles, since then. Shortly after the Los Angeles Riots, in which her office burned, she addressed the congregation at First African Methodist Episcopal Church. The following passage is excerpted from that speech.

There was an insurrection in this city before, and if I remember correctly it was sparked by police brutality. We had a Kerner Commission report. It talked about what was wrong with our society. It talked about institutionalized racism. It talked about a lack of services, lack of government responsive to the people. Today, as we stand here in 1992, if you go back and read the report it seems as though we are talking about what that report cited some twenty years ago still exists today.

Mr. President, our children's lives are at stake. We want to deal with the young men who have dropped off of America's agenda. Just hangin' out, chillin', nothin' to do, nowhere to go. They don't show up on anybody's statistics. They're not in school, they have never been employed, they don't really live anywhere. They move from grandmama to mama to girlfriend. They're on general relief and they're sleeping under bridges. Mr. President, Mr. Governor, and anybody else who wants to listen: everybody in the street was not a thug or a hood. For politicians who think everybody in the street who committed a petty crime, stealing some Pampers for the baby, a new pair of shoes ... We know you're not supposed to steal, but the times are such, the environment is such, that people behave in strange ways. They are not all crooks and criminals. If they are, Mr. President, what about your violations? Oh yes. We're angry, and yes, this Rodney King incident. The verdict. Oh, it was more than a slap in the face. It kind of reached in and grabbed you right here in the heart and it pulled you and it hurts so bad. They want me to march out into Watts, as the black so-called leadership did in the Sixties, and say, "Cool it, baby, cool it." I am sorry. I know how to talk to my people. I know how to tell them not to put their lives at risk. I know how to say don't put other people's lives at risk. But, journalists, don't you dare dictate to me about what I'm supposed to say. It's not nice to display anger. I am angry. It is all right to be angry. It is unfortunate what people do when they are frustrated and angry. The fact of the matter is, whether we like it or not, riot is the voice of the unheard.

Congresswoman Maxine Waters was elected to a tenth term in the U.S. House of Representatives in 2008.

that has been handed down through generations. Only recently have a significant number of African Americans been able to transfer wealth in this fashion. Home ownership provides a stark example, since for many families a home is the most important and most expensive purchase they will ever make. In 2005 70.7 percent of white families owned their homes, compared to 48.6 percent of African-American families. Like other racial gaps, this one is narrowing, but excruciatingly slowly.

Education is one of the key markers—and guarantors—of success in the United States. Some African Americans—giants like John Hope Franklin, Henry Louis Gates, Deborah Gray White, Neil deGrasse Tyson, Nell Irvin Painter, and many more—have achieved the highest ranks of academic superstardom. Across the board, African-American rates of education have improved since the civil rights movement. Unfortunately consistent underfunding of schools in poor urban and rural areas prevents many poor children (and African-American children are disproportionately poor) from reaching their full potential.

Though legally mandated segregation was struck down more than half a century ago (the aforementioned Supreme Court decision notwithstanding), residential segregation by race and class continues to plague the United States.

*Henry Louis Gates Jr. shown above in April 2007, holds the rank of University Professor at Harvard and directs the university's W.E.B. Du Bois Institute for African and African American Research.*

## HEALTH

The overall health of African Americans improved 1990–2008. By 2000, African-American male life expectancy had risen to 68.3 years, while black female's had risen to 75.2. The figures for white men and women were 74.9 and 80.1, respectively. Since African Americans remain poorer, and are more likely to suffer dire poverty than their white counterparts, some health problems affect African Americans more profoundly than whites. Serious health problems are more likely to go untreated among populations with less regular access to high-quality healthcare.

Don't just worry about HIV. Do something about it.

If you think you are at risk for HIV infection, now's the time to consider counseling and testing. If you test positive, work with a doctor to make decisions that are right for you. The earlier this happens, the more medical care can help.
Talk to a doctor, your health department, or other local AIDS resources. Call your State or local AIDS hotline, or the National AIDS Hotline at 1-800-342-AIDS. Call 1-800-243-7889 (TTY) for deaf access.

HIV is the virus that causes AIDS.

*This U.S. government poster promoted early treatment for HIV-positive African Americans.*

HIV/AIDS has also emerged as a serious health threat to African Americans in recent years. African Americans, who represent 13 percent of the U.S. population, account for more than 50 percent of new HIV infections. Intravenous drug use and unprotected sex are the primary modes of transmitting the virus. Some gay and bisexual African-American men have also exhibited a reluctance to reveal their sexual activities to female partners, resulting in African-American women being infected with the virus.

## THE CLINTON ADMINISTRATION

Bill Clinton, governor of Arkansas, won the 1992 presidential election, thanks in part to a large majority (78 percent) of the African-American vote. More than many white candidates before him, even Democrats who were successful at earning African-American votes, Clinton seemed to evince genuine respect, understanding, and appreciation of African Americans. African Americans supported Clinton on a political level, but also appreciated Clinton's efforts to bridge America's racial divide. The Clinton family worshiped in black churches and toured South Central Los Angeles. Bill Clinton donned sunglasses, dusted off his saxophone, and played Elvis Presley's *Heartbreak Hotel* on the Arsenio Hall show. Hall joked that it "was nice to see a Democrat blowing something besides an election."

Once elected, Clinton named Marian Wright Edelman, Barbara Jordan, Vernon Jordan, and William Gray III to his transition team. Upon taking office in 1993, Clinton appointed African Americans to many governmental posts. These appointments came at the most visible levels—Hazel O'Leary to head the Department of Energy, Alexis Herman as secretary of labor, and Ron Brown as secretary of commerce—as well as the hundreds of lesser jobs filled by each U.S. president. Bill Clinton also became the first U.S. president to pay an extended visit to Africa, when he toured Ghana, Rwanda, Botswana, South Africa, and Senegal. In South Africa, he joined Nelson Mandela on a tour of the Robben Island prison where Mandela spent 18 years for his opposition to apartheid.

The novelist Toni Morrison wrote in the *New Yorker* in 1998, at the height of the Clinton sex scandal, that "white skin notwithstanding, this is our first black President. Blacker than any actual black person who could ever be elected in our children's lifetime. After all, Clinton displays almost every trope of blackness: single-parent household, born poor, working-class, saxophone-playing, McDonald's-and-junk-food-loving boy from Arkansas." Bill Clinton was also known for his ability to seize upon the most popular parts of his political opponents' positions, a trait on display in his eager support for the Personal Responsibility and Work Opportunity Reconciliation Act, a major welfare reform initiative. The welfare reform bill masqueraded as an attempt to get families off welfare and into productive employment, but its principal effect was to slash welfare rolls with little regard for what happened to the people affected. Once the economic boom of the 1990s petered out, poverty deepened for many former welfare recipients.

## THE GEORGE W. BUSH ADMINISTRATION

Race was a major factor in the hotly contested, bizarre 2000 election. Most Americans went to bed on November 7, 2000, unsure of who had won the presidential election. The controversy centered on Florida, which, like other states, had its own rules and local practices governing elections. In the contest between Texas Governor George W. Bush and Vice President Al Gore, Florida was too close to call. By Florida law, recounts began in several counties. These recounts were stopped by the U.S. Supreme Court ruling in *Bush v. Gore*, which ensured that George W. Bush would win the election. As Democratic partisans cried foul, scant attention was paid to the Florida laws of the 1990s, passed with Democratic support, that had permanently disenfranchised hundreds of thousands of Floridians, many of them African American and Latino, because they had been convicted of a felony.

George W. Bush took over as president in 2001 with Republican majorities in both houses of Congress. Immediately upon taking office, Bush appointed several African Americans to high-ranking government posts. Condoleezza Rice, an expert on the former Soviet Union, became Bush's national security adviser, and Colin Powell, a hero of the Gulf War and former chairman of the Joint Chiefs of Staff, agreed to serve as Bush's secretary of state. Powell recognized the symbolic value of his high position in a speech at Howard University, noting that "it's always a source of inspiration and joy to see people look at me and through me see my country and see what promise my country offers to all people who come to these shores looking for a better life."

One of Bush's campaign promises, which became a major first-term initiative, was the reform of public education. The No Child Left Behind Act (or NCLB) intended to force poor schools to improve by means of regular testing, publication of test results, and sanctions for schools that failed to meet basic goals.

## POVERTY AND PRISON

African Americans are twice as likely to live below the poverty line (around $20,000 for a family of four) as the U.S. population as a whole. The African-American poverty rate hovers between 23 and 24 percent, while the United States as a whole has a rate of around 12 percent. Among U.S. racial groups, only Native Americans approach the same poverty rate as African Americans.

The situation is especially dire for young African Americans, more than half of whom live in poverty. Generational, concentrated poverty of this kind, whether urban or rural, severely limits opportunities for economic advancement. The population of U.S. prisons is disproportionately African American as well, and young African-American men are more likely than other groups to be incarcerated. According to the U.S. Justice Department in 2003, about 10.4 percent of the African-American male population aged 25 to 29 was incarcerated, by far the largest racial or ethnic group. Since many African Americans exist at the margins of U.S. economic life, they are more likely to be affected by even slight downturns in the national economy as a whole.

## ART AND CULTURE

Between 1990 and 2008, African Americans played a greatly influential role in U.S. culture, far beyond what might be expected from a group comprising around 13 percent of the population. The most visible pop culture phenomenon of the 1990s was the commercial juggernaut of rap music and the spread of African-American hip-hop culture around the world. But hip-hop is just one of the many cultural spheres in which African Americans have achieved prominence, earned worldwide acclaim, and influenced American culture as a whole.

In the fields of drama and literature, African Americans made significant strides. August Wilson, a Pittsburgh-based playwright, wrote a cycle of 10 plays about African Americans in the 20th century. The plays illuminated themes such as the intersection between race and class, and the defeats as well as the triumphs of black history. They also make good use of black

*Toni Morrison speaking in New York City on February 26, 2008. In 1993 Morrison became the first black woman to win the Nobel Prize for Literature.*

English. Two of the plays, 1987's *Fences* and 1990's *The Piano Lesson,* won Pulitzer Prizes for drama. August Wilson died in October 2005, but before he died, he managed to complete *Radio Golf,* the 1990s part of the cycle. In *Radio Golf,* the main character, Harmond Wilks, is a wealthy real estate investor who wants to redevelop a blighted section of Pittsburgh, and harbors dreams of being elected Pittsburgh's first black mayor. The redevelopment project is put on hold when one of the houses that must be torn down belongs to Aunt Esther. Aunt Esther appears in most of Wilson's plays—Wilson uses her to represent the legacy of the African-American past (she arrives with the first shipment of slaves to British North America in 1619). This plot twist hearkens back to 1991, when workers digging the foundation for a federal office building in Manhattan uncovered a colonial-era slave cemetery that was the final resting place of thousands of African slaves, and is now the African Burial Ground National Monument.

African-American writers continued to produce stunning works of literature 1990–2008. Many of these authors were awarded the highest honors in their respective fields. Rita Dove was named Poet Laureate of the United States in 1993, and Maya Angelou memorably read her poem *On the Pulse of the Morning* at Bill Clinton's inauguration. Also in 1993, novelist Toni Morrison, long recognized as a leading light of American letters, received the Nobel Prize for Literature. In 2004 Edward Jones received the Pulitzer Prize for his novel *The Known World*.

African-American actors and actresses were some of the most recognizable faces in U.S. cinema in the 1990s and 2000s. Some African Americans commanded extremely high salaries, and several won the industry's most coveted awards, including the Academy Award for Best Actor, won by: Denzel Washington in 2001 for *Training Day*, Jamie Foxx in 2004 for *Ray*, and Forrest Whitaker in 2007 for *The Last King of Scotland*. Jennifer Hudson won the Academy Award for Best Supporting Actress in 2007 for *Dream Girls*, and Halle Berry won Best Actress for her work in *Monster's Ball* in 2001. African-American directors such as John Singleton and Spike Lee made fine films 1990–2008. In another part of the entertainment world, black comics like Dave Chappelle, Wanda Sykes, David Alan Grier, the Kings of Comedy (Cedric the Entertainer, Bernie Mac, D.L. Hughley, and Steve Harvey), and Chris Rock pointed out the humor inherent in modern American life and race relations.

Rap music and hip-hop culture more generally is another area in which African Americans exerted a heavy influence on culture. From humble roots in the South Bronx in the 1970s, hip-hip culture by 2008 had become a

*Grammy Award–nominated rap music recording artist Yung Joc performing for troops on the aircraft carrier USS Dwight D. Eisenhower on April 20, 2009.*

worldwide cultural and commercial phenomenon. Rap music was commercially viable before 1990, but the 1990s and 2000s witnessed the maturation of the genre, its division between the various regions, and its export to the rest of the globe, including Europe, Africa, and Asia. Rappers like Jay-Z and record company executives like Sean Combs and Russell Simmons exploded beyond the confines of the record industry to head major U.S. corporations, with lines of apparel and high-end fragrances and liquors. However none of this would have been possible without the initial success of the music.

Rap music in the 1990s and the 2000s, while still a major force in U.S. popular music in general, was divided into at least two regional camps, the East Coast and the West Coast. Hip-hop scholars would probably add the specific styles prevalent in Atlanta, Chicago, St. Louis, and Houston to these two major camps. East Coast rap from 1990 to 2008 runs a line from seminal groups like Brand Nubian, the Jungle Brothers, De La Soul, and A Tribe Called Quest, who fused street-wise lyrics with eclectic samples and jazz musicians playing on many tracks, through the harder styles of Public Enemy to the more recent performers Jay-Z and Nas. West Coast rap, built on the foundation of N.W.A., took a different, slightly more aggressive stance and featured artists such as Tupac Shakur, Dr. Dre, and Snoop. By 2008 the East Coast/West Coast divide had become less important as other regions rose in prominence, and the business of hip-hop seemed to take over. Those who believe that homophobia and misogyny are rampant in rap music can take heart in the music of recent stars like Philadelphia-based The Roots, Brooklyn's Talib Kweli, and Common, from Chicago.

African Americans also made major contributions to many more genres of American music besides rap. The neo-soul movement has reworked many of the themes of black music from the 1960s and 1970s with a newer, hip-hop-inflected sound. African Americans continued to perform jazz and classical music at the highest levels.

## RELIGION

Since the earliest arrival of Africans to America, religion has proven an invaluable part of community-building and the transformation of diverse groups of Africans into African Americans. It is impossible to treat all aspects of black religion in the United States 1990–2008 in such a brief overview, but some general trends are apparent.

Black churches in the United States boast 25 million members, and most African Americans in the United States are Protestants. Many black churches are deeply rooted in local traditions and have served their small congregations since the 19th century, while others, reflecting the trend toward megachurches, feature massive, state-of-the-art facilities offering financial services and a variety of other activities. In the 1990s, Bishop T.D. Jakes of West Virginia grew his once-tiny congregation into the humongous Potter's House in Dallas, with a multiracial con-gregation of around 30,000 members. Jakes's ministry benefits from his huge me-dia presence, and his ability to reach out on the Inter-net. Black Christianity is not monolithic. Some black con-gregations are relatively con-servative, while some others take more progressive stanc-es on the major social issues of the day.

There are about 1.5 mil-lion African-American Mus-lims in the United States. Of this 1.5 million, 20,000 to 40,000 men and women are members of the Nation

*Participants in the Million Man March in front of the Washington Monument on October 16, 1995.*

of Islam, led by Louis Farrakhan. On Farrakhan's watch, the Nation of Islam has acquired considerable influence, through business enterprises and Farra-khan's own penchant for making headlines.

Farrakhan's leadership of the Nation of Islam has been controversial. Farrakhan has downplayed the political struggle for civil rights and equal-ity, stressing instead black economic independence. He has also repeated-ly preached anti-Semitism. In spite of all the controversy, Farrakhan was able to widen his appeal significantly in 1995 as the chief organizer of a movement he called the Million Man March. Farrakhan called on African-American men to join him in Washington, D.C., in 1995 to advocate "unity, atonement, and brotherhood." Farrakhan asked the assembled men to join him in pledging to "take responsibility for their lives and families, and com-mit to stopping the scourges of drugs, violence, and unemployment." The size of the crowd remains in dispute, but estimates range from 400,000 to 1.2 million.

Black Christianity was the cause of some controversy in the 2008 presi-dential campaign when video clips of Jeremiah Wright appeared on YouTube. Wright was the pastor of Trinity United Church of Christ in Chicago. Senator and presidential candidate Barack Obama had attended the church, and some of Wright's more incendiary sermons were used by Obama's political oppo-nents in an effort to cast doubt on his loyalty to the United States, as well as on his character and judgment. Senator Obama publicly disassociated himself from Wright, and used the controversy to make one of the most significant speeches on race in recent memory.

## IDENTITY

In the decades since the 1960s, American identity has grown more complicated. More interracial relationships have increased the number of multiracial people, at the same time as more Americans are willing to recognize
multiraciality now and in the American past. For instance, both actor Keanu
Reeves and golfer Tiger Woods could (and Tiger Woods has) self-identified
as Asian American or multiracial. Blackness and whiteness remain powerful
forces in the United States, however, so Keanu Reeves is rarely referred to as
Asian American, while Tiger Woods is often referred to as "the first African-
American golfer" to achieve various milestones.

Until quite recently, people of mixed African and European ancestry were
usually characterized as black or African American. Even after people were
allowed to choose their own racial designation on U.S. Census Bureau forms,
checking more than one box was not really an option. To complicate matters
further, the Census Bureau decided that "Hispanic" was an ethnic group that
could be used in conjunction with one of the four main racial designations.
Some opponents of this system argue that categorizing people by race tends
to perpetuate categories that have no basis in science, and should not have
any bearing on one's life chances.

Others have called for a modification of the system to reflect an increasingly multiracial United States, even though this might divide people who have
traditionally been perceived as black into smaller, and less politically powerful, groups. In the 2000 census, 1.8 million Americans chose to designate
themselves as "biracial."

The 1960s also witnessed the passage of a new Immigration Act, which
erased the quota system in place, though modified, since the 1920s. Millions
of immigrants from around the world have come to the United States since
then, and many immigrants of African descent, including those from Africa,
Latin America, and the Caribbean have come into contact with the American
way of reckoning race.

Immigrants from Africa face an interesting set of challenges when they
immigrate to the United States. In addition to the difficulties of learning a
new language and customs, not to mention securing gainful employment,
Africans come into contact with a system in which race is important. Many
societies around the world, especially those descended from European colonial regimes, have some form of color prejudice; in the United States,
racial divisions remain quite powerful. Complicating matters is the fact
that modern African immigrants are likely to construct their identity along
ethnic or national lines (for example, Kenyan or Eritrean) and not in racial
terms.

Gender and sexuality are two often-overlooked components of black identity in the United States. Black women have struggled to be recognized as a political force in their own right. As they struggled against sexism and racism in

society, they also faced sexism held over from the era of civil rights and Black Power. Gay black men and black lesbians also face hostility from some African Americans, including members of some more socially conservative black churches. Many black leaders—Julian Bond, Eleanor Holmes Norton, Jesse Jackson, and John Lewis among them—have spoken out against homophobia.

## THE RECENT PAST

In August 2005, the Gulf Coast and the city of New Orleans were hit hard by Hurricane Katrina. The natural disaster was bad enough, but the storm also touched some of America's rawest nerves as it exposed the connections between race and poverty in the United States.

Many residents in the economically depressed, heavily African-American region were unable to evacuate, and were left to fend for themselves when the New Orleans levees broke. There was a jarring cognitive dissonance between the Bush administration's assurances that everything was fine—that New Orleans had "dodged a bullet"—and the images of families huddled on rooftops awaiting rescue or taking shelter in squalor in the Convention Center.

Three years later a far different public image emerged in Barack Obama, who might seem at first an unlikely political success story—as he has noted in numerous speeches and in his two books, *Dreams from My Father* and *The Audacity of Hope*. His father was a Kenyan who had come to the United States to study, and his mother was a white woman from Kansas. Obama had little

*Evacuees from areas flooded by Hurricane Katrina listen to religious services in the temporary Red Cross shelter set up at the Houston Astrodome on September 9, 2005.*

# "Let Us Summon a New Spirit"

On November 4, 2008, Barack Obama became the first African American to be elected president of the United States. Late that night he addressed a huge crowd of supporters in Chicago's Grant Park. Excerpts from the speech follow.

*If there is anyone out there who still doubts that America is a place where all things are possible, who still wonders if the dream of our founders is alive in our time, who still questions the power of our democracy, tonight is your answer.*

*It's the answer spoken by young and old, rich and poor, Democrat and Republican, black, white, Hispanic, Asian, Native American, gay, straight, disabled and not disabled. Americans who sent a message to the world that we have never been just a collection of individuals or a collection of red states and blue states. We are, and always will be, the United States of America.*

*It's the answer that led those who've been told for so long by so many to be cynical and fearful and doubtful about what we can achieve to put their hands on the arc of history and bend it once more toward the hope of a better day.*

*I was never the likeliest candidate for this office. We didn't start with much money or many endorsements. Our campaign was not hatched in the halls of Washington. It began in the backyards of Des Moines and the living rooms of Concord and the front porches of Charleston. It was built by working men and women who dug into what little savings they had to give $5 and $10 and $20 to the cause.*

*It grew strength from the young people who rejected the myth of their generation's apathy who left their homes and their families for jobs that offered little pay and less sleep.*

*It drew strength from the not-so-young people who braved the bitter cold and scorching heat to knock on doors of perfect strangers, and from the millions of Americans who volunteered and organized and proved that more than two centuries later a government of the people, by the people, and for the people has not perished from the Earth.*

Barack Obama on January 26, 2007, in Washington D.C., just over two weeks before he announced his candidacy for president of the United States.

contact with his father, and was raised by his mother and maternal grand-parents. His and his family's perseverance paid off, and Obama received a world-class education. He became the first African-American editor of the *Harvard Law Review*, worked as a community organizer on Chicago's South Side, and lectured on constitutional law at the University of Chicago. He be-gan his political career in the Illinois State Senate, and was elected to the U.S. Senate in 2004. In 2007 Obama launched his presidential campaign on a frigid day on the steps of the Old State Capitol in Springfield, Illinois. A multiracial crowd of thousands cheered him. Over the next two years, Obama fended off strong challengers in the primaries, most notably Hillary Clinton, to secure the Democratic nomination for president.

On November 4, 2008, Barack Obama was elected president of the United States. By the start of a new decade, African Americans had cause for optimism, tempered with the knowledge of the past and a long history of oppression.

MATTHEW JENNINGS
MACON STATE COLLEGE

# Further Readings

Benjamin, Lois. *The Black Elite: Still Facing the Color Line in the Twenty-First Century*. Lanham, MD: Rowman and Littlefield, 2005.

Chang, Jeff. *Can't Stop Won't Stop: A History of the Hip-Hop Generation*. New York: St. Martin's, 2005.

Cross, Brian. *It's Not About a Salary . . . : Rap, Race and Resistance in Los Angeles*. New York: Verso, 1993.

Dyson, Michael Eric. *Come Hell or High Water: Hurricane Katrina and the Color of Disaster*. New York: Basic Books, 2006.

Dyson, Michael Eric. *Is Bill Cosby Right? Or Has the Black Middle Class Lost Its Mind?* New York: Basic Books, 2005.

Hacker, Andrew. *Two Nations: Black & White, Separate, Hostile, Unequal*. New York: Scribner, 2003.

Hine, Darlene Clark, et al. *The African-American Odyssey*. Upper Saddle River, NJ: Pearson, 2008.

Kelley, Robin D.G. *Yo Mama's Dysfunktional!: Fighting the Culture Wars in Urban America*. Boston, MA: Beacon Press, 1997.

Kitwana, Bakari. *The Hip-Hop Generation: Young Blacks and the Crisis in African American Culture*. New York: Basic Books, 2002.

Lusane, Clarence. *Race in the Global Era: African Americans at the Millennium*. Boston, MA: South End Press, 1997.

McArdle, Andrea, and Tanya Ezen, eds. *Zero Tolerance*. New York: New York University Press, 2001.

Robinson, Lori S. "Black Like Whom?" *The Crisis* (January/February 2006).

Smith, Anna Deavere. *Twilight: Los Angeles, 1992.* New York: Anchor Books, 1994.

U.S. Bureau of the Census. Available online, URL: http://www.census .gov/. Accessed July 2009.

**affirmative action**: Theory stating that African Americans and other minorities (including women) should be promoted to higher positions in order to offset the historical effects of discriminatory practices, such as the implementation of Jim Crow laws.

**Arkansas Nine**: A group of students who in 1957 attempted to enroll at the racially segregated Little Rock Central High School, but were blocked from doing so by Arkansas Governor Orval Faubus.

**"Big House"**: A slave's phrase for his or her master's manor.

**Biracial**: A person who has DNA from two races. Important cultural figures such as golfer Tiger Woods have identified themselves as biracial.

**black codes**: Laws passed in southern states after the Civil War that severely restricted the upward mobility potential of newly freed African American slaves.

**black flight**: The act of African Americans moving out of predominantly African-American, inner-city communities and into the suburbs.

**Black Loyalist**: An African American who supported the British cause during the Revolutionary War.

**Black Power**: Phrase originating in 1954 that often meant the promotion of black separatist values.

**blockbusting**: Encouraging people to sell their property with the claim that the neighborhood in which they live is becoming inundated with minorities.

**carpetbagger**: Southern slang term for a white northerner who moves to the south in search of in search of business success.

**commodification**: The act of marketing things that would not ordinarily be sold, such as human beings.

**"contraband of war:"** Major General Benjamin Butler's term for runaway slaves during the Civil War.

**cotton gin**: Farming device that increased the ease of cotton harvesting, allowing plantations to grow in both profitability and power.

**Emancipation Proclamation**: Executive order issued by President Abraham Lincoln in 1862 that declared that all slaves in the Confederacy free.

***Enfants Perdus***: French phrase meaning "lost children" that was used to describe the U.S. Army's 369th Regiment, a World War I fighting force that was comprised entirely of African Americans.

**Enrollment Act**: Conscription legislation that granted African Americans and slaves greater ease with which to join the Union Army.

**Ethiopian Regiment**: Special fighting force composed entirely of runaway slaves that fought on the side of the British during World War II.

**ethnicity**: A group of people sharing a common heritage.

**forced busing**: The act of reassigning African Americans to areas where segregation has historically been an issue.

***Freedom's Journal***: The first African-American newspaper.

**Fugitive Slave Act**: Legislation passed in 1850 that gave law enforcement agencies greater power in tracking slaves who had run away from masters.

**gentrification**: The act of wealthy people moving into neighborhoods and displacing poorer residents, thus increasing the area's value.

**Harlem Renaissance**: Period occurring during the 1920s that saw a marked increase in the number of outlets for African-American intellectual and cultural expression.

**hip-hop**: Musical genre that was created during the 1970s in the predominantly African-American community of the south Bronx.

**HIV**: Human immune deficiency virus. The disease disproportionately impacts the African-American community, as African-American youth account for over 50 percent of new HIV infections.

**Jazz**: Musical art form that originated in southern African-American communities.

**Jim Crow Laws**: A series of legislative acts that severely prevented the African-American community's ability to assimilate into mainstream white society.

**manumission**: The act of freeing slaves.

**Middle Passage**: The route of transfer of slaves from Africa across the Atlantic Ocean into the New World.

**minstrel show**: A type of entertainment where white actors would dress in blackface and often lampoon the African-American community.

**mulatto**: Someone of mixed Caucasian and African descent.

**Nation of Islam**: Black nationalist organization that was founded in 1930 by Wallace Fard Muhammad.

**negro**: Term commonly used prior to the civil rights movement to describe all African Americans, but which became pejorative in later years; inferior goods such as patchwork blankets were described as "negro blankets."

**neo-soul**: Musical style that blends soul music with other African-American genres such as jazz, funk, hip hop, and gospel.

**Pan-Africanism**: Philosophy espousing the need for a global community of native Africans and those of African heritage.

*partus sequitur ventrem*: Latin phrase meaning "the condition of the child may follow that of the mother." The phrase applies to early slave laws that stated that the children of slaves could become slaves themselves.

**paternalism**: As it applies to African-Americans, the belief that they are not fit to govern themselves and should be dominated by a white patriarchy.

**patting juba**: Traditional African-American dance that evolved into tap-dancing.

**"peculiar institution"**: John C. Calhoun's phrase for slavery.

**perpetual servitude**: Phrase used to describe African Americans who worked below sustenance wages and suffered under meager living conditions.

**plantation**: Large-scale farm, usually in the south, where African Americans were often forced to work against their will.

**poverty line**: Imaginary line established by government agencies that determines whether someone qualifies as technically impoverished. Typically, African Americans are twice as likely to live below the poverty line than the U.S. population as a whole.

**Quakers**: Religious group whose members' top priorities included the improvement of the lives of slaves.

**racial steering**: The act of real estate brokers only showing African-American home buyers neighborhoods that are congruent to their race.

**Redeemer**: A member of the anti-Reconstruction movement usually residing in the former Confederate states.

**redlining**: Denying African Americans and other minorities access to services such as loans and health care.

**Rhode Island Regiment**: Created by the passage of legislation by the Rhode Island General Assembly, the regiment was the first all-African-American battalion in the history of the Continental army.

**rhythm and blues**: Musical genre that originated in African-American communities during the 1940s.

**scalawags**: White southerners who supported Reconstruction.

**"separate but equal":** Phrase used in the Supreme Court case of *Plessy v. Ferguson* that enabled segregation to persist across the United States.

**sit-in**: An occupation of a public place for the purpose of protesting laws and policies.

**slave**: One who is forced to undergo forced labor and is often the property of someone else.

**sundown town**: Town or village designed to be exclusively white.

**Stono Rebellion**: Insurrection that began with 20 slaves in South Carolina and eventually grew to encompass 100 other slaves.

**Underground Railroad**: A community of organizers who sought to and succeeded in secretly transfering slaves from slave states to free states.

**"welfare queen":** Phrase popularized by President Ronald Reagan that was used to describe a welfare recipient who receives exorbitant funds and has no intention of returning to work. While based on a true story, the version told by Reagan greatly exaggerated the amount of wealth the "welfare queen" was receiving.

**white flight**: The act of Caucasian people moving out of neighborhoods as they become increasingly racially diverse.

# INDEX

Index note: page references in *italics* indicate illustrations or pictures/captions; page references in **bold** indicate main discussion.

woman pilot 99
woman to earn doctoral degree 99
woman to occupy a cabinet-level post 174
woman to win the Nobel Prize for literature 200
African-American Liberty Bond 90
African Free School 51
African Methodist Episcopal Church (AME) *49*, 49, 68
Alabama
  Autherine Lucy **147–148**, *148*
  Freedom Riders **152–153**, *153*
  Maxwell Air Force Base 153
  Montgomery Boycott **145–146**
  Scottsboro Boys Trials **97**, 132
  Tuskegee Institute *73*, 78
  U.S. Supreme Court decisions 97, 128, 147, 157
  violence against blacks *78*, 150, 154, 161
  voting 157, 161
Albany State College 154
*Alexander v. Holmes County Board of Education* 164
Ali, Muhammad 140, 144
Allen, Richard 49
Almond, J. Lindsay 151
American Anti-Slavery Society 51
American Campaign Against Lynching 134
American Colonization Society (ACS) 38, 41, 43
American Emigration Society 48
American Red Cross 90
American Revolution
  Black Loyalists 25–26, *26*, **27**
  *Colored Patriots of the Revolution* (Nell) 30
  Continental army 22, *25*, 25, 28, 32
  slaves viii, xii, 21, 23, *24*
American Steel 158
Ames, Alexander 23
Andalusia, port of 1
Anderson, Marian 108, 110–111, *111*
Anderson, Osborne 55
Angelou, Maya 178, 200
anti-slavery legislation 17–18
anti-slavery movement 14–15, 17–18
Apollo Theater 108
*An Appeal in Favor of that Class of Americans Called Africans*
  (Child) 51

Herman, Alexis 198
Hessian mercenaries 32
Hill, Anita 192
Hill, T. Arnold 122
hip-hop culture 188, 199, 201–202
Hirschfeld, Fritz 31–32
*History of the Negro Church* (Woodson) 105
HIV/AIDS 197, *197*
HMS *William* 25
Holcomb, Robert E. 170
Holiday, Billie 107–108
Holly, James 48
homeowners, African-American 118, *194*, 196
homosexuality 132, 133
Hoover, J. Edgar 164, 168
Hope, Lugenia Burns 83
Hopkins, Harry 120
Horne, Lena 108, 137
*Hot Chocolates* 100–101
House Committee on Un-American Activities 135
Houston, Charles Hamilton 142
Houston Astrodome *205*
Howard, Oliver Otis 64
Howe, William 22
Hubbard, William D. 99
Hughes, Langston 102, 112–113
Hughley, D. L. 201
Humphrey, Hubert 174
Hurricane Katrina *205*, 205
Hurston, Zora 102

I
Ickes, Harold 119–120
"I Have a Dream" (King) 156
*I Know Why the Caged Bird Sings* (Angelou) 178
*Imitation of LIfe* 108
*Incidents in the Life of a Slave Girl* (Jacobs) 46
indentured servants
    black 1, **3**, 5
    white xii, 3, 4, 9, 11
    *See also* slaves/slavery
Indiana 47, 49, 164, 172, 173, 187
indigo processing 10, 11, 12, 38

Louisiana
  Civil War 44, *62*, 62
  integration 163
  Louisiana Purchase viii, 44
  *Plessy v. Ferguson 62*
Loyalists 19
Lucy, Autherine 147, *148*
lynching
  American Campaign Against Lynching 134
  anti-lynching bill (1937) 106
  during Depression 106
  Dyer Anti-Lynching Bill 78, 96
  Emmett Till and 144
  Ida B. Wells and 84
  Jack Johnson and 85
  Ku Klux Klan 96
  NAACP's campaign to end 85, 99, 128
  Nat Turner's rebellion 45, *45*
  during Progressive Era 77–78, *78*
  Truman administration antilynching legislation 129
  women's club movement against 83
  *See also* violence against blacks

# M
Mac, Bernie 201
Madame C. J. Walker (Sarah Breedlove) 92–93
Maine 44
malaria 10
Malcolm X 121, 140, 159, 168
Mandela, Nelson 198
Mann, Floyd 152–153
Mann Act 89
Mansfield, Mike 157
manumission viii, 2, 7, 8, 23, 47, 51, 52
  *See also* abolitionism; citizenship; emancipation
Marshall, Thurgood 110, 141, 142, *148*, 151, 192
Maryland
  education of African Americans 49
  manumission 52
  slave trade 9, 11, 16
Mason-Dixon line 21
Massachusetts
  54th Massachusetts Infantry 60, 61, 63

# Y

*Yo! Bum Rush the Show* (Public Enemy) 188
Young, Andrew 174
Young, Coleman 173
YWCA, African-American branches 84, 90

PHOTO CREDITS. Atlantic Canada Virtual Archives: 26, 31. Black Archives of Mid-America: 109. Federal Emergency Management Agency: 205. Gutenberg Project: 8, 63. iStock.com: 194. Library of Congress: 11, 15, 18, 23, 24, 40, 42, 45, 46, 48, 49, 52, 54, 55, 59, 61, 62, 64, 66, 67, 69, 70, 73, 80, 84 left, 84 right, 86, 87, 88, 92, 96, 100, 102, 103, 106, 107, 111, 119, 120, 121, 122, 125, 127, 130, 134, 136, 140, 143, 148, 150, 153, 155, 160, 162, 168, 173, 181, 186. National Aeronautics and Space Administration: 99. National Archives: 105, 123, 124, 146. National Library of Medicine: 197. National Park Service: 2. Newport Historical Society: 33. U.S. Air Force: 169, 171. U.S. House of Representatives: 195. U.S. Navy: 201. Wikipedia: 29, 78, 178, 184, 196, 200, 203, 206. Wikipedia/Swampyank: 6.

Produced by Golson Media
President and Editor    J. Geoffrey Golson
Layout Editor    Oona Patrick
Author Manager    Susan Moskowitz
Copyeditor    Barbara Paris
Proofreader    Mary Le Rouge
Indexer    J S Editorial